MW00774153

*The
Captain's
A Woman*

DEPT. OF TRANSP., U.S. COAST GUARD, CG-5206 (4-79)　　　　　　　　　　　　FILE NO. I-42901

SERIAL NUMBER
003545

ISSUE NO.
1-4

UNITED STATES COAST GUARD

MASTER

LICENSE

This is to certify that ___ *** DEBORAH DOANE DEMPSEY ***

having been duly examined and found competent by the undersigned, is licensed to serve as Master of United States Steam or Motor Vessels of any Gross Tons upon Oceans

ALSO, RADAR OBSERVER - UNLIMITED ___ (EXPIRES MARCH 1986) ___

for the term of five years from this date

Given under my hand this ___ day of ___ DECEMBER ___ 19 84

BOSTON, MASSACHUSETTS
Port

By direction

P. F. CHASE, LCDR., USCG
Officer in Charge of Marine Inspection

SN 7530-01-GF2-9480

The
Captain's
A Woman

Tales of a Merchant Mariner

Deborah Doane Dempsey
and Joanne Reckler Foster

NAVAL INSTITUTE PRESS

ANNAPOLIS, MARYLAND

Enjoy the adventure. Foster

Joanne

Library of Congress Cataloging-in-Publication Data
Dempsey, Deborah Doane, 1949–

   The captain's a woman : tales of a merchant mariner /
Deborah Doane Dempsey and Joanne Reckler Foster.

     p. cm.

  ISBN 1-55750-164-5 (alk. paper)

   1. Dempsey, Deborah Doane, 1949– . 2. Women ship
captains—United States—Biography. I. Foster, Joanne Reckler,
1941– . II. Title.

VK140.D46A3 1998

387.5'4044'092—dc21

  [B]   97-35201

Printed in the United States of America on acid-free paper ∞
05 04 03 02 01 00 99 98   9 8 7 6 5 4 3 2
First printing

Frontispiece: Captain Dempsey's first master's license—the
first issued to an American woman. Even today, only a handful of American women hold unlimited master's licenses.

To the memory of Jack
my captain, my husband, my mentor

To Jim and Julie
for making the adventure possible

Contents

Preface ix

1 *Girl Loves Ship, Girl Saves Ship, Girl Loses Ship* 1
Landlubber's Log: 1–2 February 1994 30

2 *The* Wind Lass *Finds the Rainbow* 39
Landlubber's Log: 3–10 February 1994 52

3 *Castine, Maine—Unsettled 1976* 65
Landlubber's Log: 11–12 February 1994 84

4 *Exxon Property* 88
Landlubber's Log: 13–14 February 1994 100

5 *The Love Boat* 106
Landlubber's Log: 15–18 February 1994 120

6 *One On and One Off—Temporarily* 129
Landlubber's Log: 19–21 February 1994 135

7 *Around the World in 127 Days* 140
Landlubber's Log: 22–23 February 1994 154

8 *It's More Fun When You're the Captain* 163
Landlubber's Log: 24–26 February 1994 184

9 *If the Pilot Refuses, Dock the Ship Yourself* 192
Landlubber's Log: 27–28 February 1994 217

10 *"How Long Have You Been in the Captin Buessness?"* 220
Landlubber's Log: 1–6 March 1994 233

11 *The Best View of Alexandria, Egypt, Is Over the Stern* 240
Landlubber's Log: 7–12 March 1994 252

Epilogue: Is There Life After Lykes? 259

Glossary 265

Preface

I am a landlubber. Before January 1991, my idea of fun on water was sitting on my dock with a good book, an iced tea, and a chicken neck on a string to entice Chesapeake Bay blue crabs for dinner. Three years later, I was standing eighty feet above the water on the bridge of a freighter on my way out of Norfolk harbor—bound for the Mediterranean and forty of the most incredible days I've ever spent.

It began like this:

I went to the yacht club for spaghetti on a Saturday night, and came away with a new friend, Capt. Deborah Dempsey, and the beginning of a great adventure. During one of her breaks between trips to the Persian Gulf, Debbie was the guest speaker at a small sailing club to which my husband, Jim (the more avid sailor), and I belong. After the slides and entertaining commentary, we chatted. On the way home, Jim, also a writer, said, "What a great story she'd make. Why don't you write a book?"

"No, I don't want to write a book. Why don't you write a book?"

"No." And there it lay for a month before I called her.

We met at her home in the Northern Neck of Virginia, where the mailbox bore a colorful, painted steamship, and her Volvo's license plate read "2 CAPTS." We talked in a sunny room overlooking her pool and boats at her dock on Indian Creek. I noticed a brass plaque on an étagère inscribed, "Whether I'm Right or Wrong, I'm Still the Captain."

Debbie is a lady, sweet and compassionate. Alternately, she's tough as nails. She can hold her own in any company. "Sometimes," she says, "I'm asked how I handle the language. My smart reply is, 'English is the international language. That's no problem.' Actually, my mother might have a problem with the tough longshoremen's language, but I don't." Debbie enjoys a practical joke. She is a gourmet cook, a competitive sailor and bridge player. She was wary of reporters, but agreed—reluctantly—to collaborate.

As the only female general assignment reporter on cityside when I began my newspaper career at the *Rocky Mountain News* in Denver in the mid-1960s, I knew something about being a woman in a man's world. But I knew nothing about the life of a merchant mariner.

Among the first questions I asked her was how many gallons of fuel her ship carried. When she stopped laughing enough to answer me—in barrels—she began in earnest to educate me. The learning curve was enormous.

My overriding impression is that her job as an international ship's captain was anything but glamorous. It involved sex discrimination. It involved union hassles. It was definitely dangerous and hard work. It was lonely, with long months at sea away from family and friends. So why do it?

"I wouldn't wish this life on anybody unless they really wanted to be out there," she says. "I love working on the sea."

For three years I wrote sporadically—and the story changed dramatically. But the world of the merchant marine remained completely theoretical to me until, armed with computer, tape recorder, camera, and almost as much stamina as the captain, I was aboard the 646-foot containership *Charlotte Lykes* as the tug *Cape Henry* pushed her away from the dock in February 1994. With Captain Debbie, a crew of twenty-eight, and one passenger, the *Charlotte* sailed out in an evening snow shower.

Voyage 87 was the perfect opportunity to see what life at sea was like for a commercial ship captain, and particularly for the lone female master. As much as possible, I went where she went and did what she did, for forty days—and nights, because the ship continues its business in daylight and darkness. Each stint on the bridge was an opportunity to learn about another facet of the business, each walk around the deck another chance to see the specialized equipment in operation. Each conversation with crew revealed more about how they viewed their jobs and their relationships with the captain.

As with any self-contained community, from campers to college students to a circus troupe, for ship's crew the days blur and run together. Every nuance of weather and working part on the ship is noted. Meals, movies, and mail call take on special significance, providing the variety in a string of repetitious days. With only parts of nine days spent on land, passenger and crew alike make every minute of it count, as I soon found.

Each day as Debbie worked, I wrote. Quickly it became apparent that what the captain described so matter-of-factly as the routine of her job I saw with all-new, gee-whiz eyes. Hence, my Landlubber's Log between the chapters is the salt and pepper flavoring her meat-and-potatoes tale.

—*Joanne Reckler Foster*

It's true. Like the delicious little illustration from Kenneth Grahame's *The Wind in the Willows* tucked in a corner of my porch, there's nothing I like as much as messing about in boats. That's where my story starts. You know, there are two kinds of stories. Fairy tales start, "Once upon a time . . . " Sea stories start, "This is no bull." Believe me, this is no fairy tale.

—*Deborah Doane Dempsey*

*The
Captain's
A Woman*

The Captain's A Woman is two distinct narratives told in two distinct voices. It begins with Captain Dempsey recounting her rescue of the *Lyra*. Foster follows with the first section of her Landlubber's Log, kept during forty days spent aboard a freighter under Dempsey's command. This pattern of alternating narratives is used throughout.

1. *Girl Loves Ship, Girl Saves Ship, Girl Loses Ship*

*W*hen I sailed away from the *Lyra* that Sunday afternoon in late January 1993, I thought it was for the last time. It was not without a tinge of regret: I had hoped to captain her one last time. I also remarked to myself that we were going into a rough weather period, and I sure hoped they knew what they were doing towing that ship from Baltimore to New Orleans with no crew on board.

Little did I know I would get my last chance.

When she sailed into New Orleans, only a day late and an anchor short but leaving a lifetime's worth of adventure in her wake, it was to a hero's welcome and an almost happy ending. I was credited with averting a potential environmental disaster. And I'd saved the ship I'd captained since 1989—only to lose her again.

The story began innocently enough.

I'd been in Baltimore for two weeks, helping effect the turnover of the MV *Lyra,* a 634-foot RO/RO motor vessel, to the U.S. Maritime Administration (MARAD). After being under charter to the military during the Persian Gulf conflict, when all sorts of vehicles and helicopters were rolled on and rolled off via her road-sized stern ramp, the 1977 German-built vessel had been sold to the government. The military was buying twelve RO/RO ships at a total cost of $266 million, then planning to spend $2–4 million per ship to put each in perfect working order. Theoretically, each would be maintained permanently by a nine-man crew, be worked two weeks a year, and be ready for active duty in forty-eight hours. The *Lyra* was the first to be delivered.

I was on vacation between trips on the *Charlotte Lykes,* the containership to which Lykes had permanently assigned me in September

1992 after the *Lyra*. So Capt. Clark Seelig, my boss and then manager of Lykes Lines marine division, had asked me to help. I agreed.

The two weeks for me involved a huge amount of plain old grunt work—securing the quarters for the tow to New Orleans, for instance. It meant systematically going from cabin to cabin and making sure everything was locked up, tied down, and taped down. It also meant putting all of the lashing gear in fifty-five-gallon drums: twist locks, turnbuckles, chains used to secure the cargo, whether in containers or loose—and carrying the drums by forklift from the main deck down the ramp to the number two, or main RO/RO deck, so they'd be out of the weather, then placing them along the whole port side and securing them. It was a huge job, and I resented the port engineers asking me to do that.

MARAD's surveyors on the deck side had warned me early on: "If you're getting involved in a tow that Weser puts together, look out." Gerhard Weser, a Dutchman from Houston who often acts as middleman in arranging tows, had an experience on the Mississippi River that ended in disaster. He had gotten this job on the *Lyra* because he was the low bidder. But I was not concerned, because I didn't expect to be part of the riding crew.

The ship had been laid up in December at Bethlehem Steel's Sparrows Point Yard, so it was less expensive to tow her down the Atlantic—a common MARAD practice—than to put her back in operating condition and recrew. But in confined navigable waters a riding crew of at least two is required. In this case, a crew needed to be aboard from Baltimore down Chesapeake Bay to its mouth at Cape Henry and, at the other end, from the mouth of the Mississippi River to docking in New Orleans. Crew members don't need any particular ratings—it doesn't have to be a captain and chief engineer, just two bodies, in case you need to drop the anchor or run the emergency generator.

When I first heard about the tow, I started quizzing Lykes's head office in New Orleans. I didn't want to be part of the riding crew simply because I didn't want to be involved with MARAD and the office. I was assured there would not be a riding crew.

"Don't worry about it," Captain Seelig said. Then, in the yard, Capt. John Vickers, the Salvage Association's surveyor representing Lykes, let slip that we were to be riding crew, after all.

Saturday, 23 January, was a flat, calm day, a little chilly when we left our anchorage off Dundalk Terminal north of the Francis Scott Key Bridge about 1045. Hoisted on the flying bridge was the black cloth diamond, the day shape telling other vessels we were under tow. That was a sad sight. Along with me were Brian Norton, chief engineer, and Peter Smith, his first assistant. Ahead was the tow-boat, the tug *Mark McAllister,* with the required two Chesapeake Bay pilots aboard.

We were attached to the towboat, from her end, by two thousand feet of two and a quarter-inch braided wire cable, and from our end by one shot (ninety feet) of three-inch die lock anchor chain. That came up through an opening in the bulwark dead center on the bow—the bullnose, a two-foot circle thirty feet off the water. It was attached to the main tow bridle, two-inch chain figure-eighted around two sets of bitts on either side of the bullnose on deck. Tow bridle and tow chain were connected by a fifty-ton shackle—fifty tons being its breaking strength. The shackle alone weighs so much, more than one hundred pounds, that it takes two strong men to lift it. I can handle a twenty-five-ton shackle alone; I can only lift the pin from a fifty-ton shackle. In between was 150 feet of twelve-inch nylon-Dacron shock line, designed to maintain a catenary, its give used to absorb the strain on the taut braided wire and chain.

And the ship was towing like hell. At that point the tow cable was short, about five hundred feet, to keep the *Lyra* in the twelve-hundred-foot-wide channel until we were south of the Chesapeake Bay Bridge. After that, it was lengthened to a thousand feet, but the yaw improved very little. At times we seemed to be going one way, the towboat another. And we didn't make very good speed, maybe three and a half knots. We'd estimated five to seven knots for the twelve-day trip.

Sunset was lovely. Peter had some beer, and I had brought maybe four cans. Brian had a bottle of champagne. We all shared. We bundled up and barbecued chicken by the pool on D deck that night, eating at the picnic table. We were close enough to shore that we could get TV, and we had a nice evening. Louis Castro, Lykes's manager of maintenance and repair (MNR), had bought us three portable toilets for the ride down the Bay because the sanitation system had been drained and winterized. But Brian turned on the emergency generator, so we could use the system after all, rewinterizing before we left the ship. At one point, Brian turned off the emergency generator, concerned that it wouldn't last the twenty-eight hours down the bay. But it worked perfectly. That power meant we even had warm showers, very welcome on a raw January day, and could turn on space heaters in our cabins. It was eerily quiet on what was a "dead" ship—although the emergency generator was running, I couldn't hear it in my stateroom. When you lose the plant on a voyage, *no* vibration is what wakes you. It felt really different without that vibration, and I slept in bits and pieces, talking to the tug off and on, checking our position and progress. Finally about 0600 I got up, showered, had a bowl of Rice Krispies and a banana, also courtesy of Mr. Castro's thoughtfulness.

About 0700 I took a cup of coffee up to the bridge. And that's when I heard the conversation about the weather. The tug office was talking to the tug captain, Captain J.

"Do not anchor the vessel. Remove the riding crew from the vessel and keep going. Ignore the weather. Somebody in Lykes says to keep going."

The captain acknowledged: "All right, we'll keep going and take the riding crew off," as planned, at the pilot station at Lynnhaven.

I called Captain J, who said yes, I'd heard what I'd heard. And I was concerned. Generally, you do not leave Chesapeake Bay for open waters without a twenty-four-hour window of good weather to test the tow under calm conditions. If there will be a problem, it will show up shortly. Already the wind was twenty knots, the seas six feet—the limit recommended by the surveyor for towing—with small-craft warnings and even worse weather predicted. But because we were only bay riding crew, responsible only for running the emergency generator and dropping the anchor, we had no say.

We had several last duties, among them to lock up everything on the ship. I locked my stateroom door and my office door and gave the keys to Brian, who locked them in the desk drawer in his office. He planned to meet the ship at the other end of the tow for the ride up the Mississippi. I hadn't planned to keep any keys, but I was able to come up with an extra set. It was a damn good thing I did, because later on when Lykes couldn't reach Brian, those keys were a godsend.

I knew we were getting off on the port side, so I'd already secured the starboard pilot ladder up out of the water so it would be there when the river riding crew got aboard at the mouth of the Mississippi. That was crucial. The pilot ladder *normally* is the only way aboard. Last, off the port quarter I'd trailed a float attached to three hundred feet of nine-inch mooring line that, in turn, was attached to the emergency tow cable—six hundred feet of two-inch wire, tied off about every twenty feet to stanchions along the port side of the main deck, and attached with a twenty-five-ton shackle to a second bridle snaked around bitts on the port side of the fo'c'sle deck. It was intended to be used only if the regular tow cable broke. I was assured it never did.

I even asked the tug, "Have you ever had to use an emergency tow cable?" The answer was no.

When we reached Lynnhaven at 1420, we, along with the two pilots who had been aboard the tug, got off onto the Maryland pilot boat for the forty-five-minute ride to the pilot station just inside Cape Henry. That's a bigger feat than it sounds. The pilot ladder is made of international-orange wooden rungs fourteen inches apart, with one and a half-inch line threaded through each side of the rungs, and periodically a six-foot spreader bar to keep it from twisting. The bottom four steps are hard rubber. The rungs are tight against the ship, allowing only the toes of your shoes on them; the lacing is designed with cutouts to accept your hands. Usually a pilot ladder is lowered from a door on the number two deck, about twenty-four feet, but with nobody aboard, there would have been nobody to close the door. So we rigged it from the main deck, up one deck, increasing the drop to thirty-five feet. I was quite concerned, as neither of my crew had been on a pilot ladder before.

Out of my earshot, Mr. Castro had instructed Brian to leave last, making sure first that I got down okay. When Brian told me that, I said, "Forget it." First Peter slowly descended the thirty-five feet, then Brian, without mishap. As captain, I was the last to leave. By then, the weather was quite rough, too rough even to try to tie off the port pilot ladder to protect it on the tow south.

Strapped in the enclosed pilot boat, which had seats for six and the feel of an airplane, I took pictures of the *Lyra* as we left her. She was a sad sight, especially under tow. I thought I'd never see my ship again.

My husband, Jack, then one of Lykes's most senior captains, showed up about 1600. The pilot's dispatch tower at Lynnhaven had given him a wrong time for our arrival, several times. After we dropped Brian and Peter off at the Norfolk airport, we drove north a couple of hours to our waterfront home in the Northern Neck of Virginia.

That was Sunday, 24 January.

On Monday afternoon Captain Seelig called to see how I'd made out. I told him about the weather conversation I'd overheard. No comment. He asked the *Lyra*'s ETA (estimated time of arrival) for New Orleans, which was Friday, 5 February, and suggested I fly down and ride her up the Mississippi. No comment.

About 0930 Tuesday, Jack and I were just finishing breakfast when the phone rang. It was Captain Seelig.

"Debbie, don't go anywhere. The *Lyra* broke her tow."

Captain Seelig told me she was dangerously close to the reefs off North Carolina, fifty miles northeast of Cape Fear. She had 387,000 gallons of heavy fuel oil aboard, half her capacity, and she was threatening to go aground and foul the Carolina beaches. Lykes needed a captain and skeleton crew aboard to lower the anchors and stop her drift toward shore. Because I had just left her, I was nearby, and I was available, I was the logical captain to call.

"Can you leave immediately?" Captain Seelig asked.

"Yes!"

"It involves a helicopter ride. Does that bother you?"

"No!"

Then began the rapid but intense process of trying to get there. There isn't a really direct route from Kilmarnock, a small town, south to Wilmington, North Carolina. There was a commercial flight to Wilmington from Richmond, more than an hour's drive, at 1215. Nothing out of Norfolk.

In the meantime, Captain Seelig called back, asking about former chief mates on the *Lyra*. The best I had sailed with, Eric Wilcox, was in Maine. Too far. Pete Pizzarelli and Billy Miles were in Charleston. Curtis Hall, I thought, was in New Hampshire. Again too far. The critical point: Could we get there before dark? Without power the ship had no lights, and the helicopter couldn't land on a pitch-black deck.

At 1045 Captain Seelig called back with the go-ahead. I raced to All Seasons Travel in Kilmarnock and called Captain Seelig from there.

"I can't get to Richmond on time. If I drive like hell, I'll get there as the plane leaves."

"Start driving," Captain Seelig said. I did, then stopped and ran back to the travel agency.

"Are there any charters available?"

All Seasons called Al Pembroke, who checked with the Federal Aviation Administration (FAA) and got back to us within minutes with a plane—a twin-engine Cessna—a price—$875—and news that the weather was so bad the FAA required us to pick up a second pilot in Newport News.

Back to Lykes. I relayed the information to Nell Bourgeois, Captain Seelig's secretary. Her response: "Go!"

I told Al I'd meet him at Hummel Field in thirty minutes, and hung up. Hummel is a tiny airport in Topping, south across the Rappahannock River and around a bend. I raced home and finished packing my bag, which was still basically ready from my return on Sunday. I took foul-weather gear, wool hat and gloves, a change of pants and shirts, several pairs each of underwear and socks, thermal long underwear, a toothbrush, a washcloth, and my flashlight, and I threw in a notebook and my wallet. I deliberately didn't take my master's license—required by the U.S. Coast Guard before a ship can move under its own power—because I was afraid they might discontinue the tow and steam ahead, and I did not want to take the *Lyra* to New Orleans. I did grab my camera and my Christmas present from Jack, a SpyderEdge serrated yachting knife (aptly named the "Rescue" model), and I changed my shoes for boots, as I didn't know how cold it would be. That was it.

Jack dropped me off in Topping at 1145 and, after thirty minutes spent fueling the plane and getting ready, we were off. It was cool. I was able to sit up front to Newport News, where the other pilot was waiting for us. We filed a flight plan and proceeded to Wilmington. I paid Al with a check—he had specified no credit cards—and was later reimbursed by Lykes, no questions asked. All Lykes required was the receipt.

I was the first to arrive in Wilmington, stepping into the executive terminal for charter and private flights in my ready-to-go-to-work clothes at 1400. Jack had called the Lykes agent there with the Wilmington Shipping Co., Thomas McReedy, to meet me at Wilmington Airport. He was waiting, as was Capt. Richard Toomey, then manager of Lykes's Norfolk office. So were the newsmen, the Coast Guard—ready to be helpful in any way—and a Marine Corps helicopter, a twin-rotor troop transport, RESCUE etched black on yellow beside the door. When the commercial helicopter pilot Lykes had called became ill, the marines had volunteered. The ship chandler, O. E. DuRant, Inc., of Wilmington, was also waiting with two boxes of food—cold cuts, bread, mustard and mayo, apples and grapefruit, Coke, milk, and bottled water; four brand-new handheld VHF radios and a cellular phone, plus charts of the crucial coastal area.

At 1420 Fred Judge and George Bradley, the two port engineers who had handled the dry-docking, arrived from Jacksonville, Florida, all dressed up and carrying big suitcases. From Baltimore they had gone to Florida to oversee some problems with the *Thompson Lykes,* which had been laid up in a Jacksonville yard for more than a year. Some of her equipment and spare parts were going to auction that day. Lykes flew the two men north in a private jet, which, they said, took them "right up to 37,000 feet and right back down." I'd like to know how much the bill for that one-hour flight was! Curtis Hall, the chief mate, was expected to arrive last. He had been attending school in Baltimore, and would arrive at 1550 by commercial airliner—but we couldn't wait. Daylight would run out fast. I was acquainted with all three members of my crew, although I had never sailed with any of them.

I talked to Captain Seelig from the terminal and, in the course of the conversation, he asked us each individually to swear to James Amoss, the CEO, and Eugene McCormick, president of Lykes Bros. Steamship Co., that we were taking the assignment voluntarily. Then the marine helicopter pilot briefed us, talking about the helmets we were to wear to protect our ears; goggles (no hats, because they could blow off or catch on something), and the fact that we would be lowered to the deck of the *Lyra* in a Billy Pugh net.

My ears perked up.

Billy Pugh was chief boatswain's mate on my father's U.S. Coast Guard FS (freight supply) 198 vessel in World War II, and I'd met Billy Pugh. In fact, he lives in Corpus Christi, Texas, and I saw him now and again whenever a Lykes vessel took me there. He's in the offshore supply business, outfitting oil rigs in the Gulf of Mexico, and became a multimillionaire, partly from inventing the Billy Pugh net. He first designed it for the Apollo program, and it was adapted for the oil rigs. It is made of orange nylon netting on an aluminum frame, and is pyramid-shaped at the top, where it attaches to a hook, and rectangular in the body, with three sides and bottom ade of net and one long side open. It carries two people facing each other, hugging their knees, and it lands on the steel deck—rump first. It is not a soft landing.

With the briefing out of the way, the engineers changed into work clothes, and I put on long underwear and foul-weather gear. Then the excitement began. We climbed aboard the helicopter at about 1500 and, just as we were ready to leave, a Maryland Airways flight arrived, bringing Curtis.

"That's the chief mate," I shouted. "Get him on board."

I don't know why I wasn't scared, but I wasn't. I don't think the other crew members were, either, although none of us had ridden in a helicopter before. During the ride I was sitting next to Fred Judge, an easygoing, cool guy, and a good shipmate. He sails regularly for Lykes as chief engineer, and fills in as a port engineer in the Boston area where he lives. Except for taking some pictures, I spent the flight thinking about what came next: trying to lower the anchors. What Captain Seelig had told me and what Jack had told me were two different things. Finally I leaned over to Fred, lifted his ear flap, and yelled, "We're not going to do what Captain Seelig told me to do at all."

Fred: "What did Jack tell you to do?"

"He told me to watch my ass."

"Yeah, you better do that."

All I could think about was Captain Seelig's order: "Here's what I want you to do. Start the emergency generator and walk out the anchors, both at the same time." Jack had warned me, from his experience, that they needed to be alternated, port and starboard, one with more anchor chain out than the other, to keep from tangling.

Seldom, rarely, do you have to use two anchors. If it's the weather that might warrant using two, most ships don't anchor. They heave to, or steam slowly until the weather moderates. If it's too rough to anchor, you don't anchor. The big problem of dropping two anchors is the possibility of getting them tangled; then they lose their holding power.

After about fifty minutes, the *Lyra* came into view.

What a sight! I felt sorry for the ship. She was in the trough. No control. I thought the inside was probably totally torn apart. I'd been through weather like that before passing hurricane Lillie in the Atlantic in 1990, and I know what it can do. With the ship in a tender condition, which is the way I like it, you experience five-degree rolls in flat calm, and ten- or fifteen-degree rolls don't bother you. In that case, the center of gravity is high. But this time she was in a stiff condition, with a low center of gravity. With no cargo to balance the fuel oil and ballast, she was riding high and doing thirty-five-degree snap rolls—eleven seconds over and back. That's when things start flying.

Initially, the *Mark McAllister* had said the reason she didn't hook up to the emergency tow cable was that the float buoy had been fouled by the stern section of the ship. As the helicopter approached the ship, however, we could see the buoy floating free. Maybe it had been fouled; only later did we learn that in that terrible weather, when the cable broke, the tug had been in extremis. Her steering gear room had flooded, she'd lost a generator, and she'd nearly lost a man overboard.

The *Mark McAllister* and the Coast Guard cutter *Staten Island* were standing by, circling, keeping track of the *Lyra*'s position; the ship had been drifting about nine and a half hours since she'd broken her tow at 0730 that morning. Now she was twenty-four miles northeast of Frying Pan Shoals, southwesterly set of 247 degrees, drift of three knots.

The helicopter had considered the possibility of landing, because there was flat deck eighty-nine feet wide for about five hundred feet forward of the house, but it was just too rough—the ship was rolling thirty to thirty-five degrees in winds of forty knots, with fifteen-foot seas. In fact, the marine captain, a Persian Gulf vet, said it was the worst weather he'd ever flown in! First, one of the marines was lowered in a collar that fit underneath his arms; his job was to hold a line attached to the top of the net to help control its direction as we landed. (Buildup of static electricity in the aluminum frame precluded him from touching the net itself until it reached the deck, or he'd have gotten quite a jolt.) Next came the two port engineers in the Billy Pugh net. Next, the equipment and stores, enough for four people for forty-eight hours, were lowered in the net, along with my carry-on and Curtis's duffle. As we hovered that fifty feet above the ship's deck, I looked down once through the helicopter door while the stores were being loaded, but I didn't think about it. Heights don't bother me anyway, so I guess that helped.

Last aboard were the chief mate and I. As the crew held the bottom of the Billy Pugh net even with the door of the helicopter, we crawled into it, one at a time, on our knees, then turned so we were facing each other, knees up under our chins. Quickly we swung outside the ventilator housing—a six-foot-high box along the railing that covers the intakes and exhaust vents for the lower decks—back in, and landed on the main deck. The whole operation took maybe ten minutes, max.

Curtis and I didn't get hurt, but the two engineers weren't so lucky. George Bradley, particularly, is very tall and he hit so hard that it jarred his head between his shoulders and jammed his left hip. That night he was feeling it; he was hurting, and after working on the emergency generator, he also felt sick from the diesel fumes.

In port, the port engineers had been in charge of the *Lyra*. But when I'd talked to Lykes from Wilmington, Captain Seelig had made my role perfectly clear: "You make the decision to stay on the ship, to anchor and get off or stay, or not land at all. You're in charge. You're the captain. You call it."

Suddenly there we were on the deck. The helicopter was hovering across the deck, nose into the wind, its red-painted bottom about fifty feet above us; it could have hovered for two hours or more. The ship was in the trough, rolling like hell. As instructed, I immediately tried to use the cellular phone to call Lykes. Nothing. We were too far out of range. I asked the engineers how they felt. George said, "I'm staying out here!" He didn't want to go back in that helicopter. So I told the marines, "Go. We'll stay. We're all right."

Because we'd just run the emergency generator for twenty-eight hours down the bay, we expected it to start right up. Using its power—our only source—we'd have the anchors lowered within the hour. But when Fred and George tried to start it, they had no luck.

After several attempts, it finally started at 1800, and it was a hell of a sight. Suddenly, in the darkness, all of the lights on the ship came on. The Coast Guard, standing by a quarter of a mile away, radioed with a cheer. Drifting in 108 feet of water, we began to walk out the port anchor. The generator ran for about twenty minutes, and, with only half a shot out, it overheated, boiling over. So we shut her down. Darkness again.

At sea, if something breaks down, you work at it until it's fixed, and we looked at this problem with the same determination. Thank God I'd scrounged that set of keys in Baltimore. With those keys, I was able to get into Brian's office and take from his desk my grand master. It's a set that only the captain, chief engineer, and chief mate on a Lykes ship have—and it can open any door on her. With my grand master I was able to get into the engineers' staterooms on A deck to get the immediate necessities: tools and new fuel filters to work on the emergency generator, flashlights—our *only* sources of light—and the VHF handheld radio I'd left behind—our *only* way to communicate with the *Staten Island* and the *Mark McAllister*—

because the new ones we'd brought aboard were useless. No one had thought to charge their batteries.

The doors to the engineers' spare parts lockers, like all others on the *Lyra,* open in, not an easy task to perform with all of the jumble left by the rolling ship. But after forcing the heavy sheet-metal door open and rummaging through everything, we found new fuel filters and replaced the old ones, working on a fuel-slick deck with only flashlight beams to see by.

Even getting the water to refill the radiator on the emergency generator was an enormous task. We scrounged empty gallon antifreeze jugs, with lids and handles, and filled them from the potable water supply tanks in the engine room on the next-to-bottom deck. Just imagine you're carrying two of those jugs in one hand, a two-cell flashlight and another jug in the other hand. The path is forward through the engine control room, up a four-foot-narrow ladder—steel stairs with a sharp incline and a railing on either side—to number two deck. Usually you keep three points out of four (hands and feet) touching the ship; with both hands full, all we could do is inch our way up and try to balance as best we could. Then it's out a heavy watertight steel-plate door, careful to put it on the hold-back hooks so it won't swing. If you get hit by one of those doors, you can get hurt. Now we're on centerline atop the keel. Walk aft to the starboard side fifty feet, feeling like you're in a huge parking garage with a dinky flashlight to guide you. Now through another doorway that leads to a narrower ladder, up two decks, by the ballast control room, by the rope locker, up another half flight to the emergency generator room. Close this steel door, used to seal off the emergency generator from water—just in case—and close the steel handles or hatch dogs, two each side, one each top and bottom, to tighten the seal against the gasket.

We restarted the generator at 1930. Lights went on again. After only ten minutes the generator shut down again, white hot. By this time we'd backed out one shot of chain on the port anchor, but unfortunately nothing on the starboard anchor. That's when I started worrying. We allowed the generator to cool down again, but this time it took two hours before we could refill the radiator. The first time each of us had made three trips back and forth; this time, five or six. And with George feeling too ill to help—just trying to keep down Coke and saltines—the task loomed larger. We attempted to restart the generator a third time, with no luck. Finally, we opened the inspection plates to examine the pistons. We could see the number three piston was seized up, and it would have to be rebuilt. We all realized then we had absolutely no power. It was a sobering moment. By now the winds were fifty to sixty knots, the seas eighteen feet.

We never dwelled on "what if" we don't stop the vessel. I knew that if we got one anchor down, we'd slow the ship's drift, whether or not she fetched up. To hold, in calm weather and in less than one hundred feet of water, you need anchor chain at least three times the depth of the water. In this case, the depth was 108 feet. Anchoring overnight, you need a ratio of five to one. Storm condition, seven to one. The more chain, the more scope.

But I was concerned that if we dropped the anchors without walking them out in water that deep, with the long drop and sheer weight—the anchor alone is 11,000 pounds, plus 11 shots at 7,670 pounds each—we would be unable to stop them. Luckily, during dry dock I'd insisted that the shot markings be painted on the ranged anchor chains. A red link indicates where shots are joined together by a detachable link; the number of white links on either side of it, the number of the shot. Spotting the painted links with a two-cell flashlight was the only way we could tell how much chain was out!

I never thought we *wouldn't* be successful. But by 2200 we were closing on the shoals and I was getting very impatient. The executives were sitting by the phone at their command post on the twenty-second floor of the New Orleans office, waiting until we anchored, ready to deal with an oil spill or call a helicopter to lift us off the ship, if need be. Without direct communication, our only link with New Orleans was through the Coast Guard or the tug. I was quite concerned that we weren't getting the anchors down; I felt we were running out of time for the engineers to mess with the emergency generator. Although I never expressed my concern to the others, I didn't think the ship would survive the night if we couldn't drop the anchors.

At 2300 we four went up to the bow, and I made a decision to go with what we had.

Just before midnight, we disengaged the wildcat, which hauls the chain out of the locker a deck below or puts it back in, and put the wildcat on the brake—a four-inch-wide band designed to keep the wildcat from turning by friction—so the chain could fall freely. Turning the two-foot-diameter hand wheel, we released the brake band and, in succession, we dropped the port anchor to number five shot

. . . next, starboard to number three . . . then port to number eight . . . starboard to five.

Our last go at the starboard anchor gave us the ultimate scare: We tried to stop it after three shots, and couldn't. Sparks flew. We tightened down on the brake, burning up the brake band. Finally, I threw the riding pawl—a big, heavy piece of solid steel with a half circle cut out of the middle—over the top of the runaway chain, caught a link, and stopped it. That was the good news. The bad news was that we could not let out any more chain on that anchor until we got power.

At 2350 I relayed a message to the office via the *Staten Island:* "We're fetched—holding our position." Those gathered in Lykes's office cheered.

When the tugboat had called headquarters at 0730 to report she'd broken her tow, the *Lyra* was within fifty miles of Frying Pan Shoals; by 2400 she was only sixteen miles off—but the anchors were holding. When we had gone a full hour and our position hadn't changed, we knew we were no longer in an emergency situation. That was the best moment.

Unable to get the generator started, we set about camping out on the ship. At that point we'd been on board for eight hours, with only a short break for a snack while we waited for the generator to cool down. So our first priority was food. We had no way to heat anything, but bologna sandwiches and milk, plus cookies and such, did the trick. George was still on saltines and Coke.

Next, we set up one of the three new portable toilets that had been put aboard the ship in Baltimore. Because the toilet needed water to flush it, we set it up where the water supply was—in the lower engine room. There was another advantage to putting it at that low point in the ship—it had the least roll. On Thursday, when I finally moved to my quarters, I set up a toilet in my own head, but I had to carry up water in a bucket from the engine room to use it. It's a long way up seven decks.

We had set up headquarters in a conveniently located cabin on the main deck. That cabin is better known as the Suez Canal Workers' Room: When we transit the canal, it is occupied by three Egyptian boatmen, aboard in case we have to tie up to the bank of the canal, and an electrician, there to man the spotlight. For two days we ate, worked, and slept in there.

With the ship doing quick rolls every eleven seconds, you try to sleep what little you can while bracing yourself with your hands and feet. That first night was the coldest—about forty degrees. It gradually warmed to fifty during the week. Without electricity, the whole ship was cold, and there's nothing colder than cold steel. Except for being out of the wind, being inside didn't help. I slept in the same clothes I wore for four days: long underwear, khaki trousers, turtleneck, work vest, long-sleeved wool shirt, Patagonia Polartec jacket, and Polartec gloves and hat. It was such dirty work that I didn't change trousers or shirt all week.

The engineers had brought everything to Wilmington in big suitcases, which were left behind there; they caught up with us in Charleston. As it turned out, I was definitely the most prepared—I even ended up lending them socks and such, and was glad to do so. I was also the only one with a toothbrush. I made a lot of money renting it out!

The cabin, if none too attractive, at least had two upper and two lower bunks. George took the lower bunk on the inside set against the bulkhead; he was feeling the ill effects of his hard landing and seasickness, and without insulated coveralls on, he was quite cold. Curtis, younger than George and more willing and able to put up with the conditions, was above him. Fred was in the other lower bunk, which had no bulkhead on either side; above him we threw the survival suits and life jackets we'd collected. I had no intention of getting in that upper bunk.

I found all kinds of flashlights and batteries, and more wool blankets for everyone, then prepared my own spot on the deck. I found a mattress pad and a couple of pillows for insulation—the floor is steel with a thin carpeting on it. I catnapped that night athwartships, bundled in wool blankets and wedged in next to a table leg, checking our position periodically with the tug and the Coast Guard. The *Staten Island* was now in the lee of Frying Pan Shoals for protection—once we'd anchored, she'd headed there to get her thoroughly seasick crew out of the swells.

With the ship secure and basic living conditions addressed, I finally had time to consider my crew.

If I couldn't have Eric Wilcox, Curtis Hall was the best of the three choices available for chief mate. A Massachusetts Maritime grad, Curtis is a tall sandy blond in his mid-thirties, and a hard worker. His failing is that he tends to pit deck against engine. But that was a problem I was aware of and knew I could deal with. Toward the end of the week, he did get into a tangle with Fred that I had to stop. He got exasperated with George, too, because he didn't do much of the heavy work.

George Bradley was the only other Maine Maritime grad (class of '66) aboard besides me. If I'm type A, he's a type B personality. He moves at one speed: medium slow. As a port engineer, he is used to working over the phone, not doing physical work. He was the organizer—he took excellent notes, he's orderly, and he even offered to be the cook and organize the food. After two days in tight quarters, I finally went to my quarters to get away from him for a while.

Fred Judge, an active chief engineer, is more hands-on. When we were in the Sparrows Point Yard in Baltimore, he did legwork for George. Fred's Mass Maritime, too, class of '55, and he had also sailed with Jack, on the *Howell Lykes.* He did a lot of the heavy work with us. I could tell Fred to do something and he'd take care of it. I also knew I could count on Fred for straight answers and I could discuss things with him without their getting back to the office. He looks like a Boston Irishman, mustache and all, and he's a good shipmate—as is Brian. In fact, he was the one who had trained Brian in diesel engines, so he really was able to help Brian when he arrived on Wednesday.

With my husband, Jack, as my mentor, I'd learned a lot about dealing with crew that stood me in good stead as captain. Jack had a great reputation, and Curtis knew Jack—generally if a crew member didn't know me, he lumped me in with Jack. As for the port engineers, most captains don't give them the time of day, but Jack did, and I did. We'd do anything for them, and they would do anything for us. Jack also taught me to include the engine room in making rounds of the ship. He did, but most captains don't. It certainly makes for better rapport with the engineers if you do.

Early Wednesday morning a Coast Guard helicopter hovered to announce that it was bringing Brian (who was flying in from Boston) that afternoon. It asked us what we needed. We asked for a cellular phone; a portable gas generator to charge batteries for the phone and the VHF radios we'd brought aboard with us, and some already-charged batteries; a Coleman stove and lantern; and hamburger—the latter a request we made repeatedly through the week to no avail! The Coast Guard, despite its regulations against flying out gasoline for the generator, looked the other way and did so.

Also on Wednesday morning, we began to hear a regular, high-pitched noise made by something loose, steel grating against steel with each roll.

We thought the stern ramp might be loose. It wasn't. I even crawled up the kingpost to the catwalk on the fantail where the ramp secures to check. Then, back on the bridge, I noticed the rudder angle indicator was off twenty degrees. That was it. Unbelievably, the rudder had jumped its lock! We had another major problem to deal with: the rudder had to be locked parallel to the ship before we could get under tow again.

Waiting for the helicopter's return, we turned to cleaning up what we could on the ship, and in the afternoon we snoozed in the sun by the pool, sheltered from the wind. Actually, we were pleased that what we had done to secure the ship in Baltimore had held up pretty nicely. But the bridge was a shambles, with papers everywhere. One drawer had fallen out, and it was pretty much destroyed. A door had fallen off. In the interior of the ship, the stewards' and engineers' storerooms were really messed up, with the sea tossing equipment and pots and pans every which way.

At 1400 the *Staten Island* was replaced by the buoy tender *Cowslip* out of Hampton Roads, Virginia. About three hours later the tug *Turecamo Boys* from Charleston replaced the *Mark McAllister.* That was my first clue that we were going to be towed to Charleston rather than Wilmington, which was much closer, but Lykes had its reasons—the company had better relations with the Coast Guard there than in Wilmington. Moving the ship farther from the scene also removed it somewhat from the news.

With the ship continuing to roll, we were constantly thinking about it and we were uncomfortable all of the time. We couldn't even set a cup down. The turbulence also meant that Brian couldn't land, but had to be lowered from the helicopter along with the supplies, as we had been. He arrived about 1500, waving a sheaf of Wilmington *Morning Star* newspapers.

"You're in the news now!" he greeted us through his full black beard.

In Brian, who'd been one of two chief engineers with me on the *Lyra* since 1989, we had the experience we needed to prepare the main generators to run again. (The *Lyra* has two MAN main engines, medium-speed diesels with 16,000 horsepower, each with a generator.) Brian, a '79 Mass Maritime grad, is young to be a chief engineer—but very ambitious. He also helped us regroup and reenergize. Brian's an excellent morale booster—you see him coming and immediately start smiling. And he's a good friend.

Despite the absence of hamburger, that night Brian set up the Coleman stove he brought, using duct tape to put it in place and make sure it didn't slide off the table. Meanwhile, Fred went into first assistant Peter Smith's room and thought he had found a whole case of Bud Light. He kicked it—all empties! I scrounged in the stewards' storeroom and got some utensils, a tablecloth, and even a messman's white jacket and hat, which I put on. We had some hot chicken noodle soup for dinner, hot coffee, and that was nice.

Later that night when I was up on the bridge, checking the anchor, touching base with the Coast Guard, I got to thinking. I went back down and looked in the first assistant's refrigerator—sure enough, three beers. The five of us shared them the next day. And on the tow down the bay, Brian and I had asked Peter Smith if he had more beer, and he'd said no. Turkey!

When Brian had arrived in Wilmington Tuesday night, the first thing Captain Toomey had said to him was, "Don't say anything to the media!" But Brian, as gregarious as he is, couldn't help it. When Captain Toomey turned on his television set for late news, there was Brian, being interviewed. His part in the *Lyra* rescue?

"I gotta go out and turn on the lights."

And he did. Typical Brian—expecting to be up all night working on the portable generator, he rigged up what looked like a miner's cap, using a white safety helmet with "Visitor" stenciled on the front, and flashlights taped on each side. It was pretty useful.

Thursday, and Friday, too, were quite calm, with very little wind, although there were still swells. The tug *Turecamo Boys* was standing by; the crew of the *Cowslip* spent most of the day Thursday playing games in her inflatable, and having a good time until she departed about 1400.

The portable generator supplied by a repair yard in Wilmington weighed about fifteen hundred pounds, and Lykes was unable to locate a heavy-lift helicopter to bring it out on Thursday. But Captain Toomey asked if I thought it was worthwhile to try and bring it alongside, on the back of a launch. A definite yes. More waiting.

At 1745 an Omni Air helicopter brought out two Automated Marine Propulsion (AMP) service engineers from Galveston, David Owens and Mario Radman, to start dismantling the emergency generator so they could rebuild it. They were familiar with it; they had worked with us on the *Lyra* from Galveston to Jacksonville when we were going under charter in the Persian Gulf in 1990. But they came with only their personal gear, no generator parts. Those came on another helicopter twenty-four hours later.

About 2000, the cutter *Block Island* showed up, with blue lights flashing as if she were coming to arrest us—a comical sight in the middle of nowhere.

"*Lyra, Lyra,* where are you?"

The captain was a rookie, and what a pain in the neck the cutter turned out to be! Personnel called every two hours for updates, despite my reassurance that there was one scenario and it didn't change: We'd fried the emergency generator, we had no main generators operating, and all we could do was wait for a portable generator to start our air compressor and build up enough air to, in turn, start one of the main generators, pick up the anchors, and get back under tow.

At 2145 a commercial launch, *Scuba South Two,* came out carrying a portable generator strapped to her deck. She hooked onto our starboard quarter and we put a line to her and made it fast. Then we hauled up the shore power cable—three hundred feet of one-inch braided wire, pretty heavy stuff—on our starboard side. Meanwhile the launch was hanging on ninety feet of nylon mooring line, snapping in the swell. The engineer who had come out to maintain the generator got seasick.

We finally got hooked up, and he started the portable generator at 2310. We could hear it running, and everybody went to the engine room/control room. We were running our air compressor so we could get the air built up to supply power to start one of the main generators. The generator ran for forty-five minutes, but we had our compressor on line for only the last twenty seconds before we lost it. And they never could get the portable generator restarted: The diaphragm in the fuel pump had ruptured.

I got extremely slaphappy as we sat there watching the voltage meter nosedive, and I told every single dirty joke I had in my repertoire. I entertained the engineers and shocked them thoroughly. We had a good time. Brian had brought an army cot to the engine control room, and he was in bed while we were telling stories. Finally, the rest of us except for the AMP engineers, who worked around the clock dismantling the emergency generator, went to sleep. I'd been dozing barely an hour when the *Block Island* called for an update.

I told him in unkind words, "If I need you, I'll call you. You just woke me up. And nothing's changed."

By 0400 I'd called Captain Toomey about the failure of the portable generator, then sent word to the *Scuba South Two* to return shoreside immediately. The plan was to get this generator repaired, or locate another one and send it out via helicopter.

We'd been anchored since Tuesday night. Early Friday things began to happen.

About 0830 the Omni Air helicopter landed the two surveyors from the Salvage Association—Capt. John Vickers, the blocky British seaman who had done the original survey, and A. G. Green, an engineer. Mr. Green went back that morning, but Captain Vickers stayed with us. They came specifically to look at the rudder, and quickly headed for the steering gear room.

That rudder is about twenty feet high and about sixteen feet wide. To keep the rudder upright, atop the rudder post is a gigantic hex nut—nearly three feet in diameter and eight inches thick. Before we left Baltimore, one-inch steel plate had been welded on top of the hex nut. Then that plate was welded to the I beam above it in the steering gear room, all to lock the rudder amidships, parallel with the ship. At that time everybody thought that plate, a half-day welding job in the yard, was overkill. But what Captain Vickers found was that the nut had slipped the lock and had shifted one hex to the left, leaving the rudder about twenty degrees to starboard.

The tug's version of the story is that the slippage caused the tow cable to break, but we don't know *when* it slipped. Timing is crucial *if* the question comes up in a lawsuit. All we knew was that Wednesday morning after we anchored the vessel was the first time we heard the noise. Now the I beam was bent downward, distorted, and we couldn't go back under tow until the rudder was once more amidships. We finally locked it again with steel wedges, which fell out, and the rudder ended up fifteen degrees out. Finally we started the steering gear and left it on to keep the rudder amidships for the tow into Charleston.

At 1230 Friday, an American Airlift heavy-lift Sikorsky helicopter out of St. Louis landed the thirty-five-kilowatt generator that was hanging below it on our main deck. By 1315 we had that portable generator hooked up to our shore power connection, and we figured it would take three hours to get our main generator up and running. The helicopter left and returned at 1500 with all of the spare parts the two AMP engineers needed to rebuild our emergency generator.

Also on Friday afternoon, Captain Vickers, Curtis, and I started beefing up the emergency tow bridle, replacing its twenty-five-ton shackles with the fifty-ton shackles from the now-useless main tow bridle. And we talked the *Turecamo Boys* into making up to our emergency tow cable before it got dark, figuring as soon as the main generator was on line, we'd go. The tug didn't want to make up to us until we heaved one of the anchors, figuring they're twisted sure as heck after the ship had been swinging on them for four days. And you don't want a tug made up to you if you've got fouled anchors—that limits maneuverability for the tug.

Remember, the tow cable is a two-inch braided wire cable, six hundred feet long, tied off with small stuff along the port rail, with a float buoy trailing in the water a couple of hundred feet behind us. We threw a heaving line to the tug and attached to the heaving line we had one of our mooring lines. The tug pulled that aboard first, and it was attached to the tow cable. The tug could have broken the small lines that tied the tow cable along the port side of the *Lyra,* but we were afraid the stanchions or railing might get bent in the process, so I cut the small lines away with my knife to free the tow cable as he was hooking up. Brian finally got one of the main generators on line as we finished hooking up at about 1745, and at 1808 we began to heave the starboard anchor. Hooking up, a three-hour ordeal, had involved a lot of bull work for the three of us, and we were quite exhausted by then.

We were supposed to call Lykes at 1800, and along came George to the bow with the cellular telephone. He was always punctual with the scheduled calls to the office, which had become frequent. In very unkind words I told him what he could do with the phone. It had looked as if the starboard anchor was clear, but it wasn't; there was one round turn of port anchor chain around its shank. That was the last straw. "George," I said, "you want to play captain, you play captain." So he made the call. I didn't care what he told the office. I just thought, "Is this ever going to be over?"

That was the only time I really lost my cool, which as captain I consciously try not to do. I did call the office later, and they were all upset, because George had told them everything was hunky-dory.

What do we do now? We tried to clear the anchor. Nothing. The weather was deteriorating, the tug was made up, and she had pulled us over the top of our anchors so she wouldn't get fouled in them. The only solution seemed to be to cut away the starboard anchor.

Over the cellular phone, Captain Seelig said in haste, "Well, cut both anchors. Just get out of there."

"Okay."

Afterward, he realized what he'd said, and worried about my response. But I wouldn't have cut both, anyway!

At 2145 we got the acetylene and oxygen bottles and torches on deck and up to the bow. Next, we laid cardboard on the deck to block the wind from coming up the hawsepipe and blowing out the torches. Brian and Fred began to cut a link in the starboard anchor chain to let the anchor fall. We were able to heave the anchor, or pick it up, to the surface of the water, about thirty feet below. The usual procedure would have been to attach a buoy to the anchor first, so that we could have gone back and found it; anchors sell by the pound, and this one was about eleven thousand pounds. In this case we didn't bother, because it had to drop through the chain of the port anchor, and we thought the buoy line probably wouldn't have survived.

Cutting the link took less time than we'd expected—eighteen minutes. Now, the theory was that the freed anchor would drop right out of the round turn of the port anchor chain—a good theory for rope, but it doesn't work with chain. We began to pick up the port anchor, a shot at a time, and halfway between shot three and shot two here's the starboard anchor, still hanging from the port anchor chain. So we put the port anchor on the brake again, disengaged it, and let it go. One hundred feet, and boom, it hit bottom—we hoped the starboard anchor would fall off. Next, we put the windlass back in gear and we picked up the port anchor again, three minutes per shot. This time the starboard anchor's still entangled in the port anchor chain, but it had slid down to the shot two position. We went through the same routine again, and this time when we brought up the anchor chain, it was clear. That was at 2235.

When I had realized the anchors were fouled, I'd called the tug captain to tell him. Emphatically, he said, "I told you we shouldn't have made up until the anchors were picked up."

"If you didn't want this job," I retorted, "you shouldn't have come out here." He didn't say anything else.

Later, when we were messing with cutting the anchor, I'd set the radio down and from the tug came, "Well, honey, how're you doing?" Total silence among all of the engineers. I just picked up the radio and said, "Excuse me?" He replied, "Uh, how's everything going back there?"

By 2250 we were under tow, headed for Charleston, and I felt great!

We'd only snacked all day; in fact, we'd hardly stopped working from the time we started fixing the tow cable until we were under way. So we all were ready for some food—and drink. We were prepared with both.

Richard Toomey had tried throughout the week to send us beer. Every time he tried, the cameras were rolling and he had to back off. However, when Fred was talking to him on Thursday, Fred said, "When the helicopter comes out, please send my blue shoulder bag. It has my medicine in it."

"What kind of medicine?"

"Blood pressure medicine."

The "medicine" was a bottle of Bushmills Irish whiskey. (The request had some residual effects—on Friday the office became concerned that Fred had a bleeding ulcer and was in medical trouble!)

About 0500 Saturday we cleared Frying Pan Shoals, the word the office was waiting for. We were no longer an environmental threat or the concern of the U.S. Coast Guard. They, along with Lykes's people, had had a seventy-man task force along the North Carolina shoreline ever since the ship broke loose, just in case they were needed to deal with pollution control. And the Coast Guard expected to be reimbursed for that time by the persons responsible for the tow cable parting.

The media had been following our progress closely, and even before we got under tow Friday night, the office was making arrangements for a press conference when we reached Charleston on Sunday. They wanted to know what we needed for an interview: Did we have clean khakis, did we need shirts? And who had his or her license, and who needed one, in case we continued under our own power to New Orleans? Curtis had been at the union school outside of Baltimore, preparing to sit for his master's exam—which he didn't get to take because of the rescue. Poor guy. Curtis is a single parent and takes his job seriously. They had to send his gear and license from the school. The engineers had to get theirs, too, but Brian had had more time to prepare and had brought his. Jack sent my license by Federal Express to Captain Toomey in Wilmington; he brought it to Charleston.

Saturday morning we faced a big job. We had to pick up the 90 feet of main tow chain, 150 feet of twelve-inch shock line, and the 100 feet of broken tow cable. We couldn't enter Charleston harbor with it dragging the bottom. We started right after breakfast. Captain Vickers had a plan. We'd bring the towline up in thirty-foot bights, using one of the electric mooring line winches to do the bull work. We'd attach the eye of the mooring line to the towline with a wire strap. We'd pull up thirty feet, stopper it off, disconnect the eye, go back and reattach it for another thirty-foot bight. It was tedious. It took three of us five hours. I learned a lot about salvage from Captain Vickers that morning.

"Do you do a lot of jobs like this one?" I had asked him.

"Yeah," he said, "but they're usually not my own jobs!" As the surveyor for Lykes in Baltimore, he had approved the tow.

Finally, starting about 1630 we all had showers—all except Brian. Nice guy that he is, he turned on the water heater, watched the water level go down, and just about the time we got to him, he had to shut the pump off because we ran out of water.

Saturday night we had a great last meal—SpaghettiOs, lettuce and tomato salad. I stayed up late talking to the AMP engineers, and when I headed to my quarters for the last time, sitting in my chair was the bottle with the last bit of the Bushmills. I saved it and drank it after we finished tying up in Charleston at 0300 Sunday.

That was a real fiasco, too. When we picked up the harbor pilot, T. Peterson, at the sea buoy, I expected him to come up to the bridge. Instead, he was doing his job from the tug, *Turecamo Boys*. The docking master, Tim West, came up on the ship. I don't know whether Peterson was jealous or what, but next thing I knew, he was up on the bridge, too. Without crew aboard we had no docking hands. So before we reached Charleston, I had called and asked Jim Murray, Lykes's office manager there, to send out a mooring gang. They had come out to the sea buoy with West in one of the three tugs—four boys right out of high school, and inexperienced. Curtis had to go aft and I had to go forward, each of us with two of these boys helping.

Curtis finally told the engineers we needed help! Brian and George ran the winches. I was just barking orders. Even with three tugs working us, it took a long time to tie up. In the process, the docking master had to turn the ship around. He didn't want to do it—it's hard to move a dead ship—but we had to, because the gray-painted spare anchor was stored on the fo'c'sle deck, on the starboard side of the bow, and we needed to get at it with a dockside crane and get it reattached before we could continue coastwise to New Orleans.

I could see the Coast Guard waiting on the dock with Jim Murray, Jack, and the media, TV cameras rolling. The Coast Guard came aboard with two hours' worth of questions, but George and I didn't have many answers because we hadn't had much to do with the tow.

The next few hours passed in an exhausted blur: a couple of hours of sleep, breakfast with everybody, more Coast Guard quizzing, interviews orchestrated with crib notes by Lykes's public relations director, Ardley Hanneman; watching the Super Bowl with Jack and the crew at a sports bar, dinner at a local steak house. Monday morning the tow company showed up with a flatbed truck to haul away their equipment; the anchor was being reattached, and the emergency generator was still being reassembled. At 1000 Monday there was a full-scale press conference, with all five crew in attendance and in uniform—white Lykes ball caps, khakis, and shoulder boards. Thank goodness I'd brought clothes. Curtis had to buy khakis and a shirt, to the tune of $120. In his haste, he came up with the wrong style shirt, and I ended up taping his shoulder boards in place.

In order to get Lykes off the front pages, Mr. Amoss and Mr. McCormick decided to recrew the ship rather than tow her the rest of the way, although I think my boss and the engineers' boss were against it. It meant we had to undo all we did to lay her up in Baltimore, then redo it in New Orleans. We had to send for a full medical locker, dispersing what needed to be refrigerated to the galley, the narcotics to my safe. The galley lockers were still a mess, with pots and pans everywhere from the ship's rolling, and the steward had to contend with that, along with taking stores. Among other problems, there was dealing with what became a pickup crew because it was only for three and a half days. Everybody was brand-new to the ship. As it turned out, one of the ABs (able seamen) had never even steered—the main job of an AB. I wanted to get off right there in Charleston.

Otherwise, the coastwise trip was not too bad. We had a quartering sea that made the ship roll ten to fifteen degrees, just enough to be annoying. We had fairly nice days, and we were making wonderful speed. I'd given Captain Seelig a conservative ETA for Southwest Pass, mouth of the Mississippi, of 0800 Saturday, then improved it to 0600, then 0200. The weather held until we arrived at Southwest Pass, about 0100. On our way up the Mississippi I was working with the third mate, the channel was very busy with traffic, and the weather turned very foul and it was blowing like hell.

I was glad to see the river pilot, Don Johnson, come aboard. I didn't remember him, but he remembered me. When I was chief mate on the *Marjorie Lykes,* his Texas A&M maritime class had come to the ship when it called in Galveston for a firsthand look at handling cargo, the chief mate's main responsibility.

With the *Lyra* in good hands, I took a nap on the settee on the bridge until a phone call interrupted. The New Orleans port captain, Joe Bridges, along with Mr. Castro and MARAD representatives, planned to board an hour before docking, and we were asked to have a gangway ready. The ship had been sold at sea, based on our 0900 position Friday, and the parties wanted to sign the papers before the ship reached the dock, in case a federal marshal was there to put a lien on the ship on behalf of the towing company with which Lykes had broken the contract.

At 0800 Friday I'd had a message from Captain Seelig: "Call this office at 0830." I was in the radio shack placing the satellite call when we lost the plant, and I couldn't call until 0855 when we got it back. Before I was able to explain, Captain Seelig chewed me out. When I did explain, he just said, "Oh, yeah."

Fortunately, we were still in international waters, a criterion for effecting the sale. Several hours later this message arrived: "Attn: Master. FYIG [for your information and guidance]. Your vessel has officially been transferred to MARAD and is now property of U.S. Government effective 1100 hours Feb. 5, 1993. Regards." We felt terrible—just blah. There goes one more ship. The crew had saved the ship only to lose their jobs.

In fact, the transfer went through without a hitch at the dock, legal or otherwise, and we were very relieved when the last of the eight forward and eight aft lines was secured.

After we docked, there was unfinished work to fill the better part of the week. We had to pump off about 5,500 barrels of fuel, leaving five days' worth, or 1,500 barrels, as contracted. We had to pay off the crew and close up shop. I had paperwork galore. One day I worked with the ship engineers. Then there was a session with Captain Bridges's daughter's kindergarten class. And Jack and I attended a Council of American Master Mariners luncheon in New Orleans, where I said a few words about the rescue.

Tuesday afternoon I made the rounds of Lykes's headquarters, which was notable for several reasons, not the least of which was that it was the first occasion on which Captain Seelig called me Captain Dempsey. But the first words out of his mouth were, "I sent you out there because you're one of our better captains. I didn't send you because you were a woman."

I thought to myself, "I never thought you had." Someone must have been bugging him about it.

Ashore the men treat me like a woman. They're all gentlemen; they hold the door, hold my chair. But on the ship, the female part isn't there. In fact, I probably went overboard to have the female part *not* enter into the equation—that's not a problem Lykes needed to have. From Brian's perspective, I was "no different from a male captain." If I didn't pull my weight, the crew would have been annoyed, so I went out of my way—I carried jugs of water and cleaned diesel oil off the engine-room deck. I did as much bull work as the rest of them. Besides, I liked working with them. I like getting dirty.

I had only met Curtis once briefly, when I relieved another captain, before he became my chief mate during the rescue. But he said he had always heard about me. The previous Saturday afternoon, before going into Charleston and after we'd spent several long hours picking up all of that tow cable together, Curtis and I were relaxing out on the flying bridge for a minute. I'd offered to let him use the phone up there to call his children. "Now I know why everybody asks, 'Where's Debbie Dempsey?'" he commented.

In the long run, it will be nice when people quit asking about the female question.

I stopped by to see Capt. Rick Manchester, my former boss, on the twenty-first floor. After all of his years in crisis management, no one had asked him for his advice during the *Lyra* incident. I sensed that they didn't like him in MNR; he, in turn, was put out by all of the attention we got. His only comment: "A crisis is over in eight minutes. Then you just deal with things as they come up."

"Really." It was all I could reply.

Dressed in the obligatory skirt, I also went up one more floor to meet with Mr. Amoss and Mr. McCormick, who gave me a warm reception. They showed me the chart they had kept during the rescue, and the phone where they'd accepted our "volunteer" offers to rescue the *Lyra*. I was pleased when I found out that a six-foot model of the *Lyra*, which had been at headquarters, was being presented to Maine Maritime Academy, my alma mater.

And I picked up my paycheck—no bonus. In fact, I got the lowest pay because, according to the system, it included only the built-in daily hour of overtime, and no more. The chief mate made out much better than I did.

Lykes did, however, have quite a party for us—in conjunction with the tenth anniversary of taking the company private. About seventy guests gathered in the lovely second-floor Bella Luna Room overlooking the levee near New Orleans's French Market. Besides all of the Lykes brass, there were representatives of the tow company and the Salvage Association. A guest from the mayor's office presented us each with a proclamation. Mr. McCormick introduced us and Mr. Amoss gave us each several letters, including ones from the Military Sealift Command and the North Carolina governor's office. A third letter was a total surprise. Dated 8 February, it read:

Dear Debbie,

I am pleased to join with your family and friends in commending you for your courageous achievement of rescuing the unmanned vessel, MV Lyra.

Because of the efforts of dedicated individuals like you who place the safety and well-being of others above their own, our Nation is a better place in which to live. Your act of daring bravery not only saved a ship, but prevented a devastating environmental disaster.

Thank you for a job well done.

Sincerely,
President Bill Clinton

It was quite a letdown when Jack and I went back to our motel that night, sort of the same feeling I'd had when our wedding was over. I had been very much in the limelight, and I didn't get much chance to eat the fantastic dinner—everybody wanted to talk. I finally brought back something from a nearby restaurant!

Other honors followed.

In June 1993 the *Lyra* received one of three lifesaving awards given by the Seamen's Church Institute at its annual fund-raising dinner in New York. I was there to accept.

The following October, on behalf of the crew of five, I received the AOTOS Honored Seamen Award from the United Seamen's Service at a black-tie dinner in New York. AOTOS stands for Admiral of the Ocean Sea and is named for Christopher Columbus. The award is given to officers and crews of American vessels for outstanding seamanship in rescue operations at sea.

A year later, during a ceremony at the U.S. Merchant Marine Academy at Kings Point, New York, my team and I became the twenty-fourth recipient of the American Merchant Marine Seamanship Trophy, which recognizes extraordinary seamanship demonstrated by American mariners. The winner of the annual award was chosen by a select committee chaired by Adm. Albert J. Herberger, U.S. maritime administrator, and comprised of representatives of maritime labor and management.

On Saturday, a week after we'd safely docked the *Lyra,* I drove by to see her for the last time on the way to the airport. It's not too bad to leave a ship when you expect to return, but knowing I might never see her again made me feel rotten. Now, instead of the distinctive black hull and white house, she's painted gray, she's the *Cape Texas* out of Norfolk—and she's no longer mine.

Six months later I received a bill from a car rental company for $42.45 to repair a flat tire. I'd picked up a nail from a piece of dunnage, waste wood used to protect cargo on a ship, on the dock on that last drive by the *Lyra.* One more fond remembrance.

For Lykes, selling the *Lyra* meant, "Boy, did we get rid of a problem and are we glad to do so." She was the newest and most modern of Lykes's ships, but too expensive to operate because the company was not geared for a RO/RO operation. In fact, she and three other RO/RO vessels broke Hansa Lines, the German shipping company that was the oldest in Europe. For me, the *Lyra* represented a wonderful, specialized ship to operate with good people in a great working relationship. A *Lyra* life ring and house flag, mementos of my first trip aboard her, will always be reminders. I miss her terribly.

Landlubber's Log
1–2 February 1994

Tuesday, 1 February

We've been up since 0415, on the road since 0500 sharp with Capt. Jack Dempsey driving the van from Kilmarnock, and we arrive at the *Charlotte,* an Express class containership, about 0700. One of four Lykes Lines freighters on the liner Med service, it's scheduled to make the circuit every fifty days. The engineers kiddingly call it the "distress" class. Lots of distress calls to the engineers, maybe?

Before the stevedores begin working cargo at 0800 we are able to load all my gear aboard—up to the fourth deck of the house, or superstructure. There are three cabins, plus a room for the passengers' convenience where the washer (which alternates power with the copier down one deck) and dryer keep company with a big refrigerator. As each crew member comes along, Debbie makes introductions. That's unusual, they tell me later, and they like it. Other captains don't bother. No sooner have we—my husband, Jim; our daughter, Julie; and the captains Dempsey—had breakfast in the dining saloon than it's off to lunch at favorite Uncle Louie's, followed by a little last-minute shopping. Lots of kinds of fancy coffee, lots of bananas, and *lots* of pop (three cases of root beer and five of ginger ale that the ship chandler had failed to deliver). It's up to the captain to get it, or everyone to do without.

Debbie has thought of everything: a quick glass of champagne for the five of us, with nuts (is there a message there?), and a Lykes Bros. T-shirt and visor for me, the only passenger. Quick good-byes, and then Jim, Julie, and Jack are waving from the dock.

The tug is made fast on the stern and pushes us away from the dock, then helps us turn bow-forward to follow an Evergreen containership loaded with green boxes out of the harbor. As we glide past the navy yard, the *Seattle* is getting ready to sail. We spot the *Mark McAllister,* the tug involved in the ill-fated tow of the *Lyra.*

We leave Norfolk about 1630 in a cold, gray wind, snow flurrying and low visibility, after a very long day. I watch up on the bridge until we clear the Chesapeake Bay Bridge Tunnel, about 1730, with lights coming up everywhere.

Then I head for the dining saloon on the first deck of the super-structure, one above the main deck. Crew quarters are on the sec-ond, captain's office and quarters are on the third, passengers the fourth, the bridge the fifth. Choosing dinner from the printed menu, I eat—alone. There are four tables in an "L"—with white table-cloths, no less—where the deck officers and engineers eat. Unli-censed crew eat the same food, but have their own saloon. Meals are *early*—the sign posted in my cabin says you must be at breakfast by 0800, lunch by 1200, and dinner by 1730 in order to be served. All Lykes ships serve the same menu, and Debbie's warned me the food leaves something to be desired. We'll see. I understand already why we brought our own coffee.

I'm at the captain's table, but the captain is working. And either the chief mate, Bob Strobel, has been and gone, or he is not eating. He usually shares her table and doesn't want to move to another this trip, so we will be a threesome. Afterward, I keep Debbie company while she eats in her office (the galley crew had called her on the bridge to see what she'd like, then kept dinner warm for her) and nearly fall asleep to MacNeil and Lehrer. Off to bed—one of two small twins, its head toward the bow, wooden sides to keep the mattress from sliding off if the ship rolls, drawers beneath to hold clothes. For-ward window shades are pulled to keep the light in—it would distract on the bridge—but not the cold out. The cabin is cold, I'm cold, and, after a Dramamine, I sleep in fits and starts. At three-something I finally put the top to my sweats over my nightgown, add a third wool blanket, and sleep until "they" test gear at 0730 and wake me!

Wednesday, 2 February

Good thing the mythical "they" do. I quickly get a shower in the center passenger cabin, which I'm using for my office but which has the more desirable shower—it has walls on three sides and not just two. It's a handheld nozzle, so part of me is always cold, part warm and wet. So is the floor and bathmat outside the shower, as the water sloshes when the ship moves. Deb has provided special—larger—towels for passengers. Then I dress in my cabin, the port passenger cabin, chosen after some urging from Jim and Julie as it opens directly onto the aft deck so I don't have to go outside through a passage. The outside door lets in soot, but we put a mat in front of it to solve that problem. The cabin also contains a dressing table with mirror and chair (unused the whole voyage), a couch that makes into a bed (with wooden slats that slide into slots to keep a sleeper from falling off), and two hanging lockers with cupboards above them to hold life jackets.

Down one deck, I make the first of many pots of drip coffee using the hot pot, Melitta filters, and fancy coffee from the refrigerator in the captain's office. While it drips, I check out the captain's plants, tapes and CDs, family pictures she has brought with her to make the ship feel more like home. Then I head for the bridge for the morning ride into Port Elizabeth, New Jersey.

I'm ready for anything. I have a parka—a bitter breeze blows through the bridge when both doors to the wings on either side are open—and binoculars around my neck, pen and note pad stuffed in my jeans pocket, and coffee cup with a lid, the saving grace later on a rolling ship. In reserve is a pocket flashlight with a red shield, so the light won't interfere with anyone's night vision.

Second mate Don Josberger provides the morning's levity. What is supposed to be "go get the pilot and relieve the mate" is reversed and gives everyone a laugh—we haven't even picked up the pilot taking us into Port Elizabeth yet. Don takes third mate Amy La Cost's place on the bridge, while she heads for the stern.

I'd met Amy before, in Norfolk at an Uncle Louie's lunch during a previous trip she'd made with Debbie, but I get to know her better on this trip. Newly married at twenty-five, she has a degree in marine biology from Texas A&M, where her husband now teaches. She did a double major to get her license. Last trip she sailed second mate, but this trip she's sailing third. She's from Nebraska, but now lives in Texas. Don grew up on Long Island and feels at home here. Everyone laughs when he remarks that he gave Amy her choice and she took the stern—it's a long, cold stand down there, in bright sunshine but only seventeen degrees, until we tie up at the dock near lunchtime.

An hour before coming into New York we test the reverse gear on the engine, as required by all U.S. ports. With one warning whistle and "slow astern," it works first try. "It's not required overseas," Debbie says, "so I don't do it."

To our right is the Ambrose Light (a platform with the light atop it), to the left the pilot boat, white house with yellow "Pilot No. 1" screaming from the black hull, and beyond it the Verrazano Narrows Bridge. Dead ahead, between a white container to port and an orange one to starboard, is the World Trade Center.

The compass course is a heading of 330, then 335. An AB is at the six-spoked wheel.

Loudly and clearly, the captain calls the course change: "317." She says each number separately—three-one-seven. Sometimes there's no margin for error if the AB misunderstands what's called.

The AB begins to turn the wheel immediately. When the indicator shows he's reached the new heading, he repeats it, each number separately: "317, captain."

The captain often—but not always—acknowledges by repeating the three digits a third time: "317, thank you."

Matching "slow ahead" (nine knots) on the ship, the pilot launch starts to move away from *Pilot No. 1* toward the *Charlotte Lykes*.

Captain: "Right twenty."

AB: "Right twenty," and as the AB turns the wheel and the rudder moves, the *Charlotte* begins a turn immediately. Two indicators show that the rudder angle is twenty degrees.

"Hard right." Now the rudder angle indicator is showing the maximum, thirty-five degrees.

"Ease to ten."

We pass the four-boomed *Cotco,* anchored to starboard.

"Amidships." The rudder comes back to the ship's center line.

"Hard left . . . half ahead." Twelve knots.

A Maersk ship has fallen in behind us.

By 0857 Capt. Brian Mercereau, the harbor pilot, has climbed the pilot ladder in the lee and made his way up five decks to the bridge. The "Hotel" flag, half red, half white, flies from the halyard on the bridge wing, marking his presence. He returns Debbie's "Happy New Year" with the day's *New York Times* and *New York Post,* and the news that we'll be docking port side to at Maher Terminal, Berth 64.

Talk is very polite.

"Care for a cup of coffee, pilot?"

"Thank you, that would be very nice. Black, no sugar."

Smooth-cheeked, Captain Mercereau wears a gray knit vest over striped shirt, gray wool slacks, and sturdy brown shoes. His coat comes off, but his cap stays on. He makes sure the radios are set to monitor channels thirteen and fourteen.

Manhattan, with the fuzzy top of the Empire State Building, moves to the right as Debbie lets the harbor pilot know we have a ten-foot drag. She explains that the ship's forward bays are reserved for containers to be loaded in New York; after the cargo is loaded, the drag will be less. Visible on the deck forward of the bridge are stacked containers—blue and orange and silver and terra-cotta and black—plus an uncrated red Case International baler; along the starboard edge are ten conductor bus bars for gas and steam turbines, covered by long strips of corrugated cardboard, bound for Alexandria, Egypt. One crate way forward exceeds loading regulations, but it will only present a problem if it goes overboard. Closer to the house, military fuel pods are held in open crates that look very much as if they were put together with parts from an Erector set.

Talk turns to the weather, in particular the ice and snow of two weeks before when the *Charlotte* was there, inbound.

We follow the sea buoys or fairway buoys in. Red and white, they blink "A" in Morse code—dot, dash. Then we hit the channel buoys, red starboard, green port. The colors are reversed in every other country.

We pass a lighthouse to port, red on top, then white, sitting atop a small rocky island.

We're doing 16.6 knots—maneuvering speed, but not our top speed. Because a couple of ships are ahead of us, plus a barge, after minimal discussion the harbor pilot decides to remain at that speed.

Gone and back again, the captain announces, "The chief's got a bad piston, we've got four ballast tanks that won't empty, and they want us to carry 550 tons more than we've ever carried. How's that for a start?" Captain Mercereau suggests it's got to get better. "Well," she retorts, "my husband always says it's got to get a little worse before it gets better."

About thirty or thirty-five minutes to docking, the second mate calls all hands. The ship carries a crew of twenty-nine.

Now that the harbor pilot is aboard, he barks the orders.

"Left five."

"Midships."

"Left five."

"Steady."

It's now ten or fifteen minutes to the Verrazano Bridge, and we're coming up to buoys seventeen and eighteen.

"Heading 345."

Because we're going to the Med, there's some discussion about harbor pilots there.

"The company puts 200 cartons of cigarettes on for us and we probably use 225," Debbie says. "It takes thirty-seven and a half cartons to get through the Suez Canal." She adds, "Seven cartons and three bottles of Jack Daniels is the payoff in Haifa," noting a bottle of Jack Daniels sells there for $28.

The *Cerro* with her black hull and white house comes up starboard, the *Kleon* port.

"350."

The Statue of Liberty, her back to us, peeks out from under the right edge of the Verrazano Bridge.

"Half ahead now, please."

It's smooth sailing—the chief's isolated the bad piston so we're going in on eight instead of nine. "We'll be maneuvering big time after going under the bridge for an hour and a half until we dock," Debbie says.

January snow lingers into February along the New Jersey shore.

"Half ahead."

As we go under the bridge, it seems incongruous to see containers being carried by a truck on the bottom deck.

"348."

Ships are anchored on both sides of us—the Panama-flagged *Albe* and *Clever Duckling,* the *White Sea* from Gibraltar. The order is "slow ahead," and the tug *John Turecamo,* distinctive with her bright yellow top and black bottom, comes up on our starboard between chunks of ice. At 1005 the docking master is aboard, standing tall in a plaid wool shirt and Exxon cap. It's his turn to take charge.

"330." The AB is still steering the course.

"Left five," and we begin turning away from the Statue of Liberty.

"Right ten . . . steady now."

Passing us outbound port side is the *Chemical Pioneer,* home port New York. On the shore ahead loom many green and white fuel tanks. It's Bayonne.

The *John Turecamo* makes fast at the second chock back on the starboard side.

The chief engineer says maybe the piston is cracked. If so, we're looking at twelve hours to replace it.

Docked to our right is the *Sanko Pearl,* Monrovia-flagged, with a green hull and tan house. It's nice to see some different colors.

Deb is on the radio to the chief mate—he can't find the magnetron, although it's supposed to be among the stores the ship received.

Passing Bayonne, the docking master alternates between talking to his tug and giving orders for the *Charlotte.*

"Ease to ten."

We pass the salt works on the left. There's talk of price-gouging with the bad winter, salt going for $18 for an eighty-pound bag. The mountain that was there after Christmas is reduced to a tiny hill. Six trucks line up for what's left as we go under the Bayonne Bridge, looking into seventh-story windows of apartments off to the right.

There's some discussion about being unable to empty the water from four of the ballast tanks, which will force the ship to reduce its cargo to the Med by some 160 tons.

"*Charlotte Lykes* westbound heading for Port Elizabeth . . . dead slow . . . left ten . . . right twenty . . . ease to ten . . . steady . . . slow ahead."

On the right, we pass ice along the pier, then dredging equipment. The docks come into view on the left. First is the Sea-Land Terminal, with its black and white gantries that run on parallel tracks and support the traveling cranes that move back and forth to load and unload cargo. The *Sea-Land Expedition* has her stern to us.

"Ease to five." Manhattan is coming up again on the right.

"Left turn."

To the left is the Yang Ming Line where the *Ming Progress* is working, Hanjin and YM Line containers lining her deck, then an Evergreen container vessel. We're coming up on the Port Elizabeth channel.

"Midships . . . half to stern. Stay alongside and we'll check the headway."

We're coming up to Berth 64 at Elizabeth Terminal; it looks like we'll be wedged in behind the ACL *Companion Express* out of Göteborg. The docking master allows as how he's put her there and us behind her, so he's sure there is plenty of room at the dock. Nevertheless, he jests, "Get the shoehorns out."

"Left turn . . . stop the engine . . . half ahead," then to the tug, "All stopped, John." ("Stop the engine" means stop the propulsion.)

Debbie: "Six hundred sixty feet to go, captain."

"Half ahead, John." It's 1115 now.

The sun is bright and the breeze cool as the ship barely moves, Maher Terminal to the left, with its gray-green cranes, the distinctive blue Maersk cranes opposite.

"All stopped, John . . . dead slow ahead . . . left twenty . . . mate, we gotta come up at least a hundred feet . . . ease to ten . . . midships . . . stop engine . . . hard right . . . dead slow ahead . . . stop engine . . . slow astern . . . midships . . . stop engine . . . hard right . . . dead slow ahead . . . stop engine . . . slow astern . . . midships."

And then, to the tug, "All stopped, John."

Over the radio come welcome words, "First line," and Debbie tells the third mate to run a stern line. To a chorus of dock sounds, there's still a bit of maneuvering of ship and lines, getting the stern line out of the water, pulling up the slack forward, a warning not to heave on the head line. The call "stop engine," and with a light bump the *Charlotte Lykes* touches the dock. Finished with engines: 1136.

Just across the New Jersey Turnpike, planes come and go, oblivious.

Lunch at the captain's table turns into musical chairs as the captain eats and leaves, the chief mate eats and leaves, then the captain returns for split pea soup with the customs broker and Lykes's agent in New York, George Rolando. We exchange pleasantries. In his soft accent, Rolando tells us he left his native Ecuador when he was nine. He lives in Toms River, New Jersey, a good commute, but he doesn't do it every day. He started on cruise ships, then switched to freighters because that meant too much traveling when he had a family. He remarks that now his wife misses their yearly free cruise.

Over lunch, we learn that we might have to vacate the berth at 2150 because another ship is due to dock there before we expect to be ready to sail. Shifting the dead ship to Berth 25 at Port Newark would take three tugs and an hour, in order to give us two more hours to finish changing the bad piston. It would cost $1,000 each for three tugs, plus another $1,000 for the line handlers. Everyone agrees that's less than desirable, but it may be unavoidable.

The afternoon is spent at the Lykes dock office making phone calls. After dinner at a favorite Italian restaurant in Newark, we wend our way back to the ship from the north. We're nearly there when it seems a railroad train is blocking the way to the dock, so we retrace our drive and come back around the other way to reach the docks from the south.

At 2230 the chief mate says a few boxes are left to load, paperwork to follow. Meanwhile, the engineers are getting the piston in shape, but still need fifteen minutes to test it. The *MSC Federica* glides up past us, waiting for the berth, tug on her stern. Rolando, relaxed and sipping coffee in his Chicago Bears sweater, allows as how other Lykes ships have had to wait for a berth, so it's only a fair trade. Debbie checks with the engineers again to see how they're coming. Simon, the bearded docking master, is waiting, keeping warm in his deep turquoise Eddie Bauer jacket. The sea pilot hasn't come yet.

At 2338 we hear on the phone "last box," followed by "we found a few more boxes, and we're looking for a place to put the flat rack."

"What a beautiful sight that is," Rolando says. "Loading more cargo." Everyone agrees it looks like loading the last cargo and getting the paperwork done will take longer than finishing with the piston, so the other berth is canceled, the third tug let go. She's heading for another job nearby, and could be called back if need be.

"Three more moves and we should get that paperwork."

"Come on, pilot," Rolando says. The pilot had called at 2200, said he'd be there in fifty minutes. But not yet. At 0026, the pilot arrives and loading is completed, almost simultaneously. Only a few minutes later we ease away from the dock, stern first, and before we've turned the ship, the *Federica* has already taken our spot.

Retracing the same course we took inbound, we see a beautiful orange half moon rising over the stern, the lights of Manhattan below it. The air is cold. So is the water: thirty-seven degrees. The dredge we'd passed yesterday, which has been working in the harbor for months, is still working, smack-dab in the middle of the channel. The dredge promises to move, but stubbornly doesn't, so we make our way around it. The Statue of Liberty, now lighted, is beautiful; her green coloring makes her easy to spot. Tugs and other smaller boats crisscross around us. The docking master makes his way down the pilot ladder, waves good-bye; there's only a momentary glitch to free the ladder where it's hung up on the tug. Back out under the bridges, past the tanks and docks—spent a week in New Jersey one day. We watch as the lights of Manhattan recede and the pilot leaves in the tug. At 0424 the *Charlotte* takes departure from Ambrose Light.

And then she's outbound, compass heading 124 southeast and then due east toward Gibraltar. ETA for our first port, Leghorn, Italy: 1500, Sunday, 13 February. "Darn," somebody pipes up. "On Sunday the ice cream shop is closed!"

2. The Wind Lass Finds the Rainbow

*F*resh out of school and at sea, so to speak, I began delivering yachts. That course wasn't as random as it might seem.

I grew up in Essex, Connecticut, the middle child of five. My dad, Robert, is a pharmacist and a World World II Coast Guard veteran who had been executive officer on FS 198, a U.S. supply ship to the Philippines. My mother, Darline, is a registered nurse. I have two older sisters and two younger brothers, among them a dental lab technician, a linguist, an architect, and a civil engineer.

I was raised near the mouth of the Connecticut River, five miles from Long Island Sound, and have been on sailboats all of my life. Everybody in my family sails. As soon as we were old enough, we went to the nearby Pettipaug Junior Sailing Academy. We were raised in Blue Jays, thirteen and one-half-footers. My sister Linda and I would sail the Blue Jay on the river and camp overnight on the bank. As teenagers, she and I took off on a family friend's Pearson Electra 22 for a week. We sailed all over Fishers Island Sound and Gardiners Bay. And my brother Bob and I raced a great deal together.

We raced Blue Jays around the state and in the nationals. My family used to take cruises every summer, all seven of us. We started with a cat boat, and in 1968 my folks wound up buying the twenty-seven-foot Tartan, *Bonnie Lass,* that we all sailed wherever we could, and they still own. We'd go to Block Island, Martha's Vineyard, and on up to Plymouth, Massachusetts, where my brothers were going to race her in the Tartan 27 nationals. I don't remember how they came out, but they didn't win!

Prep school consisted of six years at the Williams School, a day school for girls in New London, where there were twenty-two students in my class. I've only attended one reunion, which came on the heels of a trip to South and East Africa. The headmistress, Marion Hamilton, introduced me as having traveled the farthest to attend. At our luncheon table later, Miss Hamilton commented that, while at school I was inarticulate and shy, "Now she's barking orders and telling sea stories nonstop."

After graduation from the University of Vermont in June 1971, I was tired of the physical sciences and never even considered graduate school. My folks were disappointed, I'm sure, that I didn't go on to medical school, but they never said so. I spent a couple of months that summer camping in the Canadian Rockies, then went back to Essex and I did what any chemistry major logically would do: I became a ski bum and a sailing bum!

Winters I lived in my folks' farmhouse in Plymouth, Vermont, with my black lab, Ebony, to keep me company. I taught skiing at Okemo Mountain in Ludlow, about a thirty-minute drive away, where I'd been teaching since I was a freshman in college. Although I never got my Professional Ski Instructors Association (PSIA) certification, the lessons did pay for my skiing.

In the spring of 1972 I'd gotten a job at Essex Machine Works, a propeller and shaft foundry—as bookkeeper! It was a good job in that it allowed me to ski and to take off on yacht deliveries, when I could get them, for three seasons.

Why deliver yachts? From the first, I just liked to be on the water. And from first to last, it was a real adventure. One yacht delivery usually led to another.

The first, in October 1971, was the *Scud,* a Morgan 35 owned by Bill and Millie Magruder. I had known them a long time—in fact, I babysat for them. For transportation and expenses, I got two crew members—the younger brother of a boy I was dating and his friend—and took *Scud* from Essex to Charleston, South Carolina.

That particular trip, it was pea-soup fog going through City Island. Same underneath the Brooklyn Bridge—we never did see the bridge. In the East River, it was so foggy that we even tied up to a buoy for a while.

I kept in touch with a yacht delivery service in Westport, Connecticut. And I answered numerous ads for yacht deliveries, enclosing the requisite photo with the response, but none ever panned out. I did have an interview in Florida (after we delivered the *Wind*

Lass) with the owner of a large brewing company, who had a forty-eight-foot ketch. He had advertised for someone to tutor his nine-year-old adopted Japanese son, but I felt that he had something else in mind, so sayonara.

My last delivery was the result of meeting Jerry and Helen Secord, the owners of a 40-foot Sparkman and Stephens yawl, *Rip Tide,* and Jerry's nephew, Ron Watson, when I was delivering the *Wind Lass.* In March 1973 I took *Rip Tide* from Miami to the Virgin Islands, then sailed her around the islands almost to the Grenadines, to the Lesser Antilles, and back to the Virgin Islands for the owner.

In late 1972 I ferried the *Wind Lass,* a forty-six-foot wooden Alden ketch, from Vermont to Fort Lauderdale. My roommate from the University of Vermont, Susie Potter, knew the broker in Shelburne who was handling the boat sale, and put him in touch with me.

According to my log, owners Jim and Bunnie Plungis, a couple from New York, entrusted their yacht to a crew consisting of me as skipper; Susan J. Potter, first mate; James E. Frech, seaman first class; William A. Giblin, seaman; Michael A. Davis, seaman apprentice.

I like getting my own crew, as I did in this case—the greener the better. That way I can train them my way.

We took off the beginning of November—winter in Shelburne—and I began a series of log entries that brings it all back.

4 November 1972
Finally raised anchor 1330 in rain and snow—first grounding off Point Bay Marina dock. Able to average 6 knots. Secured at Port Henry 1630. Celebrated with a bottle of wine. Dinner out. Bunks and gear wet and cold. To bed early. Total engine hours: 3. Distance: 16 miles.

5 November
0700 left Port Henry in cold rain—hills of Vermont and New York covered with snow! Arrived at Lock #12, Whitehall 1300 only to be greeted by the Plungises. Fuel, groceries, and a short game of football. Secured engine Lock #9, 1815. A long, cold, wet day. Total engine hours: 11$^{1}/_{4}$. Distance: 46 miles.

6 November
0630 left Lock #9. Cold but no rain. The sun finally broke through—

managed to dry some of the mattresses. Ran through eight locks! Crew improved with the practice, well, except for #3—Bill fell in and the boat ended up diagonally across the lock! Secured engine in Cohoes 1610. Arrangements made to step masts at Matton's. Total engine hours: 7 hours 40 minutes. Distance: 38 miles.

7 November
Election Day—everyone's voted except Bill—due to delay. Masts stepped 0830—quite a problem getting the stays in place. Pea-soup fog all A.M. Started engine 1200—fog lifted. Clear but windy & cold. Secured engine 1630 at Rowena Cogeman's Outboard Club. Great hospitality—"hot" showers & beer. Total engine hours: 4 hours 15 minutes. Distance: 20 miles.

8 November
Left Rowena 0610. Fog and rain. Engine trouble developed 1300. Filled gas tank. Could only run with choke out. Secured engine 1530 at The Mariner's Harbor, Poughkeepsie—refueled. Dinner at Mariner's. Gale winds developed by 2000. Part of floating dock broke loose. Kept watches most of the night. Pumped bilge twice. Bilge pump broke—had to resort to buckets. A terrible smell of gas all night. A miserable night. Total engine hours: 9 hours 20 minutes. Distance: 51 miles.

9 November
Left Poughkeepsie 0620. Still blowing and rough. Calmed down for a few hours, but really came on strong—6-foot seas and a full bilge—bucket brigade once again! A leak was discovered—hope it's nothing serious. Arrived NYC 1700 after a few groundings. Plungises met us and treated us to a good meal. All tired after a long day and night. Total engine hours: 10½ hours. Distance: 54 miles.

10 November
Spent the day outfitting the boat. A gorgeous day—figures!

11 November
The day spent finishing outfitting. Rained all afternoon and night. Laundry and shopping done. Bill and Deb took showers at Chris Kelly's, Deb's cousin.

12 November
Jim, Susie, and Mike spent the A.M. taking showers at Chris's. Jim and Bunnie said good-bye. Started engine 1145. A cloudy night with no wind and calm seas. 1945 secured engine and raised four sails. Wind held until 2300—started engine. Secured engine 2400.

13 November
Wind held until 0530. Skies cleared a bit. Secured engine 1130 at Cape Island Marina, Cape May, N.J. The night was a good experience and adventure for all. The little sailing we were able to do made it all worth it. Refueled at the Marina and reported in. Moved out to a mooring off CG station. Another cool night. Total engine hours: 15. Distance: 142 miles.

14 November
Started engine 0700. Clearance of bridges in Cape May Canal 56 feet—Bill at top of mast—rain and cold—pea-soup fog and high seas. Threw anchor 1100. Immediately cleared up a bit—raised anchor and sailed for a while. Started engine 1200—secured engine at anchor 1330. Spent the night about 20 miles off Cape May in the middle of Delaware Bay. Seas at least 6–8 feet—winds 60 MPH. A miserable night—all cold and wet. Total engine hours: 5$\frac{1}{2}$. Distance: 20 miles.

15 November
Wind, seas, and cold did not diminish, but no fog. Boys had a terrible time raising the anchor. Winds still from the NW. Set sail 0700—storm jib and mizzen. Didn't get anywhere. Started engine 0800. Secured engine 0930—made no headway against the seas and wind. Cabin by this time a shambles and full of water. Reset sail after engine died. Sailed out of channel and threw anchor 1200. Storm appeared to get worse so by 1400 decided to head back to Cape May. In raising the anchor, the chain slipped off the bowsprit and into the chock—it then ripped a 1$\frac{1}{2}$-foot section off the starboard rail. Everyone became scared. Bill frostbit all his fingers. Is it worth it? Michael decided it wasn't. Sailed back to Cape May with storm jib, double-reefed main, and mizzen. Probably doing 11–13 knots surfing on the seas. Hard to find the canal since two lights were out. But we did make it. Railroad bridge in the canal was closed and didn't hear our horn—Susie was blown to shore in the raft and got him to

open the bridge. Secured engine 2000 at Cape Island Marina. Just left the boat and had dinner at the Lobster House—food was poor but expensive. Glad to be in calm water. All physically exhausted with low morale. All the problems with the boat make it very difficult to bear such bad weather. But somehow you still feel good about having made it without more serious damage. We even tried to raise the Coast Guard only to find the radio did not work. Total engine hours: 7 1/2. Distance: 20 miles backward.

16 November
The boat from Toronto invited us to sail with them to Norfolk, but we decided we needed a day of rest. Michael departed about 1100—sorry to see him go. Did laundry and took showers. Had to pay high dockage. Left dock 1600 and picked up a mooring. A rowdy night began—shall we say Willie had just a little too much. Everyone slept well. Naturally it was a beautiful day. Total engine hours: 0. Distance: 0.

17 November
Spent the day at the mooring. Bill rowed in and got supplies. Played bridge all afternoon—the girls won, of course! Again this A.M. we tried to sail up the Bay—but the cold, wind, and seas chased us back in—engine died again on way back. Total engine hours: 1. Distance: 0.

18 November
A lazy day at the mooring. Pumped the water out of the bow and cleaned up the engine. Susie and Bill rowed in. Bill saw a doctor about his hands—report not good. Talked to Jim [Plungis] at 2000 about what happened—said not to worry. Met the townies—a fun evening. Engine hours: 1/2. Distance: 0.

19 November
Started engine 1000. Secured engine 1015 at Cape Island Marina. Not hospitable at all to sailors. Called a guy about the engine. Moved to the commercial dock where he could work on the engine. Fishermen are much nicer. The problem with the engine was only dirt and water in the carburetor. A game of bridge played and a visit by Ev. Jim called—so it's warm in Florida! Decided to leave in the A.M.

20 November

Left commercial fishing dock 0930 under sail—working jib only! Mizzen up once in ocean—small craft warnings up—blowing about 35 with high seas. Entrance to Delaware Bay was very rough. Water poured in everywhere—bilge pump, hatches, etc. Managed to control bilge pump leak with chewing gum. Seas calmed and winds died a little once we reached Delaware shore. Raised main and caught the Hinckley 38. Ev managed to keep up with us in his Hereshoff 38. Averaged 9 1/2 knots until 2000 when strong wind forced us to lower main. Six hours at 9 1/2 average—exciting. Were no more than 30 yards off the transom of the Hinckley most of that time. Able to follow the stern light of the Hinckley until 0100. Full moon and 10-foot seas and high winds. Bilge full. Total engine hours: 0.

21 November

On our own 0100. Able to pick up our buoys until 0300. Got too far out by 0500. Spotted Chesapeake Horn 0530. Headed due west. Went through Chesapeake Bay Bridge about 1000. Started engine 0945. Secured engine 1045. Sailed by Norfolk. Turned into a beautiful day. Started engine 1300. Secured engine at Atlantic Yacht Basin in Great Bridge, Virginia, 1630. Met the fellows from the Hinckley. They had gotten in about 1100. It was a long and hard trip from Cape May. All very wet and cold—and everything in the cabin soaked. Able to dry out a little once inside. A good dinner with the Hinckley crew—pool and beer. Total engine hours: 4 1/2. Distance: 177 miles!

22 November

Atlantic Yacht Basin was great—showers, electricity, and dockage for 70 cents a foot. All laundry done. Said good-bye to the Hinckley—still a little amazed that we made it in what they would not consider going outside in. Promised to go inland the rest of the way. Started engine 1000. *Snowed* all morning. Will it ever be warm and dry? Secured engine 1530 in Coinjock, North Carolina. Weather forecast not pleasant. Total engine hours: 5 1/2. Distance: 33 miles.

23 November

Started engine 0610. The decks were covered with ice. A clear, cold day. A good wind for sailing across Albemarle Sound and up the Alligator River. With engine were able to do 7 knots. If we make Belhaven there's a Thanksgiving buffet waiting. Engine conked out in

Alligator River–Pungo River Canal. Finally got it going after a half hour of dodging a wood barge and running aground. The spinnaker pole works beautifully. It sure gets dark early and quick. Secured engine at Jordan Yacht Basin in Belhaven at 1845. The buffet was great. Jim managed to finally fill himself. More bridge. Total engine hours: 12 hours 35 minutes. Distance: 66 miles.

24 November
Susie and Bill took the boat out this A.M. Started engine 0600. Another clear, cold day. Wind coming from wrong direction to sail. Trying to make Morehead City and miss the delay of closing of the Beaufort Bridge Nov. 25, 6 A.M.–Nov. 27, 6 A.M.

 Engine stopped at 1030—broken fan belt. Doing well under full sail—will try to go into Oriental. Shock cord fan belts got us into Oriental. Started engine 1430. Secured engine 1500. Got a new fan belt and assistance in putting it on. Started engine 1530. Ran hard aground 1830. Secured engine. Off at 1930—started engine. Secured engine at Morehead City 2030. A good dinner at Mrs. Willis. Skipper was unjustly angry with her crew—apologies in order. Total engine hours: 9. Distance: 61 miles.

25 November
Reunion with the Toronto boat and *Rip Tide,* who towed us to Oriental. Met the *Tara,* formerly the *Yankee Girl,* owned by Peter Schellens of Essex, Connecticut. Showers and supplies and football. Started engine 1130. Secured engine 1530 after running aground in the channel! We have not had one day without incident. Broke the spinnaker pole trying to push us off. As if that wasn't bad enough, ıt had to rain! The Coast Guard to the rescue—pulled us off easily. Started engine 1545. Secured engine 1600 at Casper Marina, Swansboro, North Carolina. Total engine hours: 4¼. Distance: 22 miles.

26 November
Started engine 0715. Overslept after dodging drips all night. Cold and windy. Jim made his own channel about 1500. *Rip Tide* tried to pull us off and finally set their anchor for us—didn't work. *Tara* finally pulled us off. At least we're getting a reputation for making an interesting day out of what would have been a boring motor day. A beautiful sunset as we pulled into Wrightsville. Secured engine 1730. Total engine hours: 10¼. Distance: 50 miles.

27 November

Started engine 0630. *Rip Tide* joined us. Said good-bye to *Tara. Luv Tub* caught us before we got to Southport. Borrowed a quart of oil from *Rip Tide.* Engine overheated 1400. Ran slower—seemed to keep the temperature down. Secured engine alongside *Rip Tide* in Little River, South Carolina, 1630. Amazing—no groundings— bumped a few times. Total engine hours: 10. Distance: 53 miles. P.S. Treated to a great dinner by Helen and Jerry Secord!

28 November

Started engine 0630. Led four boats down the [Intracoastal] Water- way. A cloudy day. Wound up being the warmest day yet. Able to take off parkas, hats, and gloves! Debbie and Jim made it to the top spreaders. Susie and Debbie enjoyed a beer on the first spreaders. A good day. Engine still ran hot, but nothing happened! Secured engine in Georgetown 1700. Charlie of *Luv Tub* doubled the water flow through the water pump—should take care of the overheating problem. Nice to have these people traveling with us. Jim and Ron rigged the burgee halyard on *Rip Tide.* Total engine hours: 10½. Dis- tance: 60 miles.

29 November

Started engine 0500. Managed to pick up most of the buoys to the cut after discovering some were out. Overcast but pleasant day. Engine running well. Choke got stuck this A.M. Temperature low. Under full sail by 1200—secured engine. A great sail into Charleston—doing over 7 knots—passed *Luv Tub* and *Rip Tide.* Started engine and dropped sails 1430. Secured engine 1445 rafted alongside two boats at the Municipal Marina, Charleston, South Carolina. At least it didn't start raining until we were in! Invited over for cocktails on *Ubique.* Total engine hours: 7¼. Distance: 65 miles.

30 November

Lazy day in Charleston—just as well—weather miserable—gale warnings up—pea-soup fog and rain. Bill saw another doctor—not much help. Met Mrs. Francie Wolff, friend of Deb's brother-in-law, for lunch and a tour of Charleston. Well-appreciated laundry done. Ron's birthday. Quite a night.

1 December

Another day spent in Charleston unexpectedly. A beautiful warm fall day—not a cloud in the sky. Took showers and dried out the boat. Looked over an interesting array of craft in the marina. Walked and played football in Charleston. Had a great dinner at Henry's and saw an amazing movie, "Lady Sings the Blues." A beautiful starlit night.

2 December

Started 0600. A beautiful clear cold morning. Seven of us left Charleston together. Engine died 1200. Charlie [of *Luv Tub*] got it going for us by 1230. A beautiful day. Christie [Charlie's daughter] played with us all afternoon. Secured engine at Beaufort Marina 1615. Total engine hours: 9 hours 45 minutes. Distance: 65 miles.

3 December

Started engine 0630. Cloudy day. Set sails in Port Royal Sound 0830. Not much wind. Many porpoises sighted. An uneventful day. Secured engine 1415 at Isle of Hope, Georgia. No one at the dock— rafted alongside *Rip Tide* at their anchor. Rain. Total engine hours: $9^3/_4$. Distance: 55 miles.

5 December

Started engine 0630. Hazy and foggy. A beautiful sunrise. A boat from Essex, Connecticut, passed us—owned by Stan Nichols. Set sail 1030—engine died anyway. Bill spent the morning trying to unclog the sink drain—no go. Boys cleaned up the spark plugs. A warm day—Susie and Debbie broke out the shorts. Started engine 1200. Engine kept dying—secured 1330. Bill drained the carburetor— chewing gum used once again. By the end of this trip he'll be quite a mechanic. Started engine 1415. Secured engine outside of Brunswick, Georgia, 1730. A fun day of sailing—everyone had their sails up. Total engine hours: $8^1/_4$. Distance: 72 miles.

6 December

Socked in by fog. Fog lifted by 1030—started engine. A stormy day but warm. Secured engine at Fernandina Beach 1715. A night to remember—testimonial last supper—awards—many truths revealed! Said good-bye to *Luv Tub*. Charlie and Elsie are the greatest. Total engine hours: $6^3/_4$. Distance: 41 miles.

7 December

Spent the morning getting money and taking showers. Started engine 1115. Set sail—not much wind. Weather forecast not good for going outside. Too bad. Decided not to wait but continue inside. Ran aground 1600 while trying to get *Rip Tide* off. Secured engine 1700 at Jacksonville Beach. A cloudy, foggy and rainy day. Total engine hours: 5³/₄. Distance: 32 miles.

8 December

Started engine 0700 after a night of heavy downpours. Foggy but warm. Turned into a cloudy, sunny, hot day—everyone in shorts! About time. Set sails. Secured engine at Marineland 1430. Everyone swam in ocean and pool. Water warm and nice breakers. Football. It's nice to get weather we've been dreaming about. The sun makes all the difference. Total engine hours: 7¹/₂. Distance: 48 miles.

9 December

Socked in by fog. Started engine 1130. Kept hitting fog every other mile. Sunny and warm. Susie rigged up her hammock. Secured engine at 1630 in Daytona. *Rip Tide* finally ran aground—in sight of their destination! Pulled them off easily. Left dock and rafted on *Rip Tide*'s anchor. A good night for dinner at The Wreck. Total engine hours: 5. Distance: 34 miles.

10 December

A beautiful warm morning with a little haze. Started engine 0630. Said good-bye to *Rip Tide* for fourth time. Secured engine 0900 at New Smyrna Beach for gas and supplies. Started engine 0932. Debbie ran aground just before Smyrna. Got off easily. Susie's overdue [to go aground]. Hot and sunny all day. Rigged the bosun chair off the boom for dunking. Water warm and fun. Secured engine in Canaveral Barge Canal 1630 alongside *Wind Song* previously owned by C. F. Chapman, Jr., of Essex. The proprietor of the dock is very nice—gave us crabs, oranges and grapefruit. A clear warm night. Total engine hours: 9¹/₂. Distance: 65 miles.

11 December

Decided to go outside at Cape Kennedy to Fort Lauderdale. Started engine 0930. Said good-bye to the great people at Tingley's Dock. Dave Tingley gave us a dozen more crabs. Susie and Bill picked a few more grapefruit. A beautiful day. Set sail 1130—secured engine—no good—started engine 1200. Engine died 1400—restarted 1430. Secured engine when it died again 1500. Sailed for an hour—restarted engine 1600. Secured engine 1730. Wind and seas picking up. Proved to be an extremely rough night. Genoa eye for sheets ripped out. Staysail gave way. Everyone and everything soaked again.

12 December
Seas about 8–10 feet. Wind about 30 MPH. Hard on the wind—moving slowly. Decided to go in at first possible inlet—proved to be Lake Worth. Started engine at Lake Worth 1130. Secured engine 1330 in West Palm Beach. Bill's given up sailing. It's too bad we had to end with such a rough trip. The crew and the boat are a complete mess. Saw a movie and had dinner in West Palm Beach. Susie and Jim slept outside—drier. Total engine hours: 8. Distance: 110 miles.

13 December
Started engine 0800. A good day for drying out. Susie finally managed to run us hard aground. Yeah! A shower and rainbow—appropriate for our entrance to Fort Lauderdale. Anchored in Fort Lauderdale 1530—secured engine. Turned the *Wind Lass* over to her owners, James and Bunnie Plungis. Hard to believe that this weather-troubled, problemed trip is finally over. Sorry it's over, but relieved we made it. Total engine hours: 7½. Distance: 40 miles.

After borrowing my log one day, Willie wrote this song in it:

Skipper Blues II
She's a mean old lady with a mighty heavy load
Sailing down a harder road than she's ever know'd
Sometimes she stands alone like a child's lonesome cry
Well, that mean old lady just won't be denied.

CHORUS
Well I'm down, yeah down
When the skipper gets the blues
I don't want to hang around.
She's got a "kidney-brained" crew that doesn't know what to do.
Too many decisions gives the skipper the blues.

She's a storm like you've never seen
When the crew runs aground she gets mighty mean
She'll curse up a gale and everything shakes
And if we don't get off soon, there's gonna be an earthquake.
CHORUS

She's a tough old lady works both day and night
Drives her kidney-brained crew all day and worries about 'em all
*   night.*
(to be continued)

Landlubber's Log
3–10 February 1994

Thursday, 3 February

Skipped breakfast—there's coffee on the bridge at 1000. Because we've been breaking in the new piston by increasing the RPM in increments of ten, we've only been at full revs (about 110) since about 0915. By 1045 we're only about ninety miles from shore, in 2,100 feet of water. We've passed two fishing fleets, then some nets with red and white floats. It's the only color we see. Then a school of dolphins crosses our port bow. Beautiful.

The wind is now force five, coming across our quarter. Soon we'll drop off the shelf; about 2200 we're due to cross the Gulf Stream. Then the water temperature will warm to seventy-two, and so will the ship's hull. Air conditioning will replace heating, sweaters melt away to be replaced by polo shirts.

About 1130 we go to lunch. Time to read *Exit the Rainmaker,* the first in a series of books brought to fill free hours, and nap—just as the winds pick up and we start to roll. It feels like a lot, but I'm told it's only ten degrees. I time seventeen seconds over and back. No nap. But then you don't have to pick up your head from the pillow to see the water out the square port on the port side, either.

We take a walk outside my cabin, past door number one (lots of electronic stuff behind it, including the works for the ship's entertainment system) and door number two (open to vent the stack gas). We promise to come back with a wire to rig up an antenna for a small radio, so I can get "All Things Considered" and "Car Talk" in the passenger quarters. The wind is now force eight (thirty-four to forty knots) and the seas are big (waves eighteen to twenty-five feet high). But the air is much warmer, and it feels good to be outside.

At 1645 it's time for what becomes the nightly ritual—cocktails and cribbage at the conference table in the captain's office. I'm the novice and, as usual, Debbie's the master—she's offered to teach me the game because she wants a partner for the trip. She's very good at cribbage, very competitive, and, as in everything else she does, she hates to lose.

As I concentrate, the extra paper holder perched on top of the copier slides off, the captain "loses" her desk, and she puts in a hurry-up call to have the stabilizers put out. She says it's unusual to have them on a freighter, but they're welcome tonight. Everyone's at dinner, however, so there's a delay. We go to dinner—it's steak night—then to the bridge. One stabilizer is working, one isn't, then both lights glow. Good. You can feel the difference.

Only red lights show on the bridge; they don't interfere with your night vision. Ahead, outside, it's all black. Lots of banter in the dark with the second mate, Don, who's got the four-to-eight watch. The captain starts to tell how the second mate showed up without his fit-for-duty slip, and all of a sudden Don's telling his version. He said, and then she said. The head on the bridge is emitting sewer gas big time, and we wonder if somebody is dying in there, but we decide the smell's so bad that if anyone were in there, he'd already be dead. Then Don moves behind the curtain, where he keeps charts; he checks the GPS (Global Positioning System) in the bright light there. He's twenty-six, so he gets a lot of ribbing from the captain about needing all that light because he has such terrible vision.

We settle into comfortable chairs in front of the TV set in the captain's office and watch the first of a nightly string of comedies on the VCR, then set the clock ahead one hour and climb the ladder one deck for bed.

Friday, 4 February

Already the days start to run together, with only the Calico Welding Supply Co. calendar on the wall to keep track. The calendar came from Brendan Gause, the second assistant engineer, after Debbie had seen his and asked him to get one for me because its decorations are pigs, my favorites. This leg of the trip is 4,130 miles, 11 days and 6 time zones, port to port.

The crew, glad to be out at sea and caught up on sleep after the coastwise run, starts to settle into a routine. The second mate has a project: putting up a basketball hoop. There's lots of talk about the movies we have on board this trip. Lykes arranges for the *Charlotte* to get a box of new movies in New York, but the ship owns about seven hundred besides. Tonight the crew has chosen one called *The Slime That Ate New York*. The second assistant engineer (of calendar fame) is in charge of making popcorn to go with it. The slop chest run by the chief mate is open for a half hour today—first time out of New York—and the crew stocks up on cigarettes.

Computer work goes fast, and at 1015 I hear the captain announce "coffee time" as she trots past my door and up the ladder to the bridge. The galley, as usual, has provided freshly baked cookies. Yesterday, oatmeal. Today, chocolate chip. We're only doing 14.4 knots—not good enough, but it seems the best we can do.

Today's conversation is about hazardous cargo and the paperwork and regulations for handling it, which, the chief mate and the captain agree, are a royal pain. The list for Voyage 87 is kept right outside the door to the bridge in a folder marked "Dangerous Cargo." It must be absolutely correct, complete with telephone numbers, or else the ship is subject to fines for every day it isn't correct. Even when *no* hazardous cargo has been loaded in port, the ship is given a load list showing this, so she won't have to keep proving she didn't receive any. And the kind of hazardous cargo makes a difference: Lithium batteries, for instance, can't be loaded next to certain things; bromide tanks—whether shipped full, or emptied and returning to be refilled—can't be next to something else. Hazardous cargo is defined in big books of regulations; not all countries agree on them. One country may say self-propelled machines are hazardous, another may not. International rules usually overrule American, but not always.

What has started as a gray day deteriorates into rolling seas coming around to the port quarter, and somehow bed and Dramamine sound better than lunch and company. The pill does the trick, and the roll subsides in time for a late afternoon walk around the deck. With the sea temperature at seventy-two and the air at sixty-seven, it's almost nice enough to bring a book outside and read (lounge chairs are stashed in protected spots here and there). But I opt for cribbage and dinner, the New Orleans–style seafood platter, a once-a-trip favorite of the crew.

We catch a little of "All Things Considered" piped over the radio in the captain's office from the ship's entertainment system—at least enough to know that Olympic skater Tonya Harding is expected to be indicted for her role in the attack on Nancy Kerrigan and that the stock market dropped ninety-six points. The captain checks the bridge, happy that our speed is now over nineteen knots, then we rerun last night's movie (again sleeping through the boring part) and turn out the lights.

Saturday, 5 February

The day dawns bright and sunny, the seas smooth (I guess the winds are force two). Everybody jokes that the passenger is bringing the good weather luck. Milton Walters, the young, black saloon messman, serves everyone breakfast. I go to my office for some work.

Chief Mate Bob Strobel quietly calls to me, down one deck from the bridge. I check the passage but don't see anyone, and go back to the computer. Too bad. He'd spotted two finback whales three to four hundred yards off the port bow about 0830. We watch for whales the rest of the day, with Amy promising that she'll call if she sees any on the twelve-to-four watch. She doesn't. The only other company is a fishing boat, westbound about 0715.

Coffee on the bridge. Peanut butter cookies today.

It's a beautiful clear day, with a wide horizon. According to Bowditch (the definitive book), we can see 9.8 nautical miles, or 11.3 statute miles, from the bridge eighty feet above the water. Because there's nothing to measure by, it's hard to tell. The chief mate says that on one trip he thought he was seeing another ship off to the right, its lights appearing and disappearing. It turned out to be airplanes taking off and landing at the airport in Naples, some forty miles away!

Lunch, a nap, and then the captain and I walk around the deck, as we do most days during the voyage. Sea temp is down to sixty-four degrees, but the air is gorgeous and warm. We spot sea grass from the Gulf Stream, and Debbie picks out a flying fish. I miss it.

Finally get a chance to find out what we're carrying from the United States. Each sheet of the manifest describes a cargo item, its shipper, and the port—and sometimes the company—for which it's bound. The cargo includes everything from select strip sirloins, StarKist tuna, and sorghum seed to various chemicals bound for the Dead Sea Bromine Co. Relief supplies for Yerevan, Armenia, and Catholic Relief Services in Israel. Cornstarch, chemicals, and whole lambskins (not dressed), suitable for furs. Bud and Coke. Plastic this and synthetic that. A big part of the cargo is military-related, whether it's household goods and automobiles being shipped over for American personnel, military parts for Egypt, or huge quantities of beverages for the Military Sealift Command in Turkey.

You can get a good idea of the cargo coming to the United States, which is even more interesting, by looking over the manifest from the previous voyage. Funny: I spot a shipment to an old friend of my parents' who has an import business in Denver. Small world.

From Alexandria, Egypt:
- Cotton fabric for Charleston.
- Egyptian cotton diapers (15,432.34 lbs.) for Atlanta.
- Ladies' clothing for Veracruz, Mexico.
- Somebody's household goods.
- Spices, including 700 multiwalled paper bags (30,864.68 lbs.) of cracked basil and 424 cartons (7,384.595 lbs.) of dill weed, for McCormick in Baltimore.

From Haifa, Israel:
- Citric acid (169,181.55 lbs.) in bags, for Norfolk.
- Grapefruit sections for Baltimore, plus one carton of apricot halves shipped as a free sample.
- Polyamide yarns for Greensboro, North Carolina.
- Tires and un-dipped tire cord fabric.
- Plastic pipes and tubes.
- Aircraft parts for Lockheed.
- Household goods for transferred military families.
- 340 cartons (11,662 lbs.) dehydrated chopped broccoli for Uncle Ben's in Fort Worth.
- Matzos (4,797.95 lbs.).
- Educational games and activity books for Miami.
- Formaldehyde for Venezuela, pharmaceuticals for Ecuador, herbicides and pesticides for Nicaragua, Ecuador, and Costa Rica.

From Izmir, Turkey:
- Bales of Anatolian kilims.
- Construction machinery for Knoxville.
- 51 sofa sets.
- Marble slabs for Miami.
- Handblown glass for Tulsa.
- Turkish towels.
- Dried, sulfured No. 4 apricots (40,741.37 lbs.) for San Jose, California, and 1,500 cartons natural, specially cleaned, Turkish No. 8 sultana raisins (46,627.71 lbs.) for Chicago, and dried figs.
- Acetaminophen (45,470.28 lbs.) in 375 fiber drums, for Chicago.

From Salerno, Italy:

- Sofa sets.
- Military household goods.
- Iron chains (21,958.01 lbs.) for Milwaukee.
- Macaroni, peeled tomatoes, balsamic vinegar, and olive oil for Antigua.

Finally, from Leghorn, Italy:

- Organs (the musical kind) for Greenwood, Mississippi.
- Olivetti printers and accessories.
- Marble and tiles, in every size, shape, and configuration, for everywhere.
- Ladies' clogs and sandals for Pic 'N Pay in Matthews, North Carolina.
- Wine, including 24,237.59 lbs. vermouth for New Orleans.
- Tractor tracks for John Deere in Chicago, and clutches and transmissions for Hampton, Virginia.
- One merry-go-round.

We opt for a longer cocktail hour than usual, then check out the movie locker. We come away with more than a week's worth of comedies, leaving behind such gems as *Can I Do It Until I Need Glasses?* The second mate kids that he's just come from the movie locker, but couldn't find anything—seems they're all gone. After tonight's viewing, we set the clocks ahead again and turn in.

Sunday, 6 February

The sun does come up in the east, for sure, but it's darker today and cloudier than yesterday. Whitecaps dot the water, and the captain says we have a head wind. The second mate says this is more typical of winter weather on the Atlantic. He's got big plans for today: He hopes to get the basketball hoop up on the second afterdeck. Because the crane there doesn't work, he's planning to use it as a framework to hold a net to capture stray basketballs.

Over breakfast, Don lets it be known that the captain is a pleasant change. "Usually they're old and grumpy, but she's always smiling," he says.

Time for work and then coffee on the bridge. Pecan cookies, the captain's favorite. The chief mate says he usually loses weight on a trip, depending on the steward. This one's good, he notes, and the captain agrees, saying every time she goes to the galley and asks how the steward is, he answers, "Fantastic." He's black and chubby and very jolly. The worst one Bob has experienced was "Bombay Joe," a steward on a long trip through north Europe, into the Persian Gulf, and around the world.

About 1045 we run through a very short rain shower, and the AB turns on the windshield wiper. Our course is 090, which Bob shortly alters to 092 to compensate for the head wind. The temperature has come up from 58 to 59, the RPM are up to 112, we're making 18.4 knots today and averaging 16.9. According to the noon slip, we're an hour and three-quarters behind, but the captain decides not to change the ETA. Maybe we can make up some time.

Lunch ends with (frozen) strawberry shortcake, minus the topping (Brendan Gause warns it will eat the enamel off your teeth). Nap time, walk the deck for 45 minutes (in shirtsleeves, but on the lee side today, out of the wind), work a bit, cocktail and cribbage time, dinner, and tonight's feature, *The Firm*. With only minutes to go—just at the exciting part—the tape borrowed from ordinary seaman (OS) Mitch King runs out. Quickly we run to the movie locker two decks down and grab the ship's copy so we can find out how it comes out! We turn our clocks ahead—again.

Monday, 7 February

Tough to get up when it's still sort of dark, after two clock advances in two nights. Although I awake at 0720 in plenty of time to shower and get to breakfast, I opt to laze and have coffee in the captain's office. The lethargy isn't caused by deprivation of sleep or rest; the motion and vibration of the ship are mesmerizing.

It's Monday, laundry day. I put mine in to wash while Janie Bodwell, the BR (bedroom steward), cleans my stateroom(s) and changes the linens for the week. With soft brown hair and a sweet smile, Janie's sixty-one, been married twice (first, for twenty years, to a navy man who, she says, changed when he got out, then for twelve years, "but it didn't work out"). She worked on the Mississippi River before going with Lykes; she really likes it, except when the weather gets to her, makes her varicose veins hurt. She owns a bar in Texas and works there when she's home. Janie tells me she had eight children in nine years, and now has twenty-seven grandchildren and three great-grandchildren.

Going to check on the laundry, I run into Milton bringing cookies (raisin) up to the bridge for coffee time. Coffee runs into boat drill—

the chief mate, who's in charge of the drill, has decided it's a good day for it: overcast, but warm. First, the crew runs firehoses, two forward and two aft. Then two squads form and lower the lifeboats on each side of the ship to the deck. I'm assigned to lifeboat two, port side, as my cabin is on that side of the ship. Passengers from the middle cabin, if there are any, are split between the two lifeboats.

I steer the ship. Really! Trying to keep the course at 091, not moving more than a few degrees left or right, watching the rudder angle indicator and keeping it amidships—it's harder than it looks. The silver, six-spoked wheel is small for such a large rudder, and there is some resistance to turning it, so it takes more effort than it would seem to turn. And it's hard to tell when to steer back, to compensate. As I steer, the captain and chief mate joke that they're going off to lunch. Afterward I see the visual record of my turn at the wheel—it's not as straight as the automatic pilot's or the AB's, that's for sure. About that time we see a freighter, a long way off our port bow.

Another first: trying on the survival suit. It's orange and has flat feet (you remove your shoes); mitts with separate places for thumb and forefinger; a hood; a big zipper (pulled up with that big mitt) with a Velcro closure atop it, and a head support—a sort of pillow that is inflated by blowing into a tube. It's very insulated and very warm, and quite heavy. One size fits all. If you are short, or big and heavy, it would be harder to maneuver. Lots of stories about survival suits: Bob said he once put his on in his cabin, all alone, then wasn't sure he could get it off. Janie went to take hers off and pulled her trousers off with it! On the *Lyra,* the crew would put the suits on, then jump into the swimming pool—once a cadet started to hyperventilate and they had to get him out of the pool.

According to the noon slip on which the third mate records each day's progress, it's 2,555 miles to Leghorn, or Livorno.

Lunch (it's McDonald's day, a crew favorite). Finish laundry. First basketball game: no lost balls. I stretch out to read, and the time change catches up with me. Finally get up to walk on the lee side of the deck. Stamp shore passes: each member of the crew and each passenger must have a pass for each port in order to go ashore. Then cribbage—a close game. The phone rings.

"Is *she* there?"

The second mate, on the four-to-eight watch, says we're going through a huge rainbow. Grab the camera and head for the bridge to capture it, and part of another rainbow shows up to its right.

Magnificent. Beans and rice for dinner—a reminder that the ship is out of New Orleans. The captain wins the interrupted cribbage game—again.

Tuesday, 8 February

Awake to rain peppering the tops of the containers, but it doesn't last long; as I'm eating toast a piece of a rainbow appears over the stern. Then the sunshine peeks through a whole sky of big, puffy clouds. No roll—that's *good* weather.

Write a while. My husband, Jim, has hooked up the computer in a perfect spot—it's tied to the table, buffered from behind with a roll of toilet paper, and it has a light above it as well as a porthole looking out over the containers and the port side of the ship. The tape recorder is plugged in, so there's music. There's even a couch next to it for when the psychiatrist is in, or the captain is dictating her memoirs.

Then it's time for coffee and cookies (peanut butter) on the bridge. Chief mate has a long face—seems there's been some talk about the captain giving preferential treatment to the third mate, because she's female. So last night when the captain wrote her required night orders, she said the chief mate and second were to follow her orders to the letter, but the third could disregard! Of course she didn't mean it, but the chief mate got his feelings hurt and couldn't be jollied into seeing that it was a joke—even after seeing other night orders written with a wink. The second and third mates agree he needs a girl. Ever polite, Bob gives me a lesson in using a sextant, which the mates use every hour to check the ship's position. I may need another lesson. He shows me the book that details changes in the positions of the stars, by the second. It's over my head. He doesn't come to lunch—maybe he's still pouting.

The noon slip shows we made 18.08 knots the past twenty-four hours, but we're only averaging 17.20. We've 2,143 miles behind us, 2,121 to go. In her daily update to Lykes, the captain betters our ETA at Leghorn, only to get a new weather report indicating we can expect head winds, so we may not do better after all. We see birds—means we're getting closer to the Azores.

After lunch write a while, read a while, and we walk the deck—three times around, or three-quarters of a mile. We check the new motor on the winch, and where other work is being done; the paint locker, the twist-lock storage room (they're steel, and heavy—watch when the longshoremen drop them three containers down to the deck, the captain says); the basketball net, connections for the fire-hoses, beer bottle tops on the deck. Also climb up a vertical ladder of about ten steps above the bridge to the flying bridge—great view up there, although it seems tippy. Good place, the captain says, to sunbathe—when she does, she puts up signs saying it's off limits.

Too warm for a turtleneck and cotton sweater; I switch to a cotton shirt and go out to read, but watch the weather and seemingly endless water with endless fascination. When clouds turn dark ahead of us, I climb up to the bridge wing (it has a covered, shielded corner with a picture window that's great for watching ahead) and visit with Amy, as we pass by another beautiful, luminous rainbow, and again see a segment of a second. The watch changes at 1600, and the second mate wanders out. "You know, passengers are allowed inside," Don offers, but it's so nice we stand outside and chat as a tanker (big white house, flat deck) passes to starboard.

A Fort Schuyler grad, Don says that maybe seven percent of his classmates were women, and he finds it unusual to have two women in the deck department on this ship. He doesn't mind, but he admits the old hands do. He says it was a shock to find out that the captain was a woman when he got aboard the previous trip. And then he found out "the old man" was riding as a passenger—he'd heard about Debbie's husband, Jack, for a long time. Don says he could only do his job the way he always does it, despite the fact that Jack was always watching. Jack must have told the captain her young second mate was doing okay, Don thinks. He likes her directness. He also remarks that Debbie has a knack of seeing a situation and being able to step outside herself. A man couldn't do that, he adds.

Don's position is different from the others on the ship—he comes from a well-to-do background. His dad is an engineer, and was disappointed when Don didn't become an engineer, too. He's been married to Raina only since June; they live in Albany, New York, where she has a good job with the state that keeps her busy when he's away.

Debbie and I decide to play a second game of cribbage while we listen to Willie Nelson tapes, then eat dinner from goodies stashed in the refrigerator in her office. Finally we go down and nibble popcorn Brendan has made for the first feature in the officer's lounge (there's always one movie that finishes before the watch starts at eight, another for the crew that comes off then) while we zap our dinner in the galley's microwave. The steward has saved us tossed salad, too—no one else eats Green Goddess dressing, so I have a whole case to myself. The captain goes to write night orders and check the bridge before we settle in to watch a movie. We turn our clocks ahead again before going to bed.

Wednesday, 9 February

Gorgeous day again—Don says he'd settle for this kind of weather if it were summer! We're about ninety miles south of Santa Maria. At breakfast, he reports that about 0530 we went through a Portuguese fishing fleet—four boats.

"You didn't alter course, mate?" the captain asks.

"No, the RPMs went crazy for a minute, but we lost him then," Don deadpans.

After more banter, the captain asks, "Do you suppose my letter [of reprimand] will reach New Orleans before we get there?" Clearly Don had the situation in hand, and the captain trusts his judgment. He's sharp and has a promising future, but he says if the contract in June drops the pay, he may be gone. He's basically sailing for the money.

Time for warm cookies (chocolate chip) and coffee on the bridge. At noon our position is latitude 36 degrees north, longitude 22 west. Our course is still 091. We're maintaining good speed, but expecting that head winds will slow us down. We talk about containers, and how the new forty-foot flat racks designed to hold two twenty-foot containers in a hatch create a stacking problem. A twist-lock hook sticks out several inches from the middle of either side, but there's no room left between rows of containers to accommodate the hooks. On a recent trip, the captain says, longshoremen pushed so hard trying to make one fit that a hook punched a hole in a container! And because of stability requirements, even the empties can't always be put in the most logical loading place on the deck. Shoreside management types who haven't been to sea just don't understand—an oft-heard complaint among those who do sail.

At lunch, conversation meanders from the buffalo wings on today's menu to animals the crew has known (and loved?) on sundry ships. Debbie's husband, Jack, once had two rhinos on his ship, and one died. He had quite a time dumping it over the side. The chief engineer recalls a cat that remained aboard after his owner was suddenly replaced. The replacement arrived without work clothes and, au naturel, began to put on some borrowed coveralls. He'd just gotten his legs in when the cat, which had perched on the refrigerator, leaped at him. Big response. Another time a crew member brought a python aboard, and he was told he could keep it in the engine room on the assumption it would be caged. It wasn't, and boy, did it surprise someone who came to check a control. Russ, a third assistant engineer, describes a pet pig a crew member was walking on the dock in Saudi Arabia, a Muslim country with pork prohibitions. Offering to let a local pet his "dog" prompted quite a to-do. Russ also was on a ship to Alaska that took horses—he had to feed them and hose the deck daily—but he says they did better than some passengers (at least the horses didn't get seasick). There's no vet aboard when there are only a small number of animals, but when a circus took its animals from Charleston to Felixstowe in 1982, a vet came along. Even though the circus had to make its way south from New York first, it used Charleston as its port of embarkation because of easy access from the train.

I read, then walk. Out the port side and then four times around the course—down several ladders to the main deck, forward to the bow, up two ladders to the next deck, around the bow, back down two ladders to the main deck and on around. That's a mile. First time around, we see a containership running parallel to us, but faster. Each time around the deck, it's farther ahead of us. Sunbathe on the deck outside the cabin—sixty-one degrees, but sunny.

At dinner we opt for a vegetarian plate. Tripe is on the menu—again—but I never hear anyone order it! When the captain goes up to write night orders, she spots a Filipino ship coming toward us on our port side and calls down to me to come watch. We change course to 095, then 100, then 110, then when we're sure what she's doing, we bring the bow back.

Thursday, 10 February

Another gorgeous day. Wake up about 0650 and decide to rest my eyes another minute—then it's 0728. Breakfast and work while the captain makes her daily rounds. Birds again.

Coffee, cookies (pecan) on the bridge, and a weather lesson from the chief mate as he fills out the slip that the radio operator sends to the National Oceanic and Atmospheric Administration—ships supply NOAA with accurate weather information from all over the world. I finally understand that the whitecaps or spray depend on where the wind is coming from. When the wind stops, so do they. Swells, however, are often the result of the previous day's weather; they take a long time in coming and in dissipating. They can be also be forerunners of a storm we will encounter tomorrow—which is why we need to care about how the weather is today in the area where we will be tomorrow.

The captain requisitions a pilot chart of the North Atlantic; I spend the afternoon with dividers and pencil, plotting on the chart our course from New York to date. When I sit at my computer, I see the Mediterranean chart taped to the bulkhead of my office. Debbie's marked the route, and it will be up to me to keep track of our location in the Med from the daily noon slips.

Time to walk—five laps around today. Earlier, Bob was wondering if the captain were my personal trainer! Too nice to stay inside, although we have some head wind today. As we're going astern one round, a whale blows—too far away for us to see more than a fluke and the blow.

Close cribbage game, interrupted by an opportunity to see another fascinating phenomenon—a "green flash." It's a nice, clear day, so just before sunset, about 1720, we head for the bridge wing and, through binoculars, we watch as bright green (no red, orange, or yellow visible) flashes around the sun for a couple of seconds as it drops below the horizon. Captain and third mate agree it was a good one. You can see green flashes at sea, maybe thirty or fourty days a year, because you have an unobstructed view of the horizon.

After dinner we write a note offering anyone who finds it (and responds) a place in the book we are writing. We put it in a wine bottle, make a wish, and pitch the bottle over the side in the dark. It makes a loud splat. After the usual movie, set clocks ahead, then read *My Secret History* and sleep.

3. Castine, Maine—Unsettled 1976

1/12/74

Hi everyone,

My first week is over and am I glad. Never have I gone through so much.

The Public Relations department is always taking my picture. The first morning at formation, Capt. Brennan introduced me—a big cheer from the guys and cameras flashing. I don't know why, but I was really feeling self-conscious! The Admiral administered the oath to me yesterday afternoon and again cameras flashed.

All this attention is making me realize what I've undertaken. It's now quite a responsibility. I can't possibly crack or give up. I must carry on and that's the biggest burden. I have no doubt that I'm capable but knowing that I can only go in one direction is demanding. I guess I really am famous, and writing that gives me chills. I'm committed and have a lot at stake.

I do feel lucky in being able to come here. Yes, I'm the first female, the "pioneer" as Admiral Rodgers called me, but more to the point, I'm doing what I want to do. I'm happy and proud of that. If I've made it easier for other gals, fine. But I can't wait for that day when I'm out on the high seas navigating! That's what I dream about.

*T*wo photos in *Trick's End,* the Maine Maritime Academy's yearbook, for my senior year give some clues to the feelings my presence brought. The first one shows a group of students posing behind a sign. It reads:

Welcome to Historic Castine
Settled 1613

Under the companion photo of students partially blocking the sign, the caption reads, "Unsettled 1976."

Castine is lovely. Located on a peninsula, it has rocky shores and cliffs, with beautiful houses overlooking Penobscot Bay and the Bagaduce River. I'll always remember an evening watch on the academy's training ship, seeing the fishing boats wander in while a spectacular sunset was displayed behind them. The townsfolk—only a few hundred during the winter, but many more when the summer houses are opened—are warm and friendly. It is a local tradition to gather at the post office on Saturday morning. I met more people there than anywhere else.

The town's big claim to fame is Maine Maritime, a state school founded in 1941. Capacity: 650 students. My reception was kind of strained: Everyone at the school was just as flabbergasted by the situation as I was!

I remember thinking right off that the middies were great—friendly, courteous, and fun. Terry O'Donnell, my big brother and a year ahead of me, was the nicest guy. At breakfast the first morning he made a point of sitting with me. Everyone knew me; even the kitchen help said, "Hi, Debbie." I had trouble remembering their names. At the end of my first week I was taken to Priscilla's in Bucksport, where I danced for an hour and a half straight with a half dozen middies. Priscilla, who loves the middies, even framed my picture and an article about me and hung it above one of her bars. That was the highest honor yet!

Breaking tradition as the first female cadet, I created a flurry of activity. Meetings with the press even made me late to class sometimes. There was a press conference my first Monday at Maine Maritime; interviews with reporters from such diverse publications as the *Boston Globe* and the *Belfast Recorder,* and television networks such as CBS, Britain's BBC, and Canada's CBC. I got fan mail (and a hate letter or two) and heard from former University of Vermont classmates. My picture showed up in *Stars and Stripes;* I knew about that because my cousin Henry Palau, who was an attorney with the U.S. Navy in Japan, spotted it and sent me a copy.

The publicity brought various responses. For instance, a write-up in *The Weekly Reader* resulted in an invitation from McFarland School in Trenton, New Jersey, asking me to talk to third graders.

I got a letter from a man doing fourteen years in the federal penitentiary in Atlanta, Georgia. He even sent me his prison number—

he thought we had a lot in common. He had been involved in a murder on a fishing vessel out of Montauk Point on Long Island Sound. I don't know how he thought we had a lot in common; I guess it was because his crime had been committed on a boat . . .

I had been quoted as saying I was attending Maine Maritime for myself, that I wasn't a flag-waver, but if what I was doing helped other women, fine. Although I got no reaction from women's liberation groups, my statement apparently prompted a woman in California to write me: "Do it in the name of sisterhood."

Was being a girl an advantage? I don't think so. I think the fact that I was older and more mature had more to do with my success.

How did I get there?

 After the three seasons delivering yachts, I was thinking about getting my "six-pack" license, which would have let me take six passengers out for charters a hundred miles offshore—the Virgin Islands, Long Island. It would have been fun, but it didn't promise a very secure future.

About that time, a friend of my father's who was an engineering graduate of Maine Maritime suggested I apply there. I didn't even know that women hadn't previously applied to the maritime academies! I was not too enthusiastic about putting in four more years of school, but I thought that with credits from the University of Vermont I could do it in three years. So in October 1973, I wrote for an application, had transcripts sent from my prep school and Vermont, and sent the application fee, so they had to take action.

Even filling out that application gave me a taste of what being the only female in an all-male school would be like. I had to change "his" to "her," "baseball" to "softball," "ice hockey" to "field hockey," and so on.

I remember when I was tackling the application in my parents' living room, my mother was showing the house to a friend. Mom commented to her friend that I was working on a job application. "No," I replied, "it's an application for maritime school." I don't think she thought I was serious.

The application completed, I took off to deliver a thirty-two-foot West Sail yacht from Vermont to Haiti. We had to stop in Annapolis, Maryland, to be the demo boat at the annual sailboat show there, and when we arrived in Annapolis, I received a message from Cdr. David Buchanan, director of admissions at Maine Maritime. He asked me to come to Castine for an interview with him and three other members of the faculty. This was on a Tuesday. I flew up. They were having a board of trustees meeting on Thursday to decide whether to admit women—they knew they were going to get hit with a woman sooner or later. I guess they figured I was a good risk: I would probably see it through, because I wasn't fresh out of high school and I knew what I wanted.

I could almost tell from the way the interview went that I would be accepted. We were all thinking I'd probably do it in three years starting in September 1974. I called them from Annapolis after the board of trustees meeting on Thursday, and Commander Buchanan said, "We voted to admit women. You can start in January '74 and do it in two and a half years, if you take every single professional course the Coast Guard requires."

I told the yacht owner to hire another captain—Annapolis was a good place to find one and, with only his young son and a dizzy blonde cook aboard, he needed one. Then I got off the yacht and headed back to Essex Machine Works to earn money to go to school.

Maritime school really was all new to me. Afterward, all of the engineers said if I'd "gone engine"—taken marine engineering rather than nautical science—I wouldn't have lasted two weeks! My father was quite concerned that I wouldn't be able to handle the military end of it. I think he expected to see me home again in a few weeks. But once I started, all I could see was going all the way—master's license.

I doubled up one semester, went to summer school, and managed to get in six months' sea time as a cadet to qualify for the third mate's license exam. I went two and a half years straight through.

But first things first.

The school didn't know what to do about a uniform for me. Initially they sent me to the Naval Exchange in Newport, Rhode Island. The 1940 Wave uniform, complete with "meter-maid hat," is what I ended up wearing. For winter, that meant a blue serge skirt or slacks and a jacket; a white blouse and black tie; a sweater like my grandfather used to wear; a pea coat; black shoes (and black socks), and a black pocketbook. In summer I switched to men's khaki slacks or a skirt, which my mother made, and shirts. Later, whenever I needed women's uniforms at school, I'd have to drive miles with

Chief Warrant Officer Fred Marzolf to the Naval Air Station in Brunswick to buy them. They didn't fit. And the male uniforms that I had to wear didn't fit either. Of course, I was twenty pounds heavier then! My work clothes consisted of men's bell-bottom jeans, a blue chambray shirt, a wool turtleneck sweater, steel-toed black boots, a green foul-weather work jacket, and a sailor cap.

The director of admissions had indicated to me that I could take my black Labrador retriever with me, and I said, "Awwwright!" So when I headed for Castine I took Ebony, with a fifty-pound bag of dog food on top of the car. After I got there they told me I couldn't keep him, so I sent him back home with my parents. For a while it was pretty lonely.

I didn't have a roommate. I also didn't have a dorm room. Because the academy had no provision for housing female cadets, I had to live off campus in an upstairs room at Peggy Gillaspy's house. Mrs. Gillaspy ran the campus book and clothing store; she had three children of her own and three foster children. I didn't like my apartment, the kids were always bothering me, and it was a bad situation. I remember Mrs. Gillaspy held a Bible class every Wednesday, and the kids had to let the evangelistic minister take their Ouija board because it was sacrilegious: Witchcraft! The work of the devil! But I didn't know how well off I was there.

There had been a kitchenette in the closet of my room, but they took it out to force me to eat in the dining hall. I agreed with that; then I could be with everybody. I kind of petitioned the school for a room—I thought I'd get along better with my classmates if I lived with them in the dormitory.

The midshipmen had been living on the 533-foot training vessel, the TV *State of Maine,* and then in Dukes, an unfinished dormitory. In the fall of 1974, as the lone female student, I became the sole occupant of a finished section of Dukes. It was on a corner of a U-shaped area where "the Wedge," the midshipmen who ran the school, later lived. And I used a head designated just for me. But living in the dorm meant putting up with more than I had to at Mrs. Gillaspy's.

Every middie, with the exception of seniors, has an assigned cleaning station. The midshipmen maintain the *State of Maine* and are responsible for cleaning their own quarters and the dorm in general. Everybody has to get up at 0600, do their cleaning stations, and then eat before morning formation and classes.

By coming in as a second semester sophomore, I missed the ten days of formal indoctrination every cadet goes through before freshman year. But I still had to prove myself. Initially there was some resentment from a few seniors, especially my company leader, Kevin Crossman, an engineering student. He gave me an especially large cleaning station that included swabbing a deck area and one head in my dorm, and dumping the trash. He criticized my uniform and made me call him "sir" and repeat things three times. He called me "third classman Doane"—often.

I expected to get that reaction all along the way. But for the most part, the first and second classmen took care of me, went out of their way to make sure I was okay. I was the little sister. (Jim Murray, class of '75, "adopted" me as his little sister, a relationship that continues even today. Jim became manager of Lykes Lines' Charleston, South Carolina, office, and in 1996 was managing the Turecamo tug company.) I went dancing with them. I played racquetball with them. Almost immediately I caught a racket right between the eyeballs, walked around with splits in the eyebrows and black eyes. I could just hear them say, "Yeah, Mom, there's the new girl. A real toughy." I had few problems with the upper classmen. I had more problems with my own class than with any other. They saw me as competition. I was six years their senior. I was on a one-to-one basis with the instructors and had no qualms about going up and asking this, that, or anything.

Some of that resentment was understandable because Maine Maritime made so much—too much, probably—of my status as the only woman, capitalizing on having a woman there at my expense. The school certainly put me in the limelight. There was a lot of unnecessary publicity, and I can sympathize with the feelings of some of my classmates. Whenever a picture was to be taken, or some other publicity, it was always "Where's the girl?"

Although the tricks began when I moved into the dorm, they didn't get too bad until the fall of 1975 when two other females entered as freshmen. The school finished another corner of the dorm, and we three were put over there. Practical and obscene jokes became common occurrences: Our head covered with laundry soap. The girls' tank suits cut up. Bras missing. When I left a note on my door, "At the library. Back at 2230," someone added, "Don't bother."

Just by being there I asked for it. Most of the time I could ignore the tricks and still smile. I had so much to learn and do in such a short time, and I refused to let anyone stop me. My goal was getting closer all the time. Besides, the good news was that I had found a companion, and a male at that! John Pfaff: the placement officer and economics instructor. As I wrote to my family, he was "smart, good looking, understanding, a gentleman, fun, a good cook, twenty-nine, and he has an interest in me." A Brown graduate, he had spent four years in the navy and was working on his doctorate in business. I thought he would do wonders for Maine Maritime, and he was determined to make a lady out of me. I liked him, and he was a great release from my other pressures. Unfortunately, a daughter of the superintendent, Rear Adm. E. A. Rodgers, also figured in the picture, and when she got too close, he escaped.

It took two years to get most of the guys in my class behind me—going to their parties and games, playing baseball with them (I earned the nickname "Slugger"), helping them with homework. I even delayed stenciling my name on the back of my jacket in an effort not to be singled out as "the girl."

There was one lousy incident my senior year. I had a car, a 1972 Dodge Polara, and I had gone to Plymouth, Vermont, to share Thanksgiving with my family. On the way back on Sunday my car broke down in Dover, New Hampshire, and it couldn't be repaired until Monday. Consequently, I didn't get back to school until Tuesday. I walked into class at 0800 to be greeted by my classmates saying, "Hey, Debbie, let's hear a cheer."

The previous Friday, the *Bangor Daily News* had carried a story in the sports section headlined, "Debbie Wins Varsity Letter at MMA," along with a picture of me from January 1974, when I first arrived. The reporter had come to interview the physical education director, Cdr. Verge Forbes, about the reasons for the lack of a varsity basketball program there, but the first two-thirds of the article he wrote was about how I had started a cheerleading squad and won a varsity letter for it. I had had nothing to do with the cheerleading squad, and I never ever was issued a varsity letter.

So, of course, I marched over to the public relations office and asked the officer, Cdr. Robert Giamatti, why. He said he supplied the picture; the physical education director, the story. And what did the physical education director have to say? Commander Forbes, who later became academic dean, said, "Debbie, you know how it is. One thing leads to another."

Actually, I didn't know how it was. Since then I've learned how to handle publicity. With Lykes Lines I directed it through the public relations office, it was controlled through them, and the resentment from my peers was controlled.

On the heels of the cheerleading incident came another at the end of finals in December. After my last exam, I returned to my room. It was during a big snowstorm, and some classmates had thrown a snowball with a rock in it through the window. The glass had shattered into the room, leaving a big hole, and snow was blowing in. I just packed my bags. Although we weren't allowed to leave the campus for the Christmas holiday until the next day, I told the duty officer about the damage, suggested they ought to fix it before the room was ruined, and announced that I was leaving the academy for vacation. I heard later that the window was fixed immediately—but nothing happened to me. I don't think they dared.

I wrote my grandmother a couple of months after my arrival: "Yes, it's lonely and I guess it always will be so—right on up the line—but I'm far from being bored or idle."

A typical day went like this: up at 0600, cleaning station at 0630, breakfast at 0700, formation at 0730, classes 0800–1200, lunch 1200–1230, classes 1300–1600, dinner 1730–1845, meetings 1900–2000, study 2000–0100. A busy, full day, but so enjoyable. At first I was exhausted every day, but soon I got used to it.

There were demerits for offenses like skipping class—one hundred a year and you got kicked out of school. That's severe. I only got eighteen—for having long hair, a new phenomenon for me since I'd always worn a pixie. When I first got to Maine Maritime, the authorities couldn't decide whether I should have a haircut. Finally they agreed I could just put it up. But one day it slipped, and I was sent to captain's mast for punishment.

I wouldn't have considered skipping class anyway, because what I liked best about the school was the instruction, and the rapport I developed with the instructors. I was at the school for one reason: I knew I wanted to learn everything I was taking. My first semester courses give some idea of the curriculum: marine economics, seamanship, rules of the road, marlinespike, naval operations, celestial navigation, oceanography, and deck drawing.

Seamanship, for instance, involved docking situations and use of tugs in docking. Deck drawing meant learning to use drafting tools and all of the projections and plans that go into a ship's design and construction. Marlinespike is knot-tying. In addition to making a knot board with samples of each variety, we learned wire-splicing, specifically the Liverpool splice that I've used on conventional ships. Even at school that skill had a practical application—the scallop fishermen paid us $30 a splice for repairing their drag wires.

My favorite subject, then as now, was celestial navigation. On a commercial ship, the second mate is considered the navigator. Using a sextant and securing the ship's position with star sights is fun, although with all of the electronic navigation equipment on the market it isn't done so much today. The navigator also has the best watches of the three deck officers: 0400 to 0800 and 1600 to 2000—sunrises and sunsets, to take morning and evening stars. And he's responsible for correcting all of the charts and publications: tide tables, light lists, sailing directions. He plots the vessel's courses as directed by the captain and maintains the equipment on the bridge.

When I was there, Maine Maritime had a reputation for turning out a hardworking, professional third mate or engineer. That was due partly to having professional merchant mariners for instructors, and partly to the school's training ship, which the cadets ran and maintained. The U.S. Merchant Marine Academy at Kings Point, New York, had no ship, so its cadets gained their sea time only from commercial shipping. I'm sorry to say that in recent years the professional maritime atmosphere at Maine Maritime has eroded, since the school has, of necessity, added more and more liberal-arts classes. The need for third mates or engineers for commercial shipping is decreasing every year as the U.S. merchant marine fleet continues to diminish, so, in order to survive, Maine Maritime now also turns out marina managers.

All of my instructors in the professional courses had unlimited master's licenses and were highly qualified. Seamanship and meteorology: Capt. L. S. Hathaway, Mass Maritime class of '36 (the last class with a *sail* training ship). A real old salt, Captain Hathaway tells the greatest sea stories; he had a few ships shot out from under him during World War II. Rules of the road: Capt. Ed Geissler, a former examiner for the Coast Guard. Celestial navigation: Capt. Sherman Sawyer. A great course and a great teacher—Captain Sawyer was also my adviser and the chairman of the nautical science department. Despite our fancy calculators, he could usually beat us solving problems the old way. He had a high reputation in the field—during the war he served as a cadet under Captain Hathaway. He had retired from the Coast Guard marine safety division, and frequently served as an expert witness for insurance companies investigating maritime accidents, mainly in the Portland, Maine, area. Admiralty law: Capt. Ed Conrad, an Annapolis grad who also served as academic dean. The year I graduated he became a Lake Ontario pilot, having sat for an original master's license after the Coast Guard waived the recent time requirement and allowed him to use his navy seagoing time.

The remaining instructors were not merchant mariners, but were experts in their fields. Their ranks were school-appointed. My marine economics instructor: Lt. Bruce Zimmerman, an MIT graduate. Oceanography: Lt. Roy Drake, a young, liberal educator more occupied with the latest teaching devices than teaching marine biology. The course was really left up to the student—I was disappointed. Deck drawing: Cdr. Joe Nichols, who had worked thirty-three years for Bethlehem Steel as a naval architect. Loved his field, loved to teach and help the students. The most organized human being I'd ever met. Marlinespike: Lt. (jg) James Buss, chief boatswain—got his high school diploma at age thirty-two! Naval operations: Lieutenant Dranchek, a '68 graduate of Annapolis—and always telling us that the navy man is so much better than the merchant mariner. I didn't care for him at all.

With such qualified teachers, how could I miss? I was so excited about taking these courses! For the first time, I knew what I wanted to do. I had a goal and was on the right track. It was a good feeling.

The initial reaction of the professors was interesting. Most treated me like everyone else. My marlinespike instructor, Lieutenant Buss, overdid it, and always called me Miss Doane whenever he made a point to make sure I didn't feel left out. The first day, I missed my first class due to a press conference and walked into my second, seamanship, late. The professor, Captain Hathaway, ignored me and just kept right on talking. Several professors said they were told to clean up their lectures. That passed.

Maybe the instructors felt sorry for me. Maybe they went out of their way to help me because I was the first girl. I could go to their homes and visit with them on a one-to-one basis, while the male cadets were more intimidated. I had to prove myself to one instructor—Captain Hathaway—before he would look me in the eye. That took several months—he sure is hard-core! But he's now a very good friend of mine. Another instructor, Captain Sawyer, who has since passed away, was a very good friend right off the bat, very supportive. I could help him put a new roof on his cabin or boil down sap for maple syrup. I felt at home, and he and his wife welcomed me. They have a daughter my age, although she wasn't there.

Before I could be eligible for a third mate's license, I needed to put in 180 days at sea. The requirement was satisfied through two separate cruises on the school's training ship and one on a commercial ship, the *Velma Lykes.*

Each cruise usually is two months long. You'd wind up with one month of summer off: May and June you're out on the ship. July or August you have off. The other month you work maintenance at the school, mostly on the ship.

There was a big buildup to my first cruise, which followed my first semester at Maine Maritime. In April 1974 the school was madly trying to get the *State of Maine* ready for the cruise and the Coast Guard inspection beforehand. The boilers on the ten-thousand-ton ship were in sad shape, and the engine crew was quitting right and left. If they couldn't pull things together, there could be a delay. But we made it. First stop: Pier 94, New York City. ETA: 1 May, 1400.

It was my job to help the cadet boatswain "dress the ship"— climb aloft and put up all the flags just before we reached New York. A metal sign, "MAN ALOFT," is always hung on the radar transmitter on the bridge to warn others not to turn it on when someone is up there—an action that can render the person sterile. You guessed it. The sign had been altered, the letters "WO" added in black tape so it read "WOMAN ALOFT."

We expected to be in New York only three days, but indecision about how to solve technical problems delayed us and, finally, we left three days late. In the meantime, I had a great time—bicycling in Riverside Park, walking through Greenwich Village, even going to the movies. I remember seeing *Over There* with a few first-class middies. It was great fun. People in the theater would try to figure out what branch of the service we were in. Needless to say, they were surprised when we told them merchant marine.

Our trip south to Norfolk was great, although we did break down for three hours off Barnegat Inlet. Luckily we didn't drift far—the seas were calm and wind light. I had some memorable watches while underway—taking azimuths, plotting, taking the helm, anchor and mooring detail, and I was learning a lot. We were heading to Norfolk for a fire-fighting class. Anchoring at Pier 7 of the naval base, where we hoped finally to get our fuel feed pump repaired, was a real experience. The base is huge and dangerous. We were the only ones in uniform at night, and the navy men let some of the middies have it. No way would I walk around the base alone.

That two-month cruise took us to Glasgow, Scotland; Helsinki, Finland; and Leningrad. Because I was the only girl, I was sent everywhere with a delegation of twenty-five students representing Maine Maritime. While we were in Russia we took an overnight train trip to Moscow and back, and even got to see the ballet *Giselle.* I must admit that I saw a lot more than some of my classmates just because I was the only female.

I was well cared for. I think I had more "fathers" aboard the ship than any other girl anywhere. The only other woman aboard was the social director, Mrs. Tenney (Mrs. "T" for short). By necessity, I had my own cabin with my own head, a real luxury; male cadets had to share.

Although now there are three classes of students at a time on the training ship, then there were only two. The students were divided into four companies; I was in Company A. One company would be on watch, rotating around the clock; one company doing training eight to five; one company doing maintenance eight to five; and the fourth company had utility—from helping with the laundry to kitchen duty, wherever general help was needed. We operated on a six-day rotation.

On the way from Norfolk to our first overseas port, Helsinki, the weather wasn't exactly optimum. We left in a terrific storm. In fact, I saw my first waterspout. We rolled a little that night, and several freshmen and galley-crew members were seasick, but the next several days we had calm seas and sunshine. Then the weather turned again, and we were in the middle of a gale with following seas. The ship was very tender, and rolled easily. No one slept that night, and we could hear crashing and banging everywhere. The following day the winds had risen and the seas were the biggest I'd ever seen. Another sleepless night. One freshman was so scared he sat on his bunk with his life jacket on for two nights. Doc Russell finally knocked him out with a sleeping pill. On the third day, we had gale force winds of up to forty knots and eighteen-foot waves. When you hear on Sunday, "Catholic services postponed until further notice," you know it's rough.

I think the galley got the worst of it. Soda machines, juice dispensers, people, glasses, everything all over the place for three days. Captain Conrad had been giving a class about the Soviet Union every night in the exhibit room; one night exhibits started falling on top of us. One morning all of the paint on the afterdeck let go and almost took the stern watch with it. He wound up painted black from head to toe.

I remember the seniors coming into our quarters puffing on cigars. "How're you enjoying the weather? Pretty sick, are you?" I wasn't. I still don't get seasick much.

During the better part of a week I was assistant to the carpenter, CWO Wescott, which I enjoyed. For two weeks I did an engine and deck sea project, which required tracing out steam lines, fuel oil lines, steering gear, and learning a bit about the engine. It was kind of scary being in the pit with relief valves going off all the time, steam coming out everywhere, all kinds of noises. But the more I learned, the less afraid I was of being down there. I missed not being able to be on the bridge, though, and was glad for the last two weeks of the cruise when I stood deck watches again.

I managed to sightsee along the way—the emerald green of Ireland through a hazy drizzle as we passed by, a training sub going by on our way to Glasgow, and fifteen sailboats racing past, colorful spinnakers flying, as we anchored for five hours at the mouth of the Clyde River waiting for the tide to rise so we could sail into Glasgow harbor. The countryside was lush, and the banks along the twenty-mile channel to the dock were lined with shipbuilders.

The scenery was different from there to Helsinki. Although it was calm and easy weather, there were rocks sticking up in the water in the middle of nowhere, and lots of traffic. We picked up a pilot to help us avoid mines lost in that area. As Captain Hathaway said, "This is where it separates the men from the boys."

As we sailed between Denmark and Norway, we came within a hundred yards of splitting a two-hundred-foot ship in half. She had only two lights showing, a red light on the stern and a white about amidships. We guessed the ship was stalled right in the middle of the channel, but we could not alter course because five ferries were crossing ahead and behind. We blasted and blasted the ship's whistle as we put the throttles full astern, slowing until it crossed. Close. Very close.

Another day, just after we entered the Baltic Sea, we talked with a German destroyer via blinker light, with help from Cdr. David McMaster, chief mate on our training ship and blinker light instructor. Initially the shade was frozen to the light, and we worked frantically for forty-five minutes to free it up while the destroyer repeatedly tried to raise us. Finally, success. I was able to read quite a bit of the German transmission, but not all. It said, "Welcome to this remote area of the world. Fair winds and smooth sailing." To which we replied, "Thank you very much and the same to you." It was fun.

Still another afternoon we were having fire and boat drill; we had the proper flag hoisted, and a Russian vessel steamed to our assistance. She sailed quite close before she realized what was happening and continued on.

Entertainment aboard ship left something to be desired. I played a few rubbers of bridge each night. And then there were the movies. I got so sick of violence, blood, guts, gore, and skin, as in *Straw Dogs, Fists of Fury, Wall of God,* and *Melinda and the Innocent Bystander.* The men loved it and cheered all the time.

In my spare time, I wrote my family: "I definitely like this life—traveling via the sea!"

As a senior I got into working on the 1952-vintage training ship, the former USS *Upshur* troop transport from the Korean War. I had wanted desperately to be the cadet navigator, the most desired job for senior deckies. You work with the navigation officer doing charts, laying out courses. Instead, I was appointed the cadet boatswain, the next best rating, working with the boatswain, Gerald Cousins, on deck maintenance under supervision of the chief mate, Cdr. Gerald Cummings. I learned how to wire splice using big stuff, one and one-quarter-inch wire. On our senior cruise we stopped first in Baltimore, Maryland, for two weeks in the shipyard. While we were in the yard, my main job was to resplice all of the eyes in the mooring lines used for permanent tie-up in Castine. And, of course, I had my pick of the Maine Maritime football players for help!

We were supposed to spend two weeks in Baltimore undergoing repairs, but we stayed forty-five days. The Coast Guard would only credit us with half of the time we were in the yard. So the academy had a problem: How do we provide the first classmen with the full six months' sea time they need to sit for a third mate's license?

We ended up sailing from Castine the day after Christmas. We sailed around San Salvador Island and back in two weeks, and didn't stop anywhere. It was freezing cold and the seas were rough, but we got our time in.

On the way back through Cape Cod Canal we were ready with our funnelators and balloons full of red and white paint to blast the Massachusetts Maritime Academy training ship in Buzzards Bay. We wound up with more paint on our deck than we ever got across the way to the *Bay State*!

To fulfill my cadet commercial shipping time, I joined the *Velma Lykes* right after the training ship cruise to Baltimore in 1975. She belongs to the Far East Clipper class: 535 feet long with six hatches, twenty fifteen-ton cargo booms and one eighty-eight-ton boom.

I arrived at Lykes Lines' office in New Orleans the morning I was to join the ship. I had on what I can only describe as a blue seer-sucker nurse's outfit, complete with my meter-maid hat. In my but-tonhole was a red rose, a gift from a nursing school friend of my mother's who had met me in the Atlanta airport.

At Lykes's office I was taken to meet Capt. Ernie Hendrix, vice president of the marine division. Next came a public relations inter-view with picture-taking, and Nell Bourgeois, Captain Hendrix's sec-retary, gave me a tour around the office. Then I just hung out there. The *Velma* was due in the Army Basin at 1600, and Captain Hendrix had a port captain transport me to meet her. As soon as he got me into his 280Z, he complained that he had been made to carry my seabag, something he'd never had to do for a cadet before. And he complained all the way to the dock. The ship was an hour late, so he took me across the street to the Ramp Bar, bought me a beer, and then told me never to go there again! I just remember standing with him on an ant hill and coming away thoroughly bitten, through my stockings, by red ants. That captain was Clark Seelig, who later became manager of Lykes Lines' marine division, and my boss.

First day on the *Velma Lykes,* they made me grease the blocks on the cargo booms—from stem to stern. Heel blocks. Head blocks. Vang blocks. All by myself. The grease, which was in a five-gallon pressurized container on a dolly, was pretty goopy stuff, like you use on your car engine. In those days I had long hair, and by the end of the day it was greased up.

The next day, hearing that I was the cadet boatswain on the Maine Maritime training ship, they had me splice some eyes in the wire cargo runners that lift the cargo from the dock to the ship. I used the standard Liverpool wire splice for a six-strand wire that I'd learned from Lieutenant Buss, using a sledgehammer and a steel marlinespike on the splice, with the wire held taut by two clamps. The process is hard work—especially when you're doing it by yourself.

On the third day Charlie Alton, the boatswain, was sandblasting. He told me to get some sand out of the locker about three hundred feet aft. When I returned with it, he just looked at me. I didn't know if I had done something wrong. Finally he said, "None of the sailors can get the sacks that size." The one on my shoulder was a hundred pounds, twice as heavy as the sacks sailors usually brought up.

The fourth day, and for the rest of the sixty-five-day cruise, they left me alone! End of story.

The yearbook, *Trick's End,* provides a good record of the makeup of my class. Of 104, 40 were from Maine, with 15 from Massachusetts and a handful each from New Jersey, New York, New Hampshire, Pennsylvania, Connecticut, and Florida. Illinois, Maryland, and Rhode Island were each represented by one student. The rest—17—came from Iran, members of the Persian Navy sent to the States to go to MMA and other maritime schools throughout the country. There was a lot of jealousy between the American students and my Iranian classmates. Each of the latter got a hefty allowance, $600 a month, and they all had brand new Camaros. On Friday afternoon, the seventeen miles between Castine and Bangor were like the Persian Grand Prix. I often wonder what happened to them when the shah got kicked out of Iran.

At the academy, the four student companies maintain a twenty-four-hour watch on a rotating basis, one company each week. Because a big percentage of the students live so close, many go home for the weekend. I worked in the library about twenty hours a week on a work-study program to earn a little money. I usually had the job of running the library on weekends—the best time, when it was very quiet.

I really liked Maine Maritime's location and the friends I made in Maine. My best friend was Jane Nesbitt, the academic dean's secretary. She and her husband, Sam, who was a local attorney, took pity on me. When I didn't have the watch on weekends, I'd go AWOL to the Nesbitts' house. At one point I was also good friends with Claire Rodgers, the admiral's twenty-five-year-old daughter, and I house-sat for them when they were away. Mrs. Rodgers treated me like one of her daughters. They were great people and very considerate of me. And I would go out with the scallop fishermen—that started one Easter vacation, when they took me out to show me how to shuck the scallops. I helped them, eating about every tenth one I shucked, raw.

Toward the end of senior year came the moment—or week—we'd all been waiting for. The seven-part U.S. Coast Guard exam, all written, all multiple-choice, comes out of Oklahoma. That's where their testing center is—no water! The exam consists of international and inland rules of the road, celestial navigation, charts and piloting, safety, general navigation (meteorology, astronomy, tides and currents) and two parts lumped under "deck general" that cover ship-handling and seamanship, cargo, ship's business and administration, stability, ship construction, and damage control. The first three are 90-percent parts—if you get less than 90 percent right, you must repeat that section—and the rest are 70 percent. If you miss only two parts, you can take them over within three months. Otherwise, you must wait at least three months and repeat the entire exam. In addition, you have to pass first aid, cardiopulmonary resuscitation (CPR), and a physical exam. You must be able to read the blinker, meaning you must catch five words, averaging five letters each, per minute, flashed with a light in Morse code. And you must get a radar endorsement. That exam, also a 90-percent part, consists of answering twenty questions about a simulated radar situation in twenty minutes. For example, the timed radar plot might simulate entering New York harbor.

Until two years before I took it, the exam had been essay questions so you could write and write and hope to get credit. With the multiple choice, it's pretty cut and dried. Either you know it or you don't. I passed the first time. So did most of my classmates.

Because I had been on the field hockey and ski teams at Vermont, I had already used up my National Collegiate Athletic Association (NCAA) eligibility, and so was unable to participate in varsity sports at Maine Maritime. But as soon as I got there, I was asked to be mat maid for the wrestling team. Wrestling is a big thing there. I had wanted to be on the sailing team, but couldn't do that either. Through the work-study program, I ended up taking care of the waterfront and the boats belonging to the sailing team—not the sort of stuff that makes the academy yearbook.

In fact, I didn't have much to do with the yearbook. Whatever they put on my page was okay with me. There's one candid of me from my first student cruise to Glasgow, Helsinki, and Leningrad, pictured between two Russian students; we were guests of their maritime school. My senior picture is coupled with a cartoon showing women's undies hanging on a line. On another page is a picture of me receiving a Maine state legislature commendation at graduation ceremonies. I also got a resolution of congratulations from the Connecticut House of Representatives. That was pretty neat.

My class had petitioned to keep me out of the yearbook. I don't know how far they went, but they didn't succeed. I didn't care. I said I'd sign the petition. I was getting what I wanted.

That was to graduate at the top of my class, top "deckie" (deck officer), with a B.S. in nautical science, and to earn an ensign's commission in the inactive Naval Reserve and a third mate's license. Because I hadn't started there as a freshman, they didn't think it was fair to make me the valedictorian, so they also named a top engineer, Paul Lenfest (who later went to Exxon with me). Together we led the class into graduation and began a tradition.

And to think that the week I started at Maine Maritime, the BBC had carried an interview with me in which they commented, "Well, that's the end of the U.S. merchant marine fleet!"

A letter included in *Trick's End* foreshadowed my future. From Rear Admiral Rodgers, USMS, then superintendent of Maine Maritime Academy, it was dated 2 May 1976:

> The year 1976 will separate the men from the boys, so to speak, amongst college graduates available in the job market. Although various voices are promising tangible evidence of recovery from the nation's worst recession since the 1930s, better times are still well out on the horizon and hence this summer you will be faced with the stiffest competition possible in finding employment. Powerful union control over a large segment of the maritime industry will further bar opportunities that should otherwise be available to you. Difficult times such as we face this year will provide the acid test of the reputation of the Academy and our graduates. Our placement efforts on your behalf will benefit from the Academy's good reputation established by previous alumni.

Good men and women can always find a job and those of us who have had a hand in preparing you for the working world are confident that our graduates will win out in this year's stiff competition. We extend congratulations on your achievement at the Academy and best wishes for success and happiness in all your future endeavors.

Landlubber's Log
11–12 February 1994

Friday, 11 February

Another lovely day, although everyone assures the passenger it's "always like this in February." Ha. Also, that we're likely to pay for it on the way back. Gibraltar midday today, and the captain says there'll be lots of navigating, lots of traffic.

"Tough?" I ask.

"Nah, piece o' cake."

Activity starts to pick up as the crossing nears its end and the crew anticipates Livorno in a couple of days. The captain carries around her list and money, in case someone wants a draw. Crew members are painting, sounding tanks to check fuel levels (we have a slight list), and getting the bow thruster in working order. A tug strike in Livorno may mean that we'll dock with only the bow thruster—if the weather's calm. Deb's done it before in a strike.

Chief engineer: "Did you tell them we'd do it anyway?"

Captain: "Yeah, right!"

Shortly after 1000, from the bridge we spot fishing buoys, then a fishing fleet off the starboard bow. When a boom ship appears to be on a collision course with us, the captain "acquires the target" on the radar screen and "locks on," as in a computer game. She follows the ship from the bridge wing with glasses and a device to measure her angle to us. The boom ship is slower, so Debbie assumes she'll pass behind us.

We pass a navy ship heading west, then a car carrier that, we guess, is on her way to Norfolk. "Ugly box," the captain says. A carrier transports as many as four thousand cars driven onto twelve decks—with lots of sail area and relatively little weight, a carrier doesn't feel very stable.

The car carrier is north of a zone of separation, designed to keep freighters going through the straits within separate lanes. A ship can only be in the separation zone if she's crossing it at a right angle, tending buoys, laying cable, fishing, or in distress. Like other ships heading east, we're south of the zone.

With the steering on automatic, Sandy, the AB, watches the traffic. "Ship three points off port bow," he tells the captain. Debbie "does" the traffic while the chief mate, Bob, navigates. A ship with a heavy center boom heads west just north of us. The visibility drops a bit about 1030. At 1040: "Steer 087." "087." The "target" drops off the radar screen, and another ship seems to take her place port side. Through the haze and glare of the morning sun, it's just possible to see the first bit of North African coast, the outline of a small mountain.

A cool breeze blows through the starboard door of the bridge; outside, two crew members with rollers on long handles are painting the bridge wing white. The wind has shifted to the south, noticeably—losing our head wind means we gain time. Across the bridge wing we spot a tower on land. There's a tiny fishing boat in the other direction.

"Tarifa traffic, this is the *Charlotte Lykes,* Whisky Papa Hotel Zulu, on channel one zero."

The captain gets no reply. It's 1110. The captain and chief mate speculate: the Tarifa traffic guy's at lunch, having cognac, or in the head. We hear other ships trying to raise Tarifa, at the southern tip of Spain, with equal success.

We see a very distinct riptide ahead. According to Bob and the GPS, the lighthouse starboard side is at Tangier. Fishing boats are all around, with two dead ahead. "Hand steering," the captain calls. "089." "089, captain." "090." Lots of tiny white fishing boats to port—we stop counting at two dozen. "091." The village of Tarifa is coming up to port, white against the mountains. A big lighthouse is visible, and a tremendous number of wind generators are lined up on the ridge. At 1145, another riptide; we slow as the wind shifts again, and we cross yet another riptide.

At noon Juan relieves Sandy. A ferry carrying passengers and cars from Tangier to Gibraltar is ahead of us. We spot two porpoises, then several small groups of them. As we're overtaking a freighter, we notice a very large sailboat with only a foresail and mizzen up—and she's moving. "063." We change course to check her out. "Anything to keep the passenger happy," says the third mate, Amy, who's taken the watch at noon. The sailboat has a light blue hull and radar, dinghy, lifeboat, the works.

Unusual in the Straits of Gibralter: We spot the spout and fluke of a finback, but it sounds and we lose it. A ferry crosses in front of us going from Rota to Gibraltar. We take photos with the rock as the backdrop—looks just like the pictures, it does. Finally, Gibraltar is on our beam, making it possible to see the man-made water catchment slope on its backside. With the current, we're doing 20.9 knots, now on a course of 076.

Lunch, finally, about 1330. The steward has saved a tuna salad sandwich—it's always tuna on Friday, on every Lykes ship. The captain loses the basketball over the side. PX, here we come! We walk, five rounds, and go down a ladder (or two or three) for a demonstration of the bow thruster being fired. It's noisy, but not much to see. The best part is the lightbulb on the wall above the telephone that is supposed to light when the phone rings, but today it's not working, despite a new bulb.

Beat the captain at cribbage—YES! She takes some kidding about that from the crew. Then after fried flounder—it's Friday, after all—and once around the engine room to give out money and check the play in the rudder, we nibble nuked popcorn at the movies.

About 2100 the captain needs to be on the bridge as we change course at Cape de Gata, Spain. It's wonderful up on the bridge at night—very dark until your night vision kicks in, then surprisingly light. Tonight's show is an oil rig under tow—the rig itself is brightly lighted, with what looks like the stationary top of a carnival merry-go-round in the center. Bob, who has the watch, says the part you can't see looks like two submarine hulls. The rig is moving very slowly, and we watch it a long time. The tug has lights—from the top, red, white, red—to show she's restricted in her ability to maneuver.

There's other traffic, which we watch on the radar, and one freighter passes about a half mile from us. That's as close as the captain likes it. I plan to get up at 0230 as we pass Cape de Palos, so I sleep in my sweats, but somehow I wake just before 0100 and again at 0345, and I miss it.

Saturday, 12 February

The water is very flat just after sunrise. The only way you can tell it's Lincoln's birthday is that after breakfast the second mate asks Debbie if he can borrow the Lincoln part of the PBS Civil War series. About 0900 the first of the Balearic Islands—Ibiza—appears off the starboard side of the ship. Its appearance coincides with the painters, who decide it's a good time to paint that side of the fourth superdeck. I finally move inside and watch behind closed doors so I won't be speckled white.

No traffic today—most ships stay along the Spanish coast, and we're heading more directly for Livorno. About 1300 we come parallel with Mallorca. High mountains, 4,700 feet, mostly hidden by a curtain of fog between them and us. We do manage to see the cut at Dragonera, then the lovely harbor with two lighthouses. Most of this side of Mallorca is quite rocky—after watching it for more than two hours, the veil of clouds lifts just as we reach the northernmost point. Good news: the radio operator, Steve Ballor, gets a message saying the tug strike is over, so we won't have that problem to contend with. Radar isn't working right, and Steve works several hours at the dirty, cool job to fix it, only to find it's still not right. A thirty-three-year-old who's on his third consecutive trip, Steve is not having a good day. In fact, some crew think he's not having a good life. They've nicknamed him "Bag o' Nuts." I leave him on the bridge, unhappy.

No time to walk today, but I lose at cribbage. After dinner and a movie, Brendan Gause gives me a puzzle ring from Izmir to practice on—the puzzle ring wins. Clocks ahead again.

4. *Exxon Property*

*W*hen I was at Maine Maritime, Exxon interviewed each senior cadet. Those the oil company was interested in went to Houston for second interviews, four cadets per day. The other three in my foursome were from Texas A&M—and among them was Susan Carter, the first female graduate from their maritime program. I was the only one from Maine: I felt like a disease around them.

The port captain who did the interview, Captain Inman, asked why I wanted to sail tankers. I told him frankly that if I had my choice, I'd probably sail deep sea, dry cargo. Dry cargo? Bag flour, grain, machinery, containers, locomotives, tanks, trucks, fire engines, cotton, rubber, wooden dowels, subway cars, even a Brahman bull—the commodities are endless!

The cargoes are more interesting, plus the runs are all around the world rather than just along the U.S. coast. You do a lot more traveling. The thing about a tanker is it's all liquid cargo. Loading and discharge are done the same way, so after a while, once you learn the piping system, it's pretty routine.

"Yes," Captain Inman said, "if I had it to do over again, I'd do dry cargo, too."

It was a very upbeat, positive interview, and I was fairly certain I would be hired. Susan Carter was not hired, although I'd assumed she would be. She went to work for Texaco, then the International Organization of Masters, Mates & Pilots (IOMM&P), the deck officers' union. I don't know where she is now.

Because the union books were closed for sailing deep sea, dry cargo, only eight of the eighty-seven Americans in my graduating class got jobs sailing on their third mate's licenses. All of those were with the U.S.-flag oil companies—all nonunion companies. If you wanted to use your license and put in the 365 days at sea required to sit for a second mate's license and the next step up, that was the only way.

When I got out of school, I had even pressed my case for a union job. Before I signed with Exxon, I went to the New York office of Masters, Mates & Pilots to meet with Capt. Hank Nereaux, vice-president for the Atlantic region.

"You have no female members, so you've got to let me in," I reasoned.

"No, I don't," he said. And he didn't.

At graduation, I won the Gulf Oil prize for navigation, a suitcase I still use. So Gulf, along with Exxon, recruited me big time. But a job with Exxon was considered the top job—it picked from the top of the class at all of the maritime schools—and it paid better than union jobs.

In addition, the company paid transportation from my door to the job, and even gave me an Exxon credit card, good for 10 percent off. Officers were nonunion, although Exxon had a company union. I didn't join right away, but was pressured into it after a while. You could buy stock options, and earn stock—when I left, I think I had seventeen shares.

Before I started working for Exxon in June 1976, I had never even seen a tanker.

So I thought Exxon's five-day, eight-to-five orientation week in Houston should have been my introduction to more than just how to be a manager on a ship. I hated it. My mother had bought me five new outfits to wear, one for each day of the training—they're still hanging in my closet, but I don't think I ever wore them again! There were maybe twenty of us, new engineers and new deck officers, including six from Maine Maritime, so at least some faces were familiar. Although we were being paid for the week, about the third day I expressed my disgust at running past five o'clock; their only response was that they'd *try* not to do it again.

One day during the training we quizzed representatives of the marine division about advancement. They let everyone know—in front of me—that they had a female quota to fill, and they were filling it.

The instructors were into role-playing and problem solving, generic skills for any job, whereas I was more concerned with more immediate needs, such as which valve to turn to do what. Instead I learned that sort of thing on the job, which was not long in coming—six hours after we walked out of the last training seminar! Like the others, I had come prepared to go to work, having brought my seabag with me, but I didn't know until the seminar ended that I had an immediate job.

My first job was on the *Exxon Gettysburg,* which carried from ten to nineteen grades of fuel. It was one of the workhorses of the seventeen-ship Exxon fleet, fifteen of which covered East Coast ports. No one wanted to work on that ship when I joined it that Friday at 2300 in Baytown, Texas, where Exxon has its main refinery, about twenty-five miles down the Houston ship channel. Why? When I arrived, the first person I met was the deck cadet. You can imagine my reaction when he said, "Good luck. When I joined up, the captain told me, 'This ship is 715 feet long, and I want 714 of it between you and me at all times.'"

The fact that the *Gettysburg* carried so many grades of fuel made it very difficult to work. The more grades, the more difficult it is to keep them separated. Although it's the chief mate's responsibility to run cargo, when it's your watch you have to be out on deck humping. Plus, it was an older ship, so you had to turn the valves physically, rather than sit in some air-conditioned office and have them closed hydraulically. The crew was very helpful in teaching me the piping system and pumping system, which was very critical.

Unlike some male classmates at Maine Maritime, the crew of the ship was very receptive to me being there. Although I was the first female officer aboard, there also was a female mess person aboard at times. And we had separate quarters with separate heads, so living conditions were not a problem.

Also aboard, coincidentally, was Sonny Perkins, an AB from Penobscot, Maine, just outside Castine. His younger brother, Bobby, who was retarded, had worked in the maintenance department at Maine Maritime when I was there. Sonny was on my watch; I knew his brother, and Sonny knew who I was.

I started telling him stories of what happened with my classmates at Maine Maritime—like getting spat on at morning formation, having mashed potatoes thrown at one side of me, gravy at the other at dinner, and getting a rock thrown through my window.

We had assigned seats in class, and I'd find some not-very-nice cartoons, articles, words, thumbtacks left for me there, and outside the door to my dormitory room.

I didn't mention any names, but Sonny said that from my description, it sounded like someone I'll call Fred.

Fred, an engineering student at Maine Maritime, was the craziest of all. Some classmates on the deck side also did perverted, disgusting, and unspeakable things, but Fred seemed to be the instigator. For one of my work-study jobs senior year, I tutored a student who rode with Fred—they both lived in the Waterville, Maine, area. He told me things Fred did, like riding around town spread-eagled on top of a car, and holding up a country store with an icicle for a six-pack of beer.

At one point, Sonny's brother Bobby was put in charge of maintenance in the new engineering building. One day he had cleaned the men's head, then the women's, and then went back to the men's head. In the meantime, Fred had smeared filth all over it, and waited until Bobby returned to see it, in tears.

As a senior, I had to sit between Fred's father and mother at an alumni association dinner in Bangor. Fred was acting like a jerk there, and his father, an engineering alum, was encouraging him.

At graduation I pointed out Fred to my family—I had quite a contingent there, about forty people. I'd rented a bunch of rooms at the Holiday House, an old house that was used as an inn in Castine, and I had a cocktail party and dance there the night before graduation, and a reception after graduation. The guys caught Fred's eye during the ceremony, and started mouthing at him, "Debbie Doane, Debbie Doane." After the ceremony, my sister-in-law Marilyn's brother, Gene Peckham, holding his young son, walked over to Fred and his mother.

He grabbed Fred by the collar and, with Fred's mother whimpering at his side about not spoiling graduation, Gene said, "I understand you have not been nice to Debbie."

Anyway, Gene let him go, and later at the reception Capt. Lou Hathaway, a favorite professor, walked up to my brother Bob and said, "I understand you [all] took care of [Fred] today."

Thinking they were being chastised, Bob said sheepishly, "Yes, sir."

Instead, Captain Hathaway shook his hand. "Way to go, Bob!"

While I was still on the *Gettysburg,* Bobby Perkins was tragically killed in a hit-and-run accident in Castine, and Sonny suspected the driver was Fred. Sonny left the ship with the promise that he would get Fred. Now, Sonny is a very large individual. It never was proved who did kill Bobby, but Sonny told me that after he broke Fred's second arm, he said, "That's for Debbie Doane."

I started as a junior third mate, more or less as a trainee preparing to assume the watch. The chief mate was Jack Stillman, who coincidentally now lives in Mathews, Virginia, not far from me—I hadn't seen him since I left Exxon, and ran into him at a Masters, Mates & Pilots union meeting in Norfolk in the early 1990s. He broke me in as far as tankers for about twenty days, two round trips maybe. When it came time for me to assume my own watch, he wrote a very nice letter saying I couldn't learn any more from dogging him. He was very supportive.

But nothing prepares you for that first watch out of school. *It was traumatic.* This tanker was 715 feet long, with a crew of about thirty, and fifty thousand tons of fuel she's carrying as cargo. I was nervous, like when you first get your driver's license and you have to pass someone on the highway. Here it is midnight, it's dark, we've made our way down the Houston ship channel, down the fairways, and we're out somewhere in the Gulf of Mexico. I think the captain probably intended to be up with me, but he was tired. Suddenly I'm all alone on the bridge, with a quartermaster on the wheel and a lookout on the bow, with the responsibility for the next four hours. There were enough ships to have to do some maneuvering for traffic, plus the ever-present oil rigs. I was relieved when I was off watch, pleased that I'd accomplished something, glad I'd gotten the first-time jitters over with—and all without the captain present.

All the captain said was, "Sorry, I meant to be up there with you."

I had somewhat the same feeling on my first foreign trip with Lykes, on the *Sheldon Lykes* in 1977. When we were at Southwest Pass at the mouth of the Mississippi River, the captain, Tom McBride, turned to me and said, "You got it." It's a big responsibility.

As a result of my experience, though, when I've had a new third mate on a ship I've been conscious of his possible apprehensions and have tried to break him in gradually. When I was on the *Lyra* and I took her on south from Charleston after we rescued the ship, I had one green third mate. I had been running the coast, I was exhausted, and I actually fell asleep on the bridge during the third's twelve-to-four watch. I felt awfully bad about that.

When you're the lowest watch officer, at sea your four hours are spent on the bridge (with two third mates aboard the *Gettysburg*, we stood the eight-to-four and four-to-eight watches, and the chief mate didn't have to stand one). You need to ascertain the ship's position, usually with hourly fixes; maneuver for traffic, using the radar if required; do azimuths to determine the gyro compass's error; and record the weather reports. You enter in the deck logbook the vessel's gyro heading, what the magnetic compass shows, the results of the azimuth, when you pass major points or navigational aids, course changes, significant weather, and a summary of the weather for your watch, including sea temperature. It's more involved when you're in pilot waters, because you have to keep track of buoys, and where the ship is in the channel at all times.

At sea, your boss is the master; in port, you're working for the chief mate on deck, sniffing fumes, taking ullages (the amount of space left in a tank) and innages (the quantity of liquid in the tank). To do that, you drop a tape until it hits the liquid, telling you how much room you have left in a tank. And you're squeezing down the valves on the tanks: When you're topping off a tank, you narrow the valve to reduce the flow of liquid, so when it's close to the top it will come up gradually, not suddenly. On older ships you have to do that physically.

On my eight hours off, I didn't need to give the operation of the ship another concern. But I spent a lot of time with the pump man, who makes sure the pumps keep running, or with the chief mate, depending on who he was, learning more.

Third mate has the least responsibility as a deck officer, but I enjoyed doing the job.

The schedule the *Gettysburg* followed was a nine-day round trip. From Baytown we'd head for Wilmington, North Carolina, where we'd discharge half the load in twelve hours. On to Charleston, South Carolina, discharge the other half, and then back to Baytown for twenty-four hours of loading. I did that for about seventy days and then went home on vacation.

I still have some sharp memories of my *Gettysburg* time.

I had a crush on an AB on my watch. He died of a heart attack while I was on vacation, and Sonny had to break that news to me when he saw me on my next ship.

To help pass the time on the twelve-to-four watch, I would blink in Morse code to passing ships. And I was pretty good at it, because I had just gotten out of school. It's one part of the Coast Guard exam you have to pass. One time when I got a ship to respond to me on the blinker, he replied, "Use VHF." That's the last time I blinked!

And when I celebrated my twenty-seventh birthday on the *Exxon Gettysburg,* the crew made a birthday cake.

There's another story about the captain from the *Gettysburg* days. He knew the third mate, on watch from midnight to 0400, was sitting in his chair. When the captain would come back up, the third mate would run onto the bridge wing; the captain would feel his chair and it would be warm. So one time the captain went down to his quarters and came back up with some Vaseline and smeared it in the chair. He told the quartermaster if he said anything, he was fired. The captain went back down and the third mate came off the bridge wing and sat down in the chair. After a while the captain came back up, the third mate got out of the chair with Vaseline all over his rear end, and the captain fired him on the spot!

When we'd be coming into port and tying up the ship, the chief mate usually was on the bridge telling us what to do. The second mate was on the stern tying up, and as the off-watch third mate, I'd be on the bow. To hold the tanker, we had to put out wires, head wires that went forward, spring wires that went back—and breast wires that ran perpendicular to the ship. Invariably, the chief mate would say, "Okay, now you can put your breast out, Debbie." Jack Stillman still tells that story, adding: "Yeah, everybody wanted to come up to the bow and see Debbie's breast."

After that first trip for Exxon, I came home with a pocket full of money. I paid off my school loan—early—which felt really good, and my sister Linda had picked out the motorcycle I intended to buy!

With Exxon, you'd receive a computerized card detailing the date and time you had to call for your next assignment. I was vacationing in Maine when I heard from my mom that Exxon was trying to reach me. When I phoned, the company wanted me to rejoin the *Gettysburg* in Charleston within twelve hours. One third mate had an emergency and needed to get off the ship. My gear and my license were in Connecticut, and I told them it was impossible for me to make the ship before she sailed. They told me to go home and report when I got my card for my next assignment. When I reported,

I was told, "Miss Doane, we consider you Exxon property. You will report when we tell you."

After vacation, in November 1976, I joined the *Exxon Washington* under Captain Frutiger for seventy-plus days. The *Washington* was a sister ship to the *Gettysburg,* but didn't carry as many grades of fuel. I joined the tanker in Newport News when she was in the yard there; from there we took her to Baton Rouge to pick up a load of heating oil bound for Riverhead, Long Island.

We went up along the coast, around Block Island—all my old sailing waters—and had to tie up to offshore buoys. Tugs had to come from New Haven. We discharged the whole load in forty-eight hours, and I called my family to tell them when we'd be by the mouth of the Connecticut River, which you can see from my folks' house about five miles away.

It was a Sunday afternoon, cold and clear; I remember seeing ice on the tanker's deck in Riverhead. Later my folks said they did see the *Exxon Washington* go by the mouth of the river. My father had powerful binoculars he'd gotten off a Japanese ship in World War II. He'd set them up on a stand outside so my nephew, John, then only a couple of years old, could watch.

"Can you see Debbie?" he asked John.

"Yes."

"What's she doing?"

"She's binocularing."

From Riverhead we headed back down to Baytown, and that's when I learned the tanker route for going around the Straits of Florida. When you're sailing south, you hug the Matanilla Shoals, the northwest corner of the Bahama-Abaco chain at the northeast end of the Florida straits, running five miles off. (You can see the difference in the color of the water; the shoal, with only thirteen feet of water, is greenish, lighter than where you are. The deeper the water, the darker the color.) In fact, it's the route I followed working freighters for Lykes. It keeps you out of the Gulf Stream, which goes against you, so although it's a greater distance, it's faster.

This particular trip, two cigarette boats were crossing from the Bahamas to Florida, barreling across our bow. The first one crossed, then stopped, waiting for his buddy. All we heard on the radio was a slow and deliberate, "You better hurry. That's a big mother."

In Baytown, Captain Mahoney replaced Captain Frutiger. Then we picked up a load of jet fuel and xylene to take through the Panama Canal to the West Coast.

That's when the chief mate overfilled the tanks. As we approached the Panama Canal and the water warmed up, we were spilling jet fuel on deck as it came bubbling out of the tanks. The weather was very rough, and sniffing the gasses from the xylene gives you a constant headache. It made me think that twenty years of that has to affect you; it gets in the tanker's ventilation system. Now, it's just diesel exhaust gas we're smelling!

On the way to the canal I went up on watch. Captain Mahoney, a former boxer with cauliflower ears, said to me, "You know, I never thought I'd see the day."

"What's that, captain?"

"Women on the bridge."

"Here I am," I said.

"Yep," he replied, "And there isn't a damn thing I can do about it."

My first time through the canal was very exciting. The size of the locks—1,000 feet long and 110 feet wide—limits the size of the ship going through. We were required to have a Panama Canal pilot on board each side of the ship; we had only a few feet to spare. It's an interesting eight- to ten-hour ride through there, seeing the lights along the banks, seeing the tropical rain forest, and the workings of the mechanical mules as we went through the locks. I'd locked a sailboat before, but never a tanker, and not there.

It wasn't all work. The second assistant engineer on the *Exxon Washington* had a crush on me. He was a young guy, not bad-looking, and we played cribbage together, but we never went out. There were a lot of money games on those ships, poker games where a crew member would even pay someone to stand his watch so he could stay in the game. I never did that. I just played cribbage for fun.

We stopped in Long Beach and got rid of the xylene, then sailed up to Benicia, California, to deliver the jet fuel. Going into San Francisco Bay, it was pea-soup fog. I'd never been there before, and the captain had me out on the bridge wing to listen for the sea buoy for the pilot station. I couldn't see anything. The only thing he said to me afterward was, "You were scared, weren't you?" I don't think I was scared, but if it suited his ego, that's fine.

My sister Timotha, who lived in San Francisco, came to Benicia to see her long-lost, gone-astray sister. Then we headed back to Baytown, and that was my last trip with Exxon. But I didn't know that when I got off in March 1977.

With the union books once again open, that spring Masters, Mates & Pilots relaxed its restrictions on applicants to allow 120 days' work before having to get off, followed by 120 days "on the beach" as it is today. Previously, I could only have worked thirty days, then would have had to get off the ship, and after thirty days ashore, stand in line again at the union hall to ship out. Because everyone would have been senior to me, it would have meant a lot of waiting and very little working.

I sent a letter to Captain Inman, reminding him of what I had said about wanting to work deep sea and dry cargo, and his reply. His response?

"I suggest you leave Exxon immediately."

I did, but certainly without the support of my friends at Maine Maritime.

Before I made the decision, I called to talk it over with my old professor and friend, Sherman Sawyer, who passed the word on to the top man at the school, Admiral Rodgers. They didn't want me to leave Exxon, for these reasons: Exxon donated money toward a tanker simulator Maine Maritime was trying to build, and I was good publicity for that cause. Further, the union companies were not giving the school any money.

Nevertheless, I felt it was the right decision for me and, severing the tie, sent back my Exxon credit card to Captain Inman, as requested, in tiny pieces.

I probably would have sailed master sooner if I had stayed—Exxon is very concerned with its public image, particularly with regard to women. The company even sent a crew to Essex to do a spread on me for its magazine, but I guess I didn't stay long enough for Exxon to use it. I later saw a nice spread in the magazine on Nancy Wagner.

Despite its efforts, Exxon has not been very successful in keeping women. Nancy, who graduated from Kings Point in '78, the first class that included women, went with Exxon out of school and stayed until 1990, but never sailed master. She then became a San Francisco Bay pilot. Susie Warren, who, with her sister, Andrea, followed me at Maine Maritime, had been a cadet on the *Exxon Washington* under Captain Mahoney. When she graduated in 1978, she made one trip with Exxon and called it quits. She didn't like it at all.

I'm not sorry I didn't stay with Exxon.

The oil companies are having their problems generally.

Look at the *Exxon Valdez.* It was an unfortunate accident, of course. But as far as I'm concerned, Exxon hung that captain, Joseph Hazelwood, out to dry. The third mate was on the bridge, but did not execute the course change properly. The result was he hit a reef. The third mate is licensed by the Coast Guard, which says he's qualified to make that course change, despite the fact that the news media reported the ship was in the hands of an unqualified third officer. That was incorrect. The captain was in his office sending out messages during the course change, and did not go back to the bridge. That was his mistake—not going back. The Coast Guard tested Captain Hazelwood for intoxication, and his blood alcohol level was above 0.04, so he was considered intoxicated. In contrast, in most states, intoxication is 0.1. An alumnus of Fort Schuyler, he is now an instructor there.

As a result of that accident, every U.S.-flagged ship now carries a Breathalyzer. We're subject to random drug testing, and each individual has to have a drug-free certificate, renewed every six months.

Crew on the *Exxon Valdez* was down to eighteen from maybe twenty-four, and the Coast Guard was going to give its approval for further reduction, to fifteen. With the increased work load, being in port and then having to sail the ship, people obviously were physically exhausted. I'm sure that was a contributing factor. Eighty percent of all accidents worldwide are caused by human error, and in this case you have to count on everyone doing his own job correctly. But the burden falls on the master.

The Coast Guard was not without its faults, however. The traffic lanes going in and out of Valdez are monitored by a Coast Guard radar tracking system, the Vessel Traffic System (VTS), and while you are in certain regions of approach channels, the Coast Guard keeps track of you by speed and course. It failed to warn the *Valdez* of any error in her track. Pilots were not required for that section of the approach, but since the accident they are. New tankers are going to be required to have double hulls, too. Perhaps that will help. The complete answer, worldwide, is properly trained personnel, and vessels constructed and maintained to standard; many foreign-flaggers are not, now.

In addition, environmental laws are killing the oil companies. It's too expensive for them to call on all the ports in the United States because of what they're subjected to—they probably have to boom a ship to protect in case she has a spill, and use tanker escorts. These and other measures are a direct result of the *Exxon Valdez* accident.

The fact is that the size of the *Exxon Valdez* oil spill was down the list from tanker spills around the world, although that doesn't make it any more right.

Jobwise, the oil companies have only a handful of ships; most everything is foreign flag. Mobil, for instance, had only one U.S.-flagged ship in 1994. A U.S.-flagged ship is required only for carrying oil from one United States port to another, and in many places pipelines are taking the place of ships—they're less expensive. And *nothing* comes from overseas on a U.S.-flagged bottom.

My short experience in the summer of 1975 as a cadet aboard the *Velma Lykes* really sparked my interest in dry cargo—and began my association with Lykes Bros. Steamship Co.

Capt. Ernie Hendrix, manager of Lykes's marine division, was on the board of visitors of Maine Maritime Academy. He had determined which ship I got on as a cadet, and he never lost sight of where I was or what I was doing. When I was thinking of leaving Exxon, I communicated with Captain Hendrix. He was delighted, and said he'd help me with trying to get jobs.

After joining the union in 1977, I worked exclusively for Lykes and have no regrets. I've seen the world, and the cargoes that we carried always proved interesting.

Landlubber's Log
13–14 February 1994

Sunday, 13 February

Dark and gray this morning, but flat again. A bit of rain. After breakfast it turns to ice pellets, a bit of snow, then sun and intermittent rain before the sun stays out for the afternoon. It's apparent that it's getting colder outside as we make our way north; even the cabin feels cold. At 0800 it's forty-eight degrees; by 1100, it's forty-four. The chief mate complains to the captain. "Head south," she replies. Yesterday Amy stood the twelve-to-four watch in shorts, but today long underwear is in order. The *John Lykes* passes, sailing from Livorno to the States, and the captain raises her on the radio. No other ships in sight.

We pass Sardinia in the distance, then, during coffee and cookies (peanut butter) on the bridge, it's Corsica to starboard. You can tell the low hills are volcanic—perfect cone shapes. We're sailing seven miles off, obeying French rules. Haze, so only outlines are visible until we get to the cut between the island and Cap Corse with its lighthouse at the northernmost point. We hear ship traffic calling the Livorno pilots, so we know we're getting there. Wind picks up after lunch; whitecaps become more numerous.

At 1330 we hear the ship ahead of us being told over the radio it'll be 1530 for a pilot, and to call back when she's five miles out. Our captain does the same: "Livorno ships' information, this is the *Charlotte Lykes* on channel one six. Over." Debbie puts our ETA at 1445, and agrees to talk to information again when the *Charlotte* is three miles from the breakwater. Then she calls the Livorno pilots. It costs $40 more if the ship picks up the pilot more than a mile outside the breakwater.

Another ship is crossing our bow in the distance. We see the lighthouse on the tiny island of Gorgona, but see little else, no beach, and it's not inviting. On the northeast corner of Gorgona is a penal colony, with a big grassy slope up the center. It's forbidden to dock there, even if we could!

"Livorno pilots—the *Charlotte Lykes,* channel one two, over. . . . We'll be three miles off the breakwater an hour from now. Will we be berthing on arrival?"

"Don't know, captain."

"We'll call you again, thank you."

Then over the radio: "Good afternoon, Captain Debbie." It's Capt. Joe O'Connor on the *Sheldon Lykes,* passing on our port side as he sails from Livorno. A little personal conversation, a little business conversation. The *Sheldon* is a mirror image of the *Charlotte.*

Suddenly ships seem to be all around us as the city with its artificial port, one of the largest in Italy, comes into focus in a wide semicircle ahead. Tom Reay, the AB from Nelson County, Virginia, goes on hand-steering. "061." We approach our arrival at 1430 after ten days, four hours, six minutes at sea and with an average speed of 17.44 knots, the ship's fastest eastbound crossing. "058 . . . 056."

"Half ahead." It's 1432. "Head right for the big light dead ahead, third mate," the captain says. There's a light haze, a little wind, and whitecaps. Houses climb the hills and travel around to the right. A few skyscrapers and some bigger buildings loom ahead.

We pass the light, painted that uniquely Italian yellow on top, black below, on a stony base to our left.

"Slow ahead. 058."

We're close enough now to see that we're following the *Zim Italia,* a containership from Haifa.

"060." Four windsurfers, white sails furled, are off our port bow. Plenty of wind. Amy raises the Italian flag on the starboard halyard.

"063." At three miles, 1445, we call Livorno pilots, and find we won't get a pilot for an hour. "Dead slow ahead . . . 065 . . . stop . . . 067 . . . hard left." With a break, we go "slow astern" and take time to test the repaired bow thruster; it's putting out good RPM now. "Midships." We see tugs coming for the *Zim Italia,* and the pilot boat, white house above a black hull, hustling toward us. The tenor on the bridge changes.

"Amy, have the boatswain rig the pilot ladder, starboard side, and call all hands at 1500. Docking starboard side to." At 1511 the pilot is aboard, and the Marlboros are lowered by line to the pilot boat. The flag indicating the pilot's presence (the signal flag for the letter H—half red, half white vertically, with the red along the halyard) is flying. It's Captain Gavi, the same pilot Debbie had during the tug strike last summer. She wishes him a happy new year, then offers coffee.

"The *John* [*Lykes*] refused to dock without tugs?" she asks. Knowing laughs. "I told them I'd do it, but only if I got you!"

It's been rain and wind, rain and wind from the northeast, the usual for Livorno. We wait; the *Zim Italia* and her tugs go in. Then we speed up, with the pilot calling the orders, third mate on watch, the AB steering, and the captain coordinating. As we head straight toward the Livorno lighthouse, a yacht club is on the right, and the sign on the Hotel Palazzo beyond it is large enough to read with binoculars. A green-painted light pole marks the right breakwater.

"Left ten, left twenty," and we see a burned ferry near the lighthouse as we turn. Just a charred hull. Three years ago in March the ferry hit a tanker at anchor in pea-soup fog at night. All on the tanker were rescued, but 140 on the ferry died. One cabin boy survived. The ferry is in that particular yard for more investigation, but the pilot says they found nothing, and she will be moved back where she was the next day.

It's a quiet Sunday, no gangs working as we come in. A palm tree sticks up between buildings. The bright yellow gantry cranes are a nice contrast against the *Zim;* the two tugs push her to the dock as we glide by. A tanker, the *Princess Ariadne,* is berthed on our left, surrounded by floating containment booms in case of a spill. A big "NO SMOKING" is painted on her house. The *Jennifer Jane,* a containership, is to our right. Ships and containers line both sides of the channel.

We stop the engine, turn the bow. It's "slow astern . . . 200 . . . clear . . . stop her," and the stern's coming around. "Hard left . . . dead slow ahead," with the tug *Tito Neri Settimo* pulling from the stern. "Slow ahead . . . dead slow . . . stop her . . . midships . . . dead slow ahead," and the bow comes around. "Stop her." The pilot turns from the radio and yells in Italian at the line handlers to come back twenty meters so the gantry can work. The stern line is set, then the ship moves back another thirty feet. Finally, "We're alongside," the captain says. She gives the pilot the obligatory carton of Marlboros, warning, "Don't smoke 'em." With a laugh on both sides, he goes down to the pilot boat.

Immediately Ilio Giocomelli comes aboard—he's the driver provided by Tecnomar, the agency that handles Lykes's ships in Livorno and Naples. Then customs. Business taken care of, about 1700 captain, chief mate, third mate, and passenger take off with Ilio for the home of his sister and brother-in-law, Anna and Mario Nannucci. Ilio is forty-three, has two children, fourteen and eighteen, and would like to go to the States, but money is a problem. For vacation he goes to the beach in Italy. He doesn't much like Pisa—too old, not enough life—but he does like Florence. His wife likes to shop there, and they go to the museums.

We drive past the hotels along the water and the naval college, about twenty minutes from the shipyard. Livorno's population is about 180,000. A couple of small skyscrapers were visible from the ship, but the rest of the buildings seem to be four, five stories. Anna and Mario live in a modest, modern flat and are nice—ply us with drinks, candy, family pictures, lots of conversation. We see pictures of a condo they've just bought on Corsica—at Bastia on the east coast, accessible by ferry.

Their daughter, Sabrina, is there, but son Alex is working in Venice. Sabrina, twenty-three, speaks good English and carries the conversation. Anna speaks none, Mario and Ilio quite a bit. Sabrina works for Evergreen as a secretary, and would like to go to the States to work—she lived in Texas for three months with a Lykes captain and wants to go back, but can't get a work permit. She says she sees more opportunity for a good life there than if she stays at home. She's impatient and distresses her mother—typically twenty-three.

When the restaurants open for dinner at 2000, Ilio and Sabrina come with us to La Parmigiana in the heart of the city, a couple of blocks from the water. A favorite of the captain, La Parmigiana is a small, cozy restaurant despite its bright lights. Dinner is a marked contrast from ship's fare: polenta with chopped shellfish and garlic garnish, spaghetti marinara with mussels, local fish barely broiled, fancy gelato (chocolate, vanilla, cherry, and coffee with a miniature ice-cream cone on top). We pass on espresso to get Amy back to the ship for her watch at 2200.

Monday, 14 February

If it's Valentine's Day, it must be Pisa. Paraphrasing the song, I spent an hour there one day. Actually I went there for bananas, or so it seems.

We wake up early thinking we will tag along and wander when

Ilio drives a crew member to the doctor in Livorno—but he misunderstood, so he came and went without us. Instead, we wander in the cold to Angelo's bar on the dock, where the seamen and soldiers hang out, and have cappuccinos (3,000 lira for two). Hits the spot. Back to the ship, and officials come and go: health, immigration, the usual. Each comes with papers to stamp and sign, and leaves with a carton of Marlboros. The captain starts to keep track, then loses count. Tug captains here have traditionally left an envelope with the captain, about $20 worth of lira. Jack always got one; this Captain Dempsey, not so far. No explanation.

Ilio returns about 1100, and in a flurry we're off to Pisa in his white taxi. There seem to be no rules of the road except drive fast, pass often, and don't have an accident. About a twenty-minute ride, and we're there. Time is short. As we drive down the narrow street, there is an older woman wearing a long fur coat and hat, walking in the street ahead. Ilio is patient, patient, patient. Finally he toots. The woman slowly, reluctantly steps right to the sidewalk.

Ilio says I must walk down "the" nice shopping street in the heart of Pisa. He drives around the block-long arcade and I walk through, glancing left and right, and meet him at the other end. Sunday and Monday morning shops are closed, but some are starting to open now. Trying quickly to take it all in, I see one shop that has nothing but Swatch watches in the window . . . a nice flower shop . . . a tobacconist . . . a lovely bookstore, with lots of American paperback novels in translation. A magnificent sweet shop has one whole window decorated for Valentine's Day with tiny wrapped boxes, clowns and mice, another window done in blue and silver. The center window has every kind of sweet and pastry. Ilio says that's the place to go, very famous, if you are having a party and want something special. The street is full of shoppers, many women in long fur coats—it's quite cold, but not unbearable. We stop at a square noted for the university and the normal school, and only blocks away is the Leaning Tower.

Debbie has given Ilio instructions to take the obligatory tourist picture of me holding up the tower. He does. No one is allowed inside it now; large blocks of poured concrete are stacked by one side, to try to bring the tower back the other way a few degrees, and it seems to be working. So we spend what little time we have in the cathedral, buy a few postcards, and leave through the old wall for the ship.

Whizzing back toward Livorno along the Arno River, we stop at a good newsstand in Marina di Pisa, quickly double back a block to a small market for bananas, and fly to the ship. It's 1320 when we arrive; after a quick call home from a phone on the ship, the *Charlotte* sails at 1400. The two tugs are standing by as we let go.

White graffiti on the concrete dock remind us Robert R. was there. The *Tito Neri Sesto* is on the stern with her Italian yellow house and black hull. A tanker, the *Dutch Sailor,* is arriving with no tugs. We head out bow first, past a fisherman on the pier. The *Jennifer Jane* and *Zim Italia* are still there to port, the *Princess Ariadne* to starboard. We maneuver out through the breakwater, drop the pilots, take bearings, finally set the course at 179 and lock it in on the mike—on automatic; take down the Italian flag and the one signaling the pilot's aboard. And we're at sea again.

At 1700 Elba, the largest, richest, and most beautiful island of the Toscano Archipelago, is on our starboard bow, with a beautiful village, white buildings with red roofs, beyond two lights at the harbor entrance. It is a big island, and takes a long time to pass. The sunset is magnificent, bright orange over the mountains, and the glow lasts a long time. The lighthouse on a tiny adjacent island is massive, but not yet lighted. On the port side, there are cities all along the coast; Piombino is quite large, large blocks facing the Mediterranean, a huge refinery. It's possible to pick out the chimneys of the steel mill.

The captain maneuvers through the Piombino Straits, between Italy and Elba; margin is only about a mile between two islands at the tightest point. Strong currents there require vigilance. Most captains choose to sail west of Elba instead; Debbie says her route saves fifteen and a half miles, an hour's sailing time. At 1745 we're past the islands, and it's time for dinner, cribbage (I win again!) and a last check of the bridge.

"So, did you see the tower?" the second mate asks. "No, I went to buy bananas," I reply sarcastically. "New York must be rubbing off on you," he says, shaking his head. We promise to share.

5. The Love Boat

*B*efore I graduated from Maine Maritime, I was asked for my description of a sailor's life as I would know it. My reply: "Challenging, exciting, demanding."

But first you have to get the job.

After I left Exxon, I "ghosted" the union hall in New Orleans, then just a second floor room in a building on Gravier Street. It was about six blocks from Lykes Center, just outside of Canal Street and the French Quarter. Job call was twice a day, at 1100 and 1400.

It works this way: You have to become an applicant within one year of getting your license, then pay an initiation fee. Mine was $2,000 then. If you didn't become an applicant within that year, it cost $3,000. Now it's at least double. As an applicant—my status—I had to work 365 days before becoming a member of Group C. Above that are groups B and A. You have to work 365 days each in C and B before you are "full book," or Group A. Group A has job priority over B, B over C, C over applicants. And within each group, you have preference by registration date: the date you got off your last ship. The older your card, the better your chances for a job in your group. Naturally, along with a couple of other applicants, I had least seniority.

The boatswain from my cadet days on the *Velma Lykes,* Charlie Alton, and his wife offered to put me up in their house in Slidell while I was looking for a job. I'd ride the bus in from Slidell to New Orleans. Charlie retired from the *Mason Lykes* in the early 1990s; he used to come see me in Norfolk when I pulled in on the *Lyra.*

After a couple of weeks, I got my first job, probably because its brief duration made it less desirable for more senior union members. It was coastwise on the *Christopher Lykes,* a Pride class ship (495 feet long, with five hatches, breakbulk) as third mate for fifteen days. I flew from New Orleans to Houston's Hobby airfield and got to the ship about 1000, when everyone was having coffee. My reception from port captain Floyd Roberts: "How the hell do you expect to work in a skirt?"

We discharged cargo around the coast and then laid her up in New Orleans. Back to the union hall.

That's when I got a job on the *Sheldon Lykes,* also a Pride class ship and sister to the *Christopher* and *Aimee,* running to South and East Africa. It was a three-month job on a conventional breakbulk ship, which carried any and every kind of dry cargo. I was pretty excited about this ship, my first foreign long-term job. The captain was Tom McBride, a fairly young Kings Point grad with a distinctively loud voice—in those days we had no walkie-talkies, so he'd shout orders to the bow and stern using a megaphone. Chief mate was Tom Grafton. Both were nice and helpful to me.

We left New Orleans, going down the Mississippi River about ninety miles in eight hours to Southwest Pass, where we took departure. I had the twelve-to-four third mate's job, so I was on watch. Although visibility was limited, oil rigs were all over the place—and Captain McBride didn't know me from a hole in the wall—he was off the bridge about two minutes after departure. I didn't see him again for the next three days!

Tom Grafton had said "If you need help, call me." I was a little anxious and I certainly had some nervous moments. I was concerned, for instance, about keeping twelve miles off the coast of Cuba as we ran north of the island. But I had no trouble. It was eighteen days from New Orleans to Capetown, and by then I was broken in. Seeing Table Mountain was a most spectacular landfall after eighteen days at sea.

Funny what you remember. It was the first time I'd seen signs for three different rest rooms: colored, black, and white. The first assistant engineer, Carl Stayton, was a nice guy, and later he took me to the Crazy Horse Saloon in Durban; I still have a picture of us there. That was fun.

We also called in Port Elizabeth and East London along the South African coast. I remember I went into the bar in the hotel in East London, and I was asked to leave because it was for men only. When it came time to sail from there, the only one who wasn't aboard was the captain. We had to hold the ship for him.

My everlasting memory of Captain McBride is stacks of paper in piles all over the deck in his office. At sea we wouldn't see him for days at a time. Now and then you'd see him come down with a coffee cup.

We took the ship back to Houston, where we laid her up at Todd Shipyard. Captain McBride was in a lot of trouble; he couldn't find his license, and he had not kept an official logbook for the *entire* voyage. A bunch of us had chartered a bus to get back to New Orleans inexpensively. When I went to say good-bye to the captain, he was sitting at the table in his office. Floyd Roberts, the port captain, was at one end, busily filling in an official logbook. The Coast Guard was there, too.

"Come on in, Debbie, have a beer," he said.

"Uh, no thanks, cap."

He died a few years later of a brain tumor, at about forty-eight.

After vacation, my next job was on the *Solon Turman* with Capt. Bill Evers in the late summer or fall of 1977. I understood that nobody wanted to sail with him because he was hard to work for; that's why I got that job. I liked him. I was still a union applicant, and I put in my full time with him on the Med run. This was in the days of Israeli ships and Egyptian ships. Before the Camp David accord, ships calling in the Middle East could not go from Israel to Egypt, so Lykes had certain ships that called at one country or the other. This was an Israeli ship.

I had the eight-to-twelve watch, and stuttering Bill Evers expected you to do it right. Sailing with him, I started getting the confidence to haul or maneuver for traffic and take care of things on the bridge by myself. He had some quirky habits—for instance, he tied a pencil to the chart table and only when it would shrink to an inch and a half, the eraser long gone, could you ask him for a new pencil. I really liked the guy, though.

He liked his coffee so strong the rest of us couldn't drink it. He drank about twenty cups a day, a pot a watch. He had a bad habit of smoking Camels—Camels and coffee. The cigarette butt and whatever was left in his coffee cup would be thrown out on the bridge wing. Pretty messy. Sailing from Houston, he asked the second mate to make coffee. Before sailing the second had been out drinking, and he insolently replied, "I don't see anything wrong with your arms." After the captain chewed him out, the second made the coffee.

We had passengers aboard, and one woman was traveling only one way and getting off in Haifa. The night before we arrived there, we had a farewell party for her, in her room. It happened to be opposite the captain's office, and he wasn't invited. It wasn't loud or anything, but we had a mother-daughter team on board from Bogalusa, Louisiana. The daughter, Susan Chapman, had won the trip through an essay contest sponsored by the Propeller Club, the largest nationwide marine organization, and she played her guitar. The chief mate was Bob Wilson, who had yet to sail master, and the captain put both of us in the official logbook for being in the passengers' quarters. It's the only time I've ever been logged!

I always liked seeing Captain Evers in the union hall, and he was always interested in my career.

During the 120 days on that ship, we came back to Mobile and put the ship in dry dock. I was on the bridge with Captain Evers when the ship was on keel blocks and they were lowering the water out from under us.

He turned to me and said, "Go down and read the draft now." I was halfway there before I realized he had set me up. No water, no draft to read.

My last trip on the *Solon Turman,* Bob Wilson sailed his first trip as master, relieving Captain Evers. We went to the Med and back, then I had to get off. Bob was a nervous captain, but I guess everybody is on the first trip.

Because jobs came through the union, I could have sailed with other companies. But Lykes was letting me know when jobs that I might be able to get were coming up, and the company was very interested in which ships I mated on and which captains I was sailing with. And because I ghosted the hall in New Orleans, where Lykes was based, it was likely I'd get on a Lykes ship.

Next came the *Joseph Lykes,* at Christmas 1977. I was pretty homesick. I even flew my sister Timotha from her home in San Francisco to Essex for Christmas, and I was the only member of my family not there. The ship was in Houston from Christmas to New Year's Eve, working cargo. One of the nicest seamen's clubs is in Houston, and we were sitting around there one night having some beers. That's when the first assistant engineer asked if I could get lobsters flown in from Maine. I thought he said he wanted $150 worth. I called my friend Sam Nesbitt in Castine to see if he could put them live on a plane. When I checked with him the next morning at 0700, he said he could—thirty lobsters would be arriving in Houston on a flight that afternoon. At breakfast, I told the first assistant how many lobsters were coming. I had misunderstood. He said, "I only wanted *$50* worth." I borrowed a car to drive to the airport that afternoon to pick them up. After the galley crew finished, I went into the galley on the ship to boil the lobsters. Three arrived dead, but I ate them anyway, for starters.

Now tied up right behind us was the *Aimee Lykes* with Capt. Jack Dempsey, whom I did not know at the time, on board. In fact, I had a blind date with the third assistant engineer on the *Aimee*. We went to Mickey Gilley's, and I killed him shooting pool. I didn't go out with him again. Jack fired him that trip.

Everybody from the *Aimee* came to have lobster, except Jack. All of the port captains—Ben Bowditch, Floyd Roberts, Ralph Krueger—came. I set up clean garbage bags on tables in the officer's lounge, but I didn't show them how to eat the lobsters. I cleared them off into a clean garbage can, and I spent the rest of the night picking out lobster, and the next two weeks eating the rest. It was wonderful.

At midnight on New Year's Eve, Capt. Archie Adams blasted the whistle and we sailed with twelve passengers, including Rep. John Dent from Pennsylvania, who was on the House Merchant Marine and Fisheries Committee, and his party of eight. Martinis and cigars started at 1000. Lykes was concerned about having a congressman aboard; consequently, Captain Adams, a cigar smoker and Scotch drinker who bets on horses, figuratively went overboard for him. I was upset because it seemed to me that he catered to Dent and his friends over the other passengers—Karl and Muriel Pogrund, and Maria Hornung and her roommate.

I had the eight-to-twelve watch, and in the morning the congressman would come to the bridge and say things to me like, "Young lady, you don't belong up here—you belong in the galley."

I gave it back. "*Mr.* Dent, I don't believe you saw the sign in the passageway. Only those involved in the navigation of the ship need to be on the bridge."

I became very friendly with the Pogrunds and Maria. They were a lot of fun and they put up with a lot of shit from Dent. The Pogrunds, from Chicago, would periodically ride one way when they went to their place in Spain, at Benalmadena, just west of Malaga. Maria Hornung was from New Orleans and taught at Tulane Medical

School. She was taking the trip by herself. Her husband, who had taught at Xavier University, had died in September of a heart attack on stage while receiving an honorary degree. They had planned the trip before he died, and she was bound and determined to do it. I stayed with Maria in New Orleans quite a bit after that. All three of them surprised us and came to the wedding, when Jack and I were married. But we'll save that story for later.

That's the trip when we got shot at off the coast of Morocco. Karl and Muriel got off in Tangier, and we were going from there to Casablanca. We were running the coast of Morocco, about five miles off, and we'd been dodging fishing boats all morning. About 0900 I spotted three naval craft, maybe eight miles off to starboard. I called Captain Adams in his office to tell him, and he said he'd also noticed them.

In turn, I asked the radio operator if he was aware of operations in the area. No.

I tried to raise the navy on channel sixteen on the VHF radio—supposedly all ships monitor that channel. No response.

I was about to haul behind what I thought was a fishing craft, crossing port to starboard in front of us. When it came time to do that, she altered course to come toward us, meeting us port to port. When we got closer, I saw three signal flags on the hoist, from the top, K, J, 2. Translation: I am towing a target. Here came the boat towing the target aboard a raft down our port side, when the first round exploded about a half mile off our starboard bow.

Captain Adams panicked. He ordered hard left, and the *Joseph Lykes* started heading for the Moroccan coast. Then the second round exploded off our port bow. Dent was on the bridge, along with his whole party. I never could get near the binoculars or radar again. When we got into Casablanca, the captain filed a complaint against the Moroccan navy.

A couple of nights out of Casablanca, when we were heading home to Corpus Christi at the end of January 1978, Captain Adams asked me to come to his office when I got off watch at midnight. I was hanging around on the bridge because I didn't want to go down there. Finally he dragged me down, and in his office he'd set out a bottle of Scotch and two glasses. We were empty, which meant we were doing a lot of rolling. On the first roll, the two glasses crashed. On the next roll, there went the bottle of Scotch!

Captain Adams had me change my statement about the naval incident to suit his needs. He was quite concerned about the congressman having witnessed it, and wanted to make sure we had our stories straight when we got back to the States. However, when we got into Corpus, no one quizzed us at all.

Because we were coming from Casablanca, where locals working on the ship openly tried to sell dope to our crew, customs agents greeted us with drug-sniffing dogs. The chief mate made me take the dogs around—checking through the crew's luggage, rooms where luggage had been stowed. I'd never experienced that before.

I wanted to get off in Corpus because I had put in my time to sit for my second mate's license, but Captain Adams talked me into riding to Beaumont because that's where they were paying off for the voyage and changing crews. I stayed with Maria Hornung in New Orleans and studied, then took my second mate's exam there. After the exam, I went to see Captain Hendrix to let him know I'd completed it, but all he did was quiz me about the shooting incident. That was okay with me. I thought that now I'd finally get some answers.

Instead, Captain Hendrix said, "Our only concern was the reaction of the congressman."

To this day I don't know whose navy it was.

I did pass my second mate's exam (after taking the rules-of-the-road section twice) and got my first job sailing second mate, on the *Aimee Lykes,* running to South and East Africa with one of Lykes's most senior captains, Jack Dempsey.

That was in April 1978. I was in Connecticut when I got the call from Lykes. I flew out at 0200, arrived in New Orleans at 0700, went to the union hall and at 0800 cleared a job that had been held over from the previous afternoon. I rented a car and, after passing the perfunctory physical exam that is a prerequisite to signing onto any ship, drove out to the *Aimee* about 1000. She was in a bad part of town, at Buck Krist's yard at the Andry Street Wharf, where she had been laid up for a month undergoing repairs.

Only later did I find out from Hank Nereaux, vice president for the Atlantic region for Masters, Mates & Pilots, that my getting the job was rigged. Captain Hendrix had called him in New York and said, "I'm gonna put her with Dempsey and if she survives that, she can make it out there."

Jack, forty-nine when I met him, had come up the hawsepipe—he started at the bottom and worked his way to captain. A native of Corsicana, Texas, he didn't have much family life and at fifteen ran away from home, forged his birth certificate, and shipped out as an ordinary seaman in 1945.

Twice before he joined Lykes he'd stayed behind when his ship pulled out. The first time was on purpose in Italy, where he had been on the *James B. Duke* and, enamored of the country and an Italian girl, he jumped ship. He spent four months there, supporting himself by selling black-market cigarettes, before the immigration authorities met up with him and sent him back stateside. The second time was accidental. As an able seaman on the *Cerro Gordo,* a Texaco Marine tanker, he was in San Pedro, the port of Los Angeles, on his way back to his ship, when he saw her sailing out—earlier than the posted sailing time due to a last-minute change of orders. He had $5 in his pocket, and no job. Times were tough in the maritime industry after World War II, and after three months he still had no prospect of a job. Anybody would buy him a drink in a bar, but that didn't include food or a place to stay.

When a fellow drinker in a bar mentioned that he was a paratrooper, thinking about reenlisting in his old unit, the need for security led Jack to join the army in 1950. And then Korea broke out. He hadn't counted on that. After his time was up, he went back to the only work he knew and signed on as an able seaman, this time with Lykes Lines. That was in 1957.

Shortly thereafter, a chief mate did him a big favor. Jack had been in trouble over the course of a year, in jail three or four times for too much drinking, or fighting in a bar. Embarrassed about it, he'd decided not to return after vacation. Just before he left the ship, the chief mate asked if he'd come up to the bridge.

"See all this stuff here? Think you could do this?" he asked. Jack had handled the wheel and done all the practical stuff, but had never thought about it. "Why don't you try for your third mate's license?"

Well, Jack had had little formal schooling, but that got him thinking and, instead of going off to Mexico to drink a bottle of tequila a day on vacation, he hied himself over to New Orleans to Page's Navigation School. Unsure if he could handle the book work, Jack explained about his lack of education.

"Can you add that column of figures?" the instructor asked.

"Sure."

"Then I can teach you." And sure enough, in six weeks Jack learned everything he needed, including trigonometry, and passed the third mate's exam. That was the break he needed.

When I arrived, Jack was leaning on the cap rail on the fantail of the *Aimee.* Both the *Ashley Lykes* and *Marjorie Lykes* were behind the *Aimee,* also undergoing repairs, and Jack just assumed I was heading for one of them. Instead, I was heading for the *Aimee.* He said to Chuck Norfleet, one of two third mates, "There's the new cadet. Better go help her with her gear." Chuck quickly reported back to the captain, "That's no cadet. That's your new second mate."

"We'll see," Jack said.

He immediately called the company. "What do you think you're doing putting a woman on my ship?"

"Just make a trip with her; you'll like her."

"We'll see."

When I gave him my papers in his office, all he said was, "I guess I don't have anything against women. After all, my mother was one."

I was very nervous about the job because it was my first as second mate, and very excited about it because the second mate does the navigation. You're dealing with the voyage charts up on the bridge, laying down the courses and correcting them, as well as keeping other records. Second mate also takes care of all of the equipment on the bridge—chronometers used for navigation time, the gyro and magnetic compasses, the LORAN electronic navigation system, the Fathometer that charts the water depth. As second mate, I got those spectacular sunrises and sunsets while taking morning and evening stars at sea. We were still using sextants; celestial navigation was it.

We spent about ten days loading the ship around the Gulf: New Orleans to Mobile, Mobile to Houston, Houston back to New Orleans.

We sat idle in Mobile for a weekend awaiting cargo. One day the chief engineer, L. G. Freund, took me out to lunch and shopping, and we went to Bogalusa to see the Chapmans, who had been passengers with me on the *Solon Turman.* All the while Jack was silently jealous of Freund, and was wondering where the hell I was. After finally loading flour, we made the two-day run to Houston.

There we worked the ship, sailed, and took departure on the twelve-to-four watch of the other third mate, John Bates. Both Chuck and John were 1976 Kings Point grads, and both were extremely jealous of a 1976 grad from Maine Maritime who was sailing as second mate. Despite my letting John use my sextant the entire voyage, he and Chuck, and chief mate Arne Olsen, all complained about my relationship with Jack.

A few years ago, Lykes sent Chuck as chief mate to Jack, and Jack sent him back—he knew it wouldn't work. Chuck subsequently lost his mate's job with Lykes, although he got a job through the union as Jack's second mate on the *Howell Lykes* a year later. His next job was for the union at $90,000 a year.

Fifty miles south of Houston, we took departure from the Galveston sea buoy with a six-hour run down the safety fairways between the numerous oil rigs and into the Gulf of Mexico. When I came up to relieve the watch at 0345, it was pea-soup fog and I couldn't see anything.

My first question of third mate Bates: "Where are we?"

He started his reply with, "I think . . ."

Uh-oh. My next question was, "Where's the captain? Don't you think he ought to be up?" He was sleeping in a bunk right off the wheelhouse in the sea cabin, designed exactly for that purpose.

I quickly looked in the three-centimeter radar and tried to piece together what we had by determining which targets were moving and which stationary, and matching the stationary patterns to the charted oil rigs. Meanwhile, the third mate did wake up the captain before he left the bridge, and Jack immediately went to the ten-centimeter radar. But I had a ten-minute head start on Jack, and had figured out we were on the wrong side of the fairway. We had oncoming traffic.

First I said to myself, "Keep your mouth shut," then thought better of it. So I said, "I think we ought to haul right."

Silence. Nothing.

Later, I learned that his first thought was, "No goddamned woman is going to tell me what to do."

After a thirty-second pregnant silence came, "I think you're right," and he hauled ninety degrees right. I finally felt I'd broken the ice.

From Houston we headed for New Orleans, where we topped off our cargo and fuel at the Nashville Avenue Wharf.

Close by is a nice waterfront bar and restaurant, Frankie and Johnnie's, which has great poor-boy sandwiches, crawfish, shrimp, Cajun food. The night before we sailed foreign, I walked out to mail letters and ran into the chief engineer and first assistant, who invited me to join them at Frankie and Johnnie's. I did. An hour or so later in walked the captain, who came over the table and asked the chief, "What are you doing with my second mate?"

Jack and I proceeded to close Frankie and Johnnie's. Johnny Laberta, who worked the waterfront for the longshoremen, gave the two of us a ride back in the cab of his pickup, and I got out and went up the gangway by myself. Later I learned Jack said to him, "I think she could be trouble."

"Oh no, captain," Laberta said. "She's fine."

Four hours later we sailed foreign.

I had a hard time waking the captain by phone the next morning. Jack smoked cigarettes then, and I just remember him standing out on the bridge wing later, smoking, obviously not feeling too well. In fact, it was my job to wake him every morning at 0600. His predictable reply: "What's the matter now, second mate?" That's because during the four-to-eight watch the second assistant engineer has to blow tubes, or clear the soot out of the stacks. Each time he did, it caused a voltage problem, which would kick out the gyro compass and start the gyro failure alarm, which meant I had to call the captain. Eventually the engineers solved the problem, and about halfway to Capetown, our first foreign port, the response when I woke him changed from "What's the matter now, second mate?" to "Good morning, second mate." Progress. Sort of.

I'd be taking evening stars, and he'd come up and make comments like "You look nice, second mate." I'd be a nervous wreck in the chart room when he was there, watching, and he'd comment on that fact: "Your hands are shaking—you must have had too much coffee." Eventually he told the chief engineer he was going to quit picking on the second mate. The chief said he shouldn't do that—I'd think he was mad at me, or something.

In Capetown, our first foreign port, the radio operator had a friend who was a nun at a hospital, and he asked if I'd like to go ashore with him. The captain had given me $100 worth of South African rand, the local currency, to go ashore, and I rode the cable car to the top of Table Mountain. When I returned twenty minutes before I was to go on watch at 1600, there was a note from the captain saying he needed to know the distance to East London—it was being added to our run. I went flying up to the bridge to figure it out for him. I worked it up in ten minutes. But in my haste, I had failed to lock the door to my room, left my pocketbook on top of my desk, open, and the rand had been stolen. Eventually Jack heard I was ripped off, and he was afraid it was more than what it was, that I'd been hit over the head or something. He overreacted in trying to find out if I was all right.

After East London, we called at Durban, which is very modern and has a reputation for a terrific yacht club, great beaches, and lots of surfing. Chuck Norfleet had his surfboard with him, and he figured when we got to South Africa, he'd be able to go surfing. The rest of us wondered who'd stand his watch—that's how much his head was up in the clouds. His quarters were small, and the surfboard stretched from floor to ceiling. It stayed there the whole time; he never went surfing. Chuck's from the white sand beaches of Pascagoula, Mississippi, but with his blond hair he could have been from California. He fit the bill.

In Durban Jack had very good friends, Dusty Miller and his son-in-law, Jamie. On the maiden voyage of the *Aimee* in 1963, Jack was the off-watch third mate when the ship hit the Aliwale Shoals just south of Durban harbor. The other third mate had misplotted the ship's position, and the *Aimee* hit the shoals doing about twenty-two knots, ripping out a third of her bottom. It was Captain Ohmstead's last trip.

Dusty Miller was the contractor who had the cleaning gang for the ship when it was in dry dock for about a month there. Dusty no longer was running the business when we were there, but he showed us all over Durban—the snake farm, zoo, aquarium, yacht club. He even sent me a huge bouquet of bird-of-paradise flowers when he knew Jack was sweet on me.

And in every port Jack bought me souvenirs. He and I were having a great trip. But the stop in Durban produced some problems. I got so sick there from bad oysters in a seafood omelet at the Durban Yacht Club that I nearly ended up in the hospital. "Surfing Boy" got hit over the head walking out of a club, and ended up with stitches. Jack stood some watches for us, and got in trouble for it later when he got back to the States.

The next memorable stop was Mombasa, one of our all-time favorite ports, where we spent about three days. It has a nice yacht club and great touristy hotels. We spent the time visiting the beaches and our favorite restaurant in the whole world, the Tamarind—where Jack proposed to me. The Tamarind sits up on a hillside overlooking the Mombasa River, and that's also where I ate Dungeness crab cooked in a ginger base, brought out in a wooden bowl a foot and a half in diameter; in fact, I spent two hours eating that one crab. It was wonderful. Whenever Jack commented on my appetite, he always reminded me of that. It was in Mombasa that I called home from the seamen's club and told my parents all about Jack.

In Kenya, Jack had bought me some skirts and halter tops. So I dressed up one night for dinner and, when we ran into the crew in an outdoor bar in Mombasa, they didn't recognize me. Mr. Kirby, an able seaman, said, "Oh, Miss Doane, it's you."

From there we sailed to Dar es Salaam, Tanzania, where we stayed a couple of weeks. First we were discharging foodstuffs, then we tied up ship to ship with the *Sheldon Lykes* to take off some heavy-lift equipment. The captain was Tom McBride, with whom I had sailed on the *Sheldon.* He was very nice to us and wished us well in what everybody knew would be a fight with Lykes.

In Dar es Salaam we picked up a great couple, Nigel and Jan Hayden-Evans. He was the harbor pilot, and we had to carry him with us to Matrawa, Tanzania, where the original *Blue Lagoon* was filmed, because he had to serve as pilot for the next port as well. Later he was a pilot in Dubai. We spent the week off-loading bagged flour, with absolutely nothing else to do except play on the beaches. I had the day watch, from 0800 to 1600, and when I got off work, Jan and Nigel would pick us up and we'd all go to their cottage or to one of the beaches.

The port has a narrow entrance, very tight, with reefs on either side, which open up into the lagoon. Only three ships could dock there at a time, and they seemed out of place—it's more suited to yachts.

When we reached New Orleans, where we had to lay up the ship, Jack went to the Lykes office to see Capt. Ernie Hendrix, vice president of the marine division, and Capt. George Price, then manager of the marine division and next down from Captain Hendrix. With his jowls that rest on his chest, Captain Hendrix was better known as Big Daddy because he was so big. He would walk down the passageway of a ship and block out the light.

Jack obviously had grown to like his second mate, as the office had predicted, and it was then that Jack told them he was going to marry me.

Now, Jack and George Price had sailed together. He is a really nice guy, and was on Jack's side. Captain Price's comment was, "Wow. The two of you in the same field: wonderful."

Captain Hendrix, on the other hand, broke the pencil he was holding. He threatened that I'd never sail chief mate, Jack and I would never sail together, and on and on. His reaction was understandable. First, he felt I hadn't yet paid my dues to him, so he went bananas. Second, Jack was not one of his fair-haired boys because he was not an academy grad. Captain Hendrix was always partial to graduates of Kings Point and Maine Maritime, where he served on the board of visitors. He'd put Jack down by saying things like, "Oh, here comes the boatswain." Everybody knew that Jack sailed ten years as chief mate, being held back by Captain Hendrix. I also think Captain Hendrix had had another problem with a woman in the office.

Eight months later, on 16 December 1978, we had a big wedding in Essex, complete with a replica of the *Aimee Lykes* for a cake.

I certainly couldn't have predicted that changing my career course from oil to dry cargo would also lead me to Jack—and union trouble for both of us.

Landlubber's Log
15–18 February 1994

Tuesday, 15 February

Day dawns gray and rainy. At breakfast, the second mate comes in with his banana. As I make coffee in the captain's office afterward, he stops in with two Andes candies—"Just our little secret," he says. "Don't tell the captain. Oh, and you got my valentine, right?"

"Invisible?"

"Right."

The steward says he's going to the "lady captain" with a crew problem; there's always something to deal with. To get ready for arrival in Egypt, all of the papers required by officials there must be in order—from crew and passenger lists to stores lists and hazardous cargo lists and regular cargo lists and more. Before lunch we pass the island of Stromboli, with its single volcanic cone. Bob says he's sailed by it in the dark and seen the reddish glow. Today we just glimpse the top before it's obscured by clouds. Stromboli is where Ingrid Bergman apparently became pregnant by her director, Roberto Rossellini, while making a film there. The side we see has a lovely little village; the ferry crosses in front of us and heads toward a landing on the east side of the island.

After a quick lunch, the captain takes a short nap in her chair on the bridge before we start through the Straits of Messina, which connect the Tyrrhenian Sea on the north with the Ionian Sea on the south. Very little traffic today, but because there have been accidents, a pilot is required on any ship more than fifteen thousand gross registered tons (GRT). Cost: $1,000. The *Charlotte*'s record time through the straits: nineteen minutes, a minute more than Captain Jack's. To our right, we start seeing huge blocks of buildings at the north end of Sicily, all facing the sea. At 1445, we begin watching for the pilot, through the rain. Usually the ship doesn't slow down, but we're getting wind, so we'll have to go half ahead, or twelve knots, when we pick him up. At Capo Peloro, a big metal tower marks the turn—we're only three-quarters of a mile off land at the turn, so it's possible to see features of Italy, left, and Sicily, right, quite clearly.

"Whoever spots the boat first gets a quarter," the captain says. She spots the speeding dot first—third mate says she saw the boat, but didn't say so!

We move half ahead for four minutes until the pilot's aboard, then full ahead. It's foggy, with light rain and cold wind; we watch the scenery, and the pilot watches the traffic. Not much today, but ferries crossing require attention. Messina is large, with many massive blocks built up the hills, very reminiscent of a Hong Kong I remember from living there some twenty years ago. Lots of white buildings with red tile roofs, boats in backyards, everything facing the water. Here and there you can see what can only be a new superhighway going through the mountains. A big pink dome must be the Mausoleum of the War Dead, according to the *Sailing Directions (Enroute) for the Western Mediterranean*. That blue paperback, put out by the Defense Mapping Agency's hydrographic/topographic center, part of a comprehensive series, is a wealth of information as a sightseeing guide from the water—noting landmarks, towers, domes, and so forth, so the tourist knows exactly what she's seeing. Among other things, the ship uses it for positions. It's too expensive for the average sailor to have, and requires continual updating.

The pilot, warning us to keep off the shoals going around the point, goes down to the main deck and catches the pilot boat on the fly, waving to signal that he's safely aboard. We'll have to try for a record next time—twenty-seven minutes today.

On the mainland side are buildings of towns and cities all along the coast, with some houses built into the side of the hills, lots of terracing, an aqueduct, many tall blocks with picture windows. There's snow in the high mountains, and we think we see a ski trail.

Finally, we reach Point Raineri and head for Alexandria, Egypt, course 120 all the way to the approach there. Too bad: Mt. Etna is totally hidden by black clouds. At 1530 it's time for fire and boat drill for the week.

The passenger wins at cribbage—AGAIN! Popcorn, again courtesy of the second assistant, with tonight's feature. Clocks ahead for the last time.

Wednesday, 16 February

The day dawns bright and sunny. Two naval ships are off the port side—but whose navy? No other traffic in sight. After breakfast comes work, coffee and cookies (chocolate chip), and conversation with the chief mate about shipping. Bob, thirty-four, a Texas A&M grad, says he'd planned to be a game biologist, but learned about the Aggies' marine biology program as a high school junior. After a summer studying and working one meal a day aboard the school's training ship, he decided there was a lot more money in shipping. If it declines to the point that he loses his job, he doesn't want a shore-side shipping job. An agent's hours are too erratic, a pilot's job too stressful. Maybe he'll go into the tractor salvage business with a buddy, maybe get an MBA. On-board management experience doesn't seem to transfer to another industry, he says.

Lunch, time for a literary stroll through *Jurassic Park,* then a walk. Warm but windy, so we walk on the lee side (out of the way of the painter and the new black paint as we lurch along the rail).

After twelve lengths, the captain asks, "Enough for today?"

"Yes."

"I was hoping you'd say that!"

Nap time, then cribbage (captain's turn to win), dinner, and ice cream from our stash with the movie.

Thursday, 17 February

It's a swell day. Sometime in the night I awake to an easy rolling ship. Can't be as much as the last time, because when it rolls to port I can't see the water from the bed. Just have to be a little more careful showering, for instance, or walking without holding on.

Cookies (oatmeal raisin) on the bridge, followed by a long talk about cargo. The system the chief mate uses to keep track of what's where for which port is color-coded by port. The chart shows several boxes that will be off-loaded and later re-stowed in Alex, probably because it's cheaper there than in Haifa. It's not his decision, but he has no reason to question it. In Naples the stevedores remove one container, then replace it with an outbound one. Other places on the run they off-load all of the cargo for that port before they load. Not all container ports work around the clock; Alex does.

This morning's message from the Lykes agent in Alexandria says we're eating dinner aboard and not at the long-anticipated

Khadoura restaurant—we'll have to anchor until at least midnight, because the berth we're slated for is tied up.

After lunch it's up to the bridge, and by 1415 the city begins to materialize ahead. On the radar, the captain counts twelve ships in the waiting area. Noses into the wind, they're at anchor, not moving. We're still six miles out. Four small fishing boats are off our port side. A seagull lazes overhead.

About fifteen minutes ahead of time the third mate warns the engine room so the bow thruster will be ready, and with three miles to go, Mr. Reay goes on hand steering. The captain and third mate are keeping track of our position, measuring our anchorage position from the black-striped light at Ras el-Tin. At 1442 we take arrival. Total miles from Livorno: 1,241. Total sea time: two days, twenty-two hours, forty-two minutes.

"122 . . . 123 . . . half ahead." Two little fishing boats are off our starboard bow. "122."

Alexandria is a huge, wide city. Two mammoth gantry cranes like pointed metal domes are the most prominent feature, with another large building alone to the right.

"120 . . . 115 . . . 113 . . . slow ahead." Great Pass Beacon, marking the entrance, is almost dead ahead. A Greek tanker lies at anchor on the port side as the captain calls, "Dead slow ahead."

With 1.8 miles to go, "Stop . . . 110." As we continue gliding forward, Amy reminds the captain that "you have the bow thruster if you need it."

We're going dead slow ahead at 109, 108, 105. On the radio to the chief mate, who is up on the bow, the captain says, "Okay mate, you can walk out one shot starboard anchor."

At 1.2 miles out, our bearing is 109, then 110. "One shot is out and it's back on the brake," the chief mate reports back.

"Have you got a spot picked out [to anchor]?" Mr. Reay asks Amy.

"Yes," she replies. "We put the course and bearing in the GPS and when it beeps, we're there."

"Left ten," the captain says. "Stop engine . . . hard left," and the nose starts turning into the wind. "Dead slow ahead . . . midships . . . left twenty." Beeps from the GPS, and from Amy, "We're there." Finally, the captain says, "Midships . . . stop engine . . . slow astern." She watches over the side of the ship until the stern wash is amidships, signaling that the *Charlotte* is totally stopped.

"Okay mate, let 'er go," the captain says; the clatter of the anchor chain follows immediately. Chief mate reports that the first shot (ninety feet) made no strain, then two are out, and, with intermittent clatter, he acknowledges the captain's order to put "six in the water." Then: "She's stretching out real good right now." At 1518 we're anchored.

To Mr. Reay's "Are you finished with the wheel?" the captain nods, and calls the engine room to tell the first assistant to shut her down and turn off the steering gear.

Then she turns her attention to the obligatory call to Alexandria Port Control. No answer. "I didn't give 'em cigarettes last trip," she notes. We see at least eleven other ships anchored, waiting to go in; smoke rises from the stern of one nearby as she burns trash. The third mate puts up the Egyptian flag, calls the chief mate to put up the American flag only to find out it's already been done, an hour and a half ago. "Thank you, mate."

Finally Port Control comes back with its questions: ship's name, anchorage position, number of crew and passengers, last port and before that and before that, number of tons of cargo for Alexandria, and hazardous cargo. And signs off with instructions to call back in an hour for more information on berthing.

After a quick call on the radio to the agent, all the ship can do is wait. Despite earlier plans, the steward has to make dinner for everyone. Chief mate remarks you only remember when you take arrival at meal time, in the middle of the night, or in weather. Tonight will be one of those times.

After steak and spaghetti, we watch *Once Around* and try to catch some sleep before shifting to a berth.

Friday, 18 February

Suddenly it's 0200, and Port Control calls: "Let's go."

"Time to go into my act again," the captain remarks.

The chief mate heaves the anchor; in five minutes, two shots of anchor chain are up.

"That's pretty good," the captain says. Chief mate calls for water on deck from the fire hoses to wash away residue the anchor has brought up. The lights shining on the bow, on the cargo deck, against the stack, go out, and it's dark once again.

"Hard right," the captain calls, then, "Here we go, ready or not."

Sailing dead slow ahead, we pass a navy vessel starboard, but otherwise all is still. "Ease to ten . . . midships." The anchor is home and water on deck is secured (shut off) as we glide slowly and silently forward toward the sea buoy.

"It's a starry, starry night over exotic Alexandria," the captain remarks.

In the black stillness the captain wanders first to the radar, then to the window with powerful binoculars, back and forth, as the *Charlotte* slips ahead more, more, more. Finally, "Stop engine," and wait for the pilot, Capt. Meha Hanna. The captain's usual quarter offer for the first to see the pilot boat is on the table again.

When we're two miles from Great Pass Beacon, Port Control is on the radio again. "He's calling to see if I'll give him a present. If I forget, all the way in he'll be calling me," the captain explains.

It's tricky here, because the ship can't afford to get east of the sea buoy, and although the engine's stopped, we're still moving. With a series of maneuvers using the engine and bow thruster, the captain keeps the ship where she wants her. Finally, she says, "I see the ship; I win."

"I was just about to tell you," Amy answers predictably.

At 0330 the pilot comes aboard via the starboard pilot ladder, along with the doctor and his three cohorts for health clearance. The *Charlotte* is heading for the range, two lights in the harbor that, when lined up, reassure the ship she's heading exactly right. Captain Hanna apologizes for the delay, but due to Ramadan he is the only pilot on duty.

He asks that both anchors be ready for an emergency. We're going "starboard to, and all the way in." Alexandria harbor is immense as the tugs *October* and *Hamus* come to help us to the dock. Many ships are moored Mediterranean style, stern in. Many are anchored inside the breakwater, and tugs are needed to push two out of our way in the narrow harbor channel as we proceed to the berth.

Ten bollards for tying lines help us line up our position along the dock. A line boat stands by. The two tugs, port side, don't make up but only push us up to the dock. The captain calls for "three and two" (three head lines and two spring lines forward, three stern lines and two spring lines aft), and even before we are finished with engines at 0448, we can hear the singsong Egyptian music piped everywhere through the loudspeakers. "Lock *everything!*" is the captain's final order.

There seems to be no point in going to sleep now. At 0600 the cranes start working cargo; it's time to get cleaned up in preparation for the day. A string of people meander through the office, and about 0700 Mohamed Saad Mohamed, otherwise known as Farouk, the driver for Mahoney Marine Services Co., comes aboard. Half an hour later we are on our way with Farouk to Cairo. The third mate and Janie, the BR, also are making their first foray there.

We stop to pick up two sailors from another ship who are tagging along. They seem at first to be bad news, hung over from a night ashore, but in the end don't cause any problems. Amy and Janie talk about their female captain, and one of the sailors asks, "Is everyone on your ship a woman?"

No, it only appears that way.

Alexandria is an exotic city of eight million. Predominantly the people dress in the old style: men with head coverings and long robes, women all in black or in bright colors with their heads covered. It's very crowded, with people and traffic everywhere. The port itself seems to be enormous, and it takes quite a while to leave the city behind.

Riding through the countryside is an experience. It's a divided highway, two lanes each side of a median planted for miles with oleander, but no one seems to stay in a lane—drivers are passing often, honking each time, and apparently always exceeding the ninety- or hundred-kilometer-an-hour speed limit. What looks like sagebrush dots the sand between palm and olive trees. Large poinsettias grow outside, reminiscent of a winter's worth I saw in Cambodia as a newlywed.

Along the highway, as well as in Alexandria and Cairo, are soldiers and police, all with guns slung over their shoulders. But the rest of the people seem to be throwbacks to earlier times. They ride camels, or on colorfully painted flat carts pulled by donkeys, carrying greens or fruit or wood. At one spot a painted pickup truck passes, with twenty, thirty, forty people standing up in the back, packed like sardines. Here and there women are herding goats or sheep or water buffalo—or camels.

And what's a trip to Cairo without a camel ride to the pyramids? Debbie's idea, once again—she's stayed behind to work, but she's planned ahead! Camels lie down; you mount using a stirrup, as you would a horse (but from either side), then lean back so the camel can rise. Mine is tied to the back of another camel, but also is being led by a five-year-old boy who keeps flicking it with a switch and talking to it in Arabic.

"How we doing, Mama?" the little boy asks repeatedly.

From experience, I found it about as comfortable as riding an elephant.

We alight and descend into the smallest of the three large pyramids. The ceiling is very low; handrails run along each wall, but the slope down is only covered with boards; slats nailed across serve as steps. Seventy steps down is a landing with a tall ceiling, then it's possible to descend about twenty steps more to another room. After endless climbing on the ship, I'm certainly in condition for these! Off the landing is one small room that is bare; another, larger, that is partitioned, we assume to hold sarcophagi. It reeks of urine; we turn and make our way back up to the top and outside.

The camels retrace their steps, and after about an hour all told we're back on the street, past black-garbed Egyptian women returning from a funeral, and back to the car. Walking may never be the same.

It's a short drive to the Sphinx Restaurant; it's huge, with two floors at least and a big pavilion where they serve outside. We are the only guests for lunch today—it's Ramadan, and all Muslims fast during the day, party at night. But tour buses bring their loads to the Sphinx, our view through the picture window as we eat lunch. Hummus, pita, baba ganoush, grilled lamb and chicken, lots of fresh and cooked vegetables, pink pickled turnips, and oranges for dessert. And always Coca-Cola. It definitely beats Friday's tuna fish on the *Charlotte*. We climb to the top to take pictures.

Driving down a back street, through mud, winding all around, Farouk takes us to a store where, we have been told, he gets a cut. Nothing is too appealing. Amy orders two silver cartouches; the store promises them in ten minutes. Farouk calls the office, and we find we won't be sailing until after dinner, instead of at 1600. Good! The ten minutes are long gone and the cartouches are not ready, so it's on to the Cairo Museum for a quick once-around—it's already after one when we arrive and it closes at three. Ramadan.

So much to see, again, and so little time. Without a guidebook, we finally find a sign for the King Tut exhibit. Magnificent—all of the small pieces that came to the States and many more. I finally find a blue hippopotamus I've been seeking, plus many more blue animals and figures of many descriptions from many periods. I purchase a hippo replica and a book on Egypt before the door is locked and we must leave.

We retrace our route and claim Amy's purchases. Then we return from our twelve-hour tour. One stop—Farouk leaves with Marlboros and comes back without them—then we're up the gangway, into the captain's office. "Are you ready to go to the Khadoura for dinner?" she asks. With a nod, back out the door, down the gangway, and a quick drive through the streets to a building on the far side of the street facing the waterfront.

It's a small restaurant on a corner, and we enter on the first floor, where there are just a couple of tables. Debbie's been promising dinner at the Khadoura as long as we've talked about making this trip together. I'm not disappointed. We pick out raw prawns (they come cooked, unshelled, in tomato, onion, and pepper) and barboni (a sweet, red Mediterranean fish, fried perfectly in a thin salty batter and just barely done inside), order a salad, then climb winding marble stairs to the second floor. It has a many-faceted, glass-covered ceiling. Of the eight or ten tables, a large one in the center accommodates a tour tonight. We sit by the huge glassless picture window and watch Alexandria pass by as we wait for dinner. A load of tires is delivered on the sidewalk, and put away. Pita with hummus is divine, also with another, spicier dip. We also try cold mashed potato flavored with fresh dill—wonderful. Farouk's treat.

On our way to the ship we drive by the Cecil Hotel, and the Metropole, where the captain stayed for three days one time waiting for Jack. Back just after nine, we don't sail until nearly midnight, two hours late. Immigration doesn't come until the last minute to check the shore passes and receive the signed statement that the stowaway search is completed and there are none on board. In exasperation, the captain asks the waiting pilot if he'll take the paperwork. The answer: "No!"

Finally the captain tells the mates to "single up"—leave one head line and one spring line forward, one stern line and one spring line aft. We make up the tugs, *Ahmas* on the stern and *October* on the bow, let go all the lines, and at 2345 we're backing away from the dock, sixty-four cartons of Marlboros poorer. That's a record; last time it was sixty.

Debbie, about age ten, sails in the family's Blue Jay with brother Bob on the bow, young cousin Philip Fryberger, and her father.

Midshipman Doane with two Russian maritime students in Moscow during the training ship cruise (1974).

Rigging a fifteen-ton boom with the deck utility on the Velma Lykes as a cadet (1975).

Graduation from Maine Maritime Academy. From left are her parents, Darline and Bob Doane; Debbie; brother Bob and his wife, Marilyn; sister Linda with daughter Jennifer; and brother John. Foreground is Linda's husband, John Crown, and son John.
Photo by John D. Hyde

Wedding day, 16 December 1978.

A ship-shaped wedding cake.

The Marjorie Lykes, a breakbulk ship the captains Dempsey sailed together.

The captain's favorite cargo shot, aboard the Marjorie, marrying a 35-ton boom to a 15-ton rig to lift a 49.8-ton locomotive.

The captain and Chief Mate Eric Wilcox chat with L. L. "Chip" Harris, left, who was chief engineer on the Cygnus when Debbie was the chief mate in 1988. Photo by Craig Moran

In a 1990 house ad, Lykes Lines features Captian Dempsey's role during the Persian Gulf conflict.

The MV Lyra, drifting toward Frying Pan Shoals (1993). Photo by The N. Pham, Wilmington Morning Star

The Lyra rescue crew in a quiet moment: from left, George Bradley, Curtis Hall, Brian Norton, Fred Judge, and Captain Dempsey.

The captains Dempsey, Debbie and Jack, on their sailboat at home
in Kilmarnock, Virginia, in 1993. Photo by Craig Moran

Even on her vacation, the merchant seaman takes to the water in a pleasure craft. Photo by Marny Emanuel

Captain Dempsey with one of the two Columbia River Bar pilot boats.
Photo by Karl Maasdam, The Daily Astorian

6. One On and One Off— Temporarily

*I*n January 1979, Jack was permanently assigned to the *Marjorie Lykes,* and I stayed in New Orleans. I was living with Maria Hornung, going to two job calls a day at the Masters, Mates & Pilots union hall, trying for two and a half months to get a job. In mid-March Jack sent me a message that he expected to be in Alexandria, Egypt, for thirty days and if I didn't get a job, I should meet him there. No luck—I even attended job call the morning I flew out of New Orleans.

I'd never been to Egypt before. I flew from New Orleans to Kennedy, where my mother and sister Linda saw me off. I went on to change in Geneva, then Rome, and on to Cairo. I had tried to reserve a hotel room before leaving the States, but couldn't because everything was filled in expectation of Jimmy Carter's arrival the next week. On the plane to Cairo I met some Amoco oil people who worked on rigs in Suez, changing out every month or so, and I told them I'd never been to Cairo.

First they helped get me through customs, which cost me $10. Then they took me to the hotel where they stayed—by now it was about 2300—and I was able to get a room there. Dinner came with the room, even at that hour. A half dozen raucous British oil rig workers celebrating a birthday at the bar saw me eating alone, and asked me to join them. I drank with them until 0200, and had to get up four hours later to get on the diesel train to Alexandria. The clerk had to knock on my door for about twenty minutes to get me up!

I was told to ride first-class, but the train personnel said "There's no such thing." So I rode second-class: a four-hour ride on a straight-backed bench, in a jam-packed car that reeked of urine, with windows that didn't open—and I was hung over. I finally got to

Alexandria, carrying the address of Mahoney Marine Service, which handled Lykes's ships. Alkaid Mahoney was a good friend of Jack's. I got a cabby to understand where I wanted to go, but it was an old address. I also had the address of the Lykes agency, Abu Simbel, and eventually I got there and made them understand I was trying to hook up with Jack on the *Marjorie.*

But the port was closed because of bad weather, Jack was at anchor five miles out, and there was no way to communicate with him. This was Wednesday. Again, every nice hotel was booked because Jimmy Carter was coming that weekend. I couldn't get into the Cecil Hotel, the oldest and nicest downtown, and ended up at the Metropole. I was scared to leave the hotel. My room had floor-to-ceiling windows, and the whole situation reminded me of the movie *Casablanca.* At 0500 everyone was called to prayer, and I could hear horses walking down the alley. I had no communication from the Abu Simbel office—except one night when I was visited by a runner who kept telling me, "I'm your brother, you my sister." He tried to force himself on me, and wound up getting fired.

On Friday I watched President Carter and Egyptian President Anwar Sadat come down the thoroughfare along the waterfront. The weather was horrible, with blowing seas coming over the seawall. On Saturday morning I took lots of toast, Coca-Cola, and hot tea back to my room and settled in. Then, about 1000, a runner arrived, and I found out Mr. Mahoney had been trying to reach me.

"The ship's coming in," the runner said. "Let's go."

I was on the Mahoney launch and actually boarding the ship before she was cleared. It felt great—and I finally felt safe.

The ship was there only eight days instead of the expected thirty. But in the meantime I had sent my old friends and former passengers Karl and Muriel Pogrund a telegram—because they had no telephone—saying I'd see them in thirty days in Spain. After a positive reply from them, midweek I cabled again and said I'd be there in eight days.

Capt. Eugenio Campanini, chairman of the Lykes Mediterranean office in Genoa, was scheduled to arrive in Alexandria midweek. He was coming to handle the *Almeria,* one of the new Seabee class barge ships, which required special care because there wasn't room in the inner anchorage for her to swing. It was a big deal. The evening before he was due, Mr. Mahoney was in Jack's office drinking Scotch about eight. There was a knock at the door, and it's Captain Campanini. Mr. Mahoney quickly hid the Scotch, then gave him the British salute. Formalities out of the way, Captain Campanini asked for a launch to go to the *Almeria*.

Now, Mr. Mahoney owned one blue suit and he always wore a white shirt. Coincidentally, the *Marjorie* was off-loading bagged flour. Flour dust was all over the decks, and the dew at night created a paste. It was pretty slick. When Mr. Mahoney came back with the launch twenty minutes later, his blue suit was white. It was all Captain Campanini could do not to laugh.

"Your launch is ready, sir," Mr. Mahoney said, and away they went.

I visited with Captain Campanini the rest of the week Jack was there. It came time for the *Marjorie* to sail for the States, without homebound cargo, and I still hadn't heard from Karl and Muriel. Captain Campanini said that when I stopped in Geneva, I should call him in Genoa before I committed myself to going to Spain. He thought maybe the *Marjorie* might get orders to change course and head for Livorno to load cargo for the return trip, instead of sailing back to the States empty. In that case I could ride the train from Geneva to Pisa, about a half hour from the port in Livorno, and meet the ship there.

In the meantime, I had to change the return flight on my round-trip ticket anyway. Abu Simbel offered to use my Z card, or U.S. seaman's card, to reduce my airfare, and did. I was now in their hands, sitting in their office with Mr. Mahoney, as someone from Abu Simbel was going to drive me to Cairo. Mr. Mahoney was dealing with a passenger who had an accident aboard one of his launches and broke a hip, to see about getting it fixed in Alexandria. He was deep in negotiations with Captain Rashad, the general manager of the agency, about insurance for the passenger.

In the midst of all that, somebody came in and handed Rashad a telegram. As the two Egyptians puzzled over it, I got its message:

"Debbie, come anytime. Love K & M."

So I was on to Cairo, where the driver for the Abu Simbel agency put me on the plane. With a cut-rate ticket all the way to New York, I flew to Geneva. In Geneva I called Captain Campanini, who replied that the *Marjorie* was indeed coming into Livorno. So I planned to spend the night there, then take the train to Pisa. I sent *another* telegram to Karl and Muriel. Captain Campanini said he'd have the agency's driver, Mario Nannuci, pick me up in Livorno, and when I arrived, Mario was there.

"Do you want to stay in the fancy St. James Hotel or the Gran Duca?" he asked.

Staying at the St. James was Capt. Danny King, the port captain for Lykes New Orleans in charge of the Seabee division, who was awaiting the arrival of the *Almeria* from Alexandria. I chose the Gran Duca, which was very nice. It was located smack dab downtown overlooking the small boat harbor and the main entrance to the harbor. The first floor of this quaint building, itself maybe two hundred years old, was a restaurant and bar, with two floors of rooms above that, and a statue of Christopher Columbus right outside.

Jack did not know I was going to be there.

When I pulled up the blind at 0730 the next morning, the *Marjorie* was coming in through the breakwater. Mario picked me up and took me to meet the ship just as it docked. Jack and I were together there for three days, and we had a wonderful time. The telegrams worked great, and I changed my ticket again. I flew to Madrid, then Madrid to Malaga, where Karl and Muriel met me. I stayed nine days before flying back to the States—and despite all of the changes in route and schedules, the travel never cost me a cent more.

It was when Jack came home from that trip, only a few months after we were married, that our legal problems with Lykes began.

His second mate was getting off the *Marjorie* when he returned to the States, and agreed to get off in Port Arthur, Texas, knowing I wanted the job. I was only in group C, so I had to give way to B and A, but I had a better chance of getting a job at Port Arthur because it's a tanker port, not a freighter port. It worked exactly that way, and I took the job, a 180-day one at that time. Jack called George Price, manager of the marine division, and told him what happened.

"You know what Hendrix said," George warned Jack.

Three days later, Captain Hendrix sent Clyde Smith to the ship as captain, and pulled Jack off. Jack was permanently assigned, so legally he couldn't be removed without just cause.

Seeking union help, we called an official of Masters, Mates & Pilots for the Gulf region, in New Orleans. He was in Lykes's hip pocket and didn't want anything to do with us. Jack was so irritated and annoyed with Lykes that he called Lykes and said we both quit. That's just what they wanted to hear!

I remember that we tied one on in Port Arthur that night. We met Bill Spencer, a radio operator from Des Moines, and he went to a club with us. The owner of the lounge took me aside and offered to tell me stories—which I had already heard—about the time when Jack had been a poker dealer at a private club in Port Arthur in the 1950s. Jack got drunk, and Bill helped me carry Jack back up the gangway.

The next day we called the union's vice president in New York, Hank Nereaux, whom I knew from when I had tried to join the union out of school. I told him the whole tale.

"Don't quit," he said, concerned that we had already signed papers to that effect. We hadn't. "We want to fight this. We anticipated something like this happening and we're ready to take it to arbitration," Hank said.

So Jack called Lykes back and said, "We don't quit."

It was a difficult time. I had to make the trip to the Med with Clyde Smith as captain. He's a great guy, and he was concerned about getting in the middle of the situation. At the same time, Jack lived with my parents in Essex, driving back and forth to New York for hearings on his job. Lykes representatives rarely showed up; if one did, it was always George Price, who in private was more sympathetic to Jack than to Lykes.

On my return, because I had just completed a round trip, I was eligible to take a one-trip leave of absence during that six months, so I did. During that time, the union arranged a luncheon with the National Organization for Women (NOW) in New York, which probably was the genesis of a subsequent threatening letter: Afterward, NOW wrote to the president of Lykes, James Amoss, objecting to what the shipping company had done to Jack and me. I guess NOW thought it could help the situation. But Mr. Amoss never saw the letter; I know it was intercepted by George Price, because we received it in a personal, confidential envelope overseas.

When my sixty-day leave was up and it came time for me to rejoin the ship, Jack was still shuttling back and forth between Essex and New York.

The ship sailed back up into the Great Lakes, and I had to fly to Calumet, just south of Chicago, to rejoin. The union told Jack to pack his bags and go there, too. Hank Nereaux flew out to Chicago with us. The ship wouldn't sail without Jack, Hank said.

The *Marjorie* was in Calumet for four days, working cargo. Masters, Mates & Pilots warned Lykes that none of the mates were allowed to sign articles to go to work, the pilots were not going to sail the ship, and the tugs were not coming until Jack was back in the captain's chair.

The union and Lykes argued the entire four days the ship was working cargo. Captain Hendrix took his whole argument about why we couldn't sail together from Lykes's blue book, the *Ship's Officers' Guide*. Among the rules, under the section dealing with "Carriage of Passengers": "Under no circumstances shall women relatives or close friends of Masters, officers or crew be transported on the same vessel where the Master, officer or crew concerned is serving." We kept saying that rule didn't apply because I wasn't being transported: I was not a passenger. I was crew! When it came time to sail the ship, Jack was reinstated and we made the round trip to the Med, sixty-five days. Chief mate was an old friend, Mark Robinson, I was the second mate, and there were two thirds.

That argument lost, Captain Hendrix turned to another: He would say Jack was showing favoritism. On our return from the Med to the Great Lakes, Jack had to call the office twenty-four hours before we arrived in the first port, Montreal.

"How many mates are getting off?" Captain Hendrix asked.

"None," Jack returned. "They're all making another trip."

End of argument.

Although Lykes fully expected us to sue them, we didn't. But a year later, Captain Hendrix was asked to retire from Lykes. Captain Price moved up, and Capt. Richard E. Manchester became manager of the marine division. Once Captain Manchester took over, he tried to help me keep a permanent job on Jack's ship.

Then the bottom fell out of the market, and I didn't have the union seniority to hold a permanent job on any ship.

When we spent Christmas in Waco a couple of years later, Jack was talking to Joan Urban, manager of Lykes's passenger department and a friend, and Captain Hendrix's name came up. He was very sick and was living out his days in a home in Tampa. In conversation with Joan, he'd asked, "Do you ever see the Dempseys? . . . I always knew Jack Dempsey was one of our better captains, and would you please pass that on to him the next time you talk to him?" He was trying to clear his conscience before he died.

Landlubber's Log
19–21 February 1994

Saturday, 19 February

Today is laundry day. It's also shirtsleeve weather; even the earlier wind seems to be gone and the swells seem smaller as we anticipate Haifa. Pedro, an AB, steers on a heading of 076 degrees. There's nothing on the radar, then about 1535 a mountainous shape is barely visible ahead. At 1605 the Israeli navy calls, asking our position: bearing to Rosh ha Karmel is 108, and we're twenty-five nautical miles off. The captain tells Don, "The hospital is the best thing to take a bearing on. I may be wrong, but I'm not usually." Not this time, either—it's a big block that is visible for a long way, in fact all the way in.

The captain orders a steering gear test, ducks to her cabin for a ten-minute shower, and returns. The engine room gets its one-hour notice before arrival, the steering gear test is gotten through, and with a heading of 100 and steering "in hand," the captain reports from the radar that "there are a lot of ships at anchor, but we're supposed to be docking on arrival."

At 1720, speaking with the pilots, she says we'll be at the pilot station in thirty minutes and is assured that yes, we will be berthing on arrival. The heading is now 107, the pilot ladder is rigged starboard side, and at 1730 we take arrival—296 miles in sixteen hours, fifty-four minutes. At six miles from the breakwater, the lights are just coming on in the city, and the buildings look very white, the surroundings very desertlike and bare. It's very wide, and quite the prettiest harbor we've come into yet.

The wind was thirty knots earlier, but, the pilot says, luckily it's gone down. It's the hardest harbor to get in and out of on this run (except for Pelican Spit at Izmir, where the light is often out) due to the combination of wind and so little protection from the breakwater. Last May the ship nearly wiped out a fence separating the container docks at the western terminal from the navy ships. Today we're heading for the eastern terminal, definitely the shortest distance to a berth on this run; New York is the longest.

The paperwork—the least amount of any port—is quickly finished, and it's time to play. David Beiten from Ardo Shipping, the Haifa agent, drives the gruesome threesome—captain, friend, and second mate—to another of Deb's favorite restaurants on the Med circuit, the Dolphin. Only one other table is taken. Dinner is wonderful: Greek salad and bread with garlic sauce and fresh fennel, prawns three ways (sesame batter, grilled, and tiny ones in the same garlicky sauce), grilled fish, and dry white Israeli wine.

We walk to a bar along the beachfront for a Carlsberg and a dose of MTV, then Morris and his cab take us up the hill to Club Chaplin in the basement of a hotel. Several hours later, after much beer and terrific live Israeli music, we fall into bed.

Sunday, 20 February

Today is a gorgeous, warm day. The view from my stateroom is of the northern part of the port and up the coast. I'm up and dressed before 0800, finally awaken the captain so she can get herself together before the ship chandler is due at 0900 with stores for the ship and seven cases of wine that we and other crew have ordered. Finally, around 1100 we grab passport and shore pass and get a ride with a delightful young Israeli girl from Ardo Shippers. Wearing high-topped lavender tennis shoes, she drives us a quick mile from the ship to near the port exit. We walk through a turnstile, over the railroad tracks, and into lower downtown Haifa.

The third largest city in Israel, with 245,000 people, Haifa has many things to see, but it is definitely not a tourist town. At least where we are we hear little English spoken, and many places do not take dollars. Because I am Jewish and Hebrew is familiar to me, it's disconcerting to see it written everywhere and hear it spoken everywhere, yet not understand much. I find my comfort level in leafing through a women's magazine written in Hebrew, read back to front, and seeing a page of patterns for making menorahs. The pastry shops have hamantaschen because next week is Purim. Although it's Sunday, everything is open, all businesses, banks, the post office. It's a good thing for us—we have a list to finish.

Everything is quite expensive (2.9 shekels to $1 U.S.), especially imports. Pastry is 25 shekels a kilo. Two lithium batteries for the camera are 76 shekels. We're not hunting souvenirs anyway.

First we find a place that develops film in one hour. Next stop is the bookstore for current news magazines. No time to browse. We wend our way several blocks to the fruit market, buying two boxes of huge strawberries, in season, and a bag of Jaffa oranges, for $5 U.S. The *Charlotte* loaded all the fresh fruit for Voyage 87 before we left the States, and by now it's long gone. If we want any, we have to buy it. Debbie has her hair cut by a barber while I wander. I find the post office in a dingy building being remodeled, post office boxes in one room to the left, the place to buy stamps around a corner in another tiny room to the right. After standing in line, I discover only shekels buy stamps. Ardo finally takes my postcards.

Meanwhile, the crew has had to shift the ship on lines once today because the middle crane was broken; there could be another move. The agent, Ari Angel, presents us with two big bags of Jaffa oranges, which we must eat before we reach New York and immigration. He says the sailing board is still posted for 1400. But if cargo isn't finished, we will be delayed because stevedores change shifts and there is a break. We head back, showing our passes, passport, and Z card at the turnstile, then confirm what Ari has predicted. Sailing board has been changed to 1600, but we won't get a pilot until 1700. Quickly we retrace our steps with Ari and climb the hill several blocks, where he buys us tickets from a machine and points us in the direction of the tram that runs to the top of Mt. Carmel.

Beautifully tiled in red and white and gray, the station is clean and the three linked cars immaculate, the seats plush gray with maroon and yellow geometric designs, the gray metal trim unscratched. Seats near the doors automatically fold back to allow more room for entering and exiting. The ride up takes only six minutes, with Hebrew Muzak. The track is all inside, like a tunnel, with one place where cars can pass each other, but the view at the top overlooking the city and harbor is quite wonderful. We walk the overlook, duck back through a two-level shopping arcade at the base of one of a pair of huge skyscrapers, and wander into a lovely shop with silver filigree, silver and yellow gold menorahs, leather goods, beautiful tiny silver sculptures. Time is short, as usual. We barely glance at the park, reluctantly skip the zoo, and after taking the cable car down, stop briefly for pastry and head for Ardo Shipping, then the ship. So much for sightseeing in Israel!

The delay is good for the ship, because it means the barge that takes slops—drippings from the engine, oil leaks, bilge water, all collected in the ship's slop tank—is able to come back. The oily stuff rises to the top of the slop tank, and at sea the ship decants the watery slops from the bottom until the concentration of oil in the tank is fifty parts per million (the limit is one hundred parts). It's okay to do this in the Atlantic, but not in special places like the Red Sea or the Mediterranean. In port, the slops are pumped onto the barge from the bottom of the tank; the oily "good stuff" is pumped last, and it's sold to be refined again. In Haifa, Ardo uses two slop-barge companies, but no longer tries to alternate them on the same ship—the two had an argument. This barge can take one hundred tons, then must dump it before she can pump again. First call at the *Charlotte* she only had time to take 80 tons; with the sailing delay, she was able to take a total of 150 tons.

That leaves about twenty-five tons of the good stuff on the ship. The ship generates five tons of slops a day, dead weight that can be traded pound for pound for cargo in the last three ports, so it's important to get rid of as much as possible. Another reason to pump it at Med ports is that it's too expensive to do it in the States, according to Lykes management in New Orleans. Haifa cost: $16 a ton. It's actually less expensive to pump it in Izmir ($10 a ton), Ari says, but it's not always possible to get a barge there.

With port business completed, the pilot, looking much older than his forty-six years and, he says, at the bottom of the list, arrives right on time. Shortly the lines are off, the tug with her Israeli flag flying pulls us aft until we can make the turn. The tug backs off and we head out past the breakwater and into open sea. Another containership is waiting to take our place. The lights of Haifa fade; the steward has saved dinner, which we devour in the captain's office, top off with fresh strawberries, and, by 2000, it's lights out.

Monday, 21 February

It's an American holiday, Presidents' Day, although every day seems the same out here. But the crew is on overtime, so they make the distinction. There's talk of cherry pie for dinner. The captain also says the good weather is over—we are awakened by a quick shower this morning, but the wind has picked up to about thirty knots and the seas have bigger swells. So far so good. As the morning wears on, another quick dousing, then sun again.

The number nine piston was fixed in New York; now number eight looks as if it's having problems with the cylinder liner. The choices seem to be to baby it all the way back to New York, or try to fix it in the Med (the latter being the captain's choice), but it's New Orleans's decision. It's a twenty-four-hour job, and Izmir's the likely place because it usually takes that much time to load and unload there. But the crew members like to party in Izmir, big time. They'd prefer working in Livorno, but we might not need to be there that long. We'll see.

About 1130 there's some discussion on the bridge, where Sandy is steering 297. Seems one ballast tank was pumped, although it shouldn't have been; we will need to have the ballast back in it this afternoon. There's that much-talked-about tension between deck and engine (captain and mates versus engineers). The chief mate, shaking his head, comments on the chief engineer, Don Forbes: "It's his engine, but it's nice if he tells us what he's doing."

The captain gets along with Forbes, a large man, remarkable for his white socks and sandals, T-shirt and jeans. He's a father figure to his crew, and does look out for them. For instance, he's asked the captain if he can reinstate barbecues, and got her to order sixty pounds of charcoal from the ship chandler in Haifa at a cost of $45. Outrageous. And he ordered wheels of cheese there, at his expense, a nice treat for the crew. Unlike Brian Norton, one of the captain's favorite chief engineers, Forbes does mind a bit that the captain's a woman. But he likes sailing with her better than with some other captains, because she cares more about doing her work.

Today's the day to play catch-up because at 2100 we hit the Khios Straits, and that's it for writing until we leave Izmir.

About 1315 a school of dolphins, playing in the rain, comes along the starboard side, leaping out of the water in pairs and trios. Wonderful to see. We're faster, and we leave them behind. At 1700 we take time to watch the island of Rhodes go by.

After supper, it's time for cribbage, and that peaceful feeling of being on the bridge in the dark, watching islands go by starboard side under a cloudy sky. Ahead of us is rain with big lightning, but it seems to stay ahead of us, and we get only brief showers. Knowing we'll have an early morning followed by a long day, we head for bed about 2130. I expect to dream about *Jurassic Park,* but don't.

7. *Around the World in 127 Days*

"*G*ary," who had been chief mate on one of my first foreign trips, was responsible for my sailing chief mate. I had passed the exam in 1981, but continued to sail second mate for two more years.

Then, in 1983, Gary was chief mate on the *Marjorie* with Jack as captain. I was second mate. Gary hadn't been able to get a fit-for-duty slip from his preemployment physical for a couple of years before that. Jack had fired him as second mate a long time before, and didn't want him then. At six-feet-two and 137 pounds, he had a lot of health problems. His hands were so arthritic that he couldn't climb ladders in the hatches when we were loading bulk grain for the Med in the Gulf, and we other mates had to do that for him. He had skin cancer, and he was so sick with emphysema from fifty years of smoking he couldn't walk from his office to the officers' saloon, about a seventy-foot walk, without being winded. He was worthless on deck because he couldn't get there in time, taking ten minutes to walk to the bow.

Usually the chief mate is the medical officer, but Gary didn't want to be bothered and I had recently completed the union's medical course at the Maritime Institute of Technology and Graduate Studies (MITAGS) in Linthicum Heights, Maryland, so I became medical officer that trip. A couple of times already that crossing Gary had called me when he needed medical attention. The third time was the worst. I was on watch at 0400, about four hours before we reached Haifa, our first foreign port, when I got a phone call from him, saying he couldn't breathe. I used up all of our medical oxygen on him. I gave him Valium to relax and calm down until he got to a doctor. The doctor adjusted his medication and told me he'd be fine in two weeks. We went on to Alexandria, then Livorno, where he refused to see a doctor because he knew he'd be taken off the ship, and he needed two more years for his pension.

The day after we left Livorno for the Great Lakes, the twelve-to-four oiler went to Gary's office to check out a movie, and found him flat on the deck. Again I was called off watch, and I started CPR on him immediately. Palma de Mallorca was the closest place we could get him medical attention, and Jack made maximum speed. Even so, it was three hours later when the *Marjorie* pulled into Palma and anchored, and the Spanish medics boarded. All of that time I did CPR. The medics put a long sodium bicarbonate needle into his heart, but it didn't help. Even when they prepared to lower him over the side on a Stokes litter, they wouldn't let me quit CPR. He was pronounced dead an hour later. The authorities kept his body for two weeks doing an autopsy before they would release it to his wife.

That's how I got my first chief mate's job. I was chief mate back to the Great Lakes, where Jim Christian came aboard to relieve me. Everybody wondered, "How would she handle the job?" I handled it just fine, and for the next six years I sailed mate, always returning after vacation to a different ship with a different captain.

Chief mate also sells cigarettes, toiletries, cards, and other incidentals from the slop chest. He or she is the department head of the deck department and, therefore, has charge of maintenance of the ship. In port, the chief mate is responsible for overseeing loading and off-loading of cargo, an all-consuming responsibility; once the ship sails, it's up to the chief mate to check the cargo and make a log-book entry every day to indicate that the cargo's okay.

Sometimes it isn't. Take the trip on the *Marjorie Lykes,* going into Mombasa with a load of bagged rice. The rice had been loaded both in Galveston and in Houston. The first rice, which we loaded in Galveston, had been through a hurricane and was wet and moldy, but it was loaded anyway. It was all done with U.S. Department of Agriculture approval, too; we had to get holds inspected, but then they ignored the wet rice! By the time we reached Houston, maggots were crawling on top of this rice. I called the port captains, wondering what would happen on the other end four weeks hence. Their response was to give me a backpack sprayer, with which I was to spray insecticide directly onto the bags of rice once a day to kill the weevils! Anyway, we loaded fresh rice on top of it in Houston, then doubled back to Galveston and finished loading with more new, dry rice.

Now, the port engineer on duty this rice-loading weekend in Houston was Paul Ross; he wasn't very well liked, to say the least. On Friday he was on board while we were testing the hatch covers for watertightness. You test using a fire hose with pressure behind it. I told him I didn't want to water-test number six, because we knew it had a leak—we could climb down into the hatch and see daylight above through it. He said we're going to do it anyway, so I told him to bring his umbrella. We got drenched.

Chief engineer this trip was Carl B. Carver, a huge man who had had an operation to reduce the size of his intestines to keep from eating so much. He was the kind of a guy who went out of his way to please Jack as captain, but a cloud kept following him—things just kept going wrong.

After the Friday fiasco, we had a hydraulic oil leak about 1600 Saturday night. Carl had closed the cover of the number three hatch on the main or weather deck, and in the process the hydraulic oil hose had burst and the oil had drained on top of all of this rice in the lower hold. Instead of fixing the leak, the chief engineer just filled the oil pump again and, because it's pressurized to open the hatch, another hundred gallons sprayed all over everything.

When Paul Ross arrived about 2000, I was having coffee with Jack, who was captain that trip. Paul took stock of the problem and told me I'd better get a crew to clean it up. We had no crew on board; they all lived in Houston, and we were not moving until Monday. All I had was one drunk ordinary in his rack, sleeping. I replied that he'd better get a shoreside cleaning gang to come clean up this mess. Then I made him follow me into the hatch to see the mess. We had to climb up onto a winch platform, down through a manhole. All this time he's talking to me, and as I went down into the hatch, I called him some choice names. He climbed out of hatch, furious, called the port captain, Ralph Krueger, and finally word got back for Jack to call Ralph.

Ralph greeted him with, "What is going on down there?" Jack told him. Ralph's reply: "We'd better get a shoreside cleaning gang to clean up."

By the time I got to New Orleans, the story had reached Bill Mendheim, who worked in the engineering department as hull and tank inspector, and was a very good friend of Jack's. Even though he didn't believe women could go to sea, we became very good friends.

Bill asked me, "Did you call him a fucking asshole?"

"Yes, I did."

"Well, he is."

Paul Ross did his twenty years and retired.

When we got to Dar es Salaam, the people were starving to death and didn't care about mold, worms, pesticides, or hydraulic oil. But when we arrived at Mombasa, the officials wanted to fumigate the ship before they discharged the rice. Finally, we talked them into putting it in the barges and then fumigating it.

My most memorable job as chief mate lasted 127 days and took me around the world.

It began on 22 December 1986, in New Orleans. I spent Christmas at the home of Capt. Benson Bowditch, Maine Maritime '64 and port captain with Lykes.

This time I was on the *Shirley Lykes,* a Pacer class ship and sister to the *Marjorie,* with six hatches serviced by twenty fifteen-ton booms, four thirty-five-ton booms for numbers three and four, and one sixty-six-ton jumbo at number two hatch. On a containership, the cargo is boring. Not so breakbulk. The cargo included ten thousand tons of bagged flour for Port Louis, food for Tamatave, breakbulk machinery for Capetown and Durban, bagged rice for Mombasa, twelve tons of condoms for the Philippines, and a huge thirty-nine-ton heavy-lift generator for Singapore, as well as containers.

The captain was Frank Smith, one of the older captains. He was a hollerer and very excitable. A very proper gentleman, he drank Guinness and felt quite at home in East London, Manila, and the old Raffles Hotel in Singapore with its Somerset Maugham flavor. Coming aboard, I relieved a drunk mate, Robert Jordan; he'd been up celebrating Christmas in the captain's office.

Prior to this assignment, Frank Smith had been captain of the *Jean Lykes*. He had waived the pilot going across Lake Ontario, went on the wrong side of a buoy, and put the ship aground. In order to refloat the ship, the stevedores there had to off-load locomotives. Captain Smith also had served as the former executive officer at Texas Maritime when Texas and Maine shared one training ship.

Second mate was a guy from the Seattle area by the name of Richard English, who was very heavy. I'm not sure how he got a fit-for-duty; he couldn't make it in and out of the manholes of the hatches. He had a relationship with the captain that went on behind my back. Consequently, when English and I disagreed, the captain wouldn't back me up, but repeatedly said, "Couldn't you two just get along?"

There were two third mates. One was Arthur Holderman, who was seventy-nine in 1995 and still serving after several years as regional vice president of Masters, Mates & Pilots for the Gulf. Arthur was extremely fair. The companies didn't like him because he held them to the rules; likewise, the higher-ups in the union didn't like him because he didn't allow them to get away with anything. He's extremely dedicated to helping anybody in the union, at all levels. He's been messing with union politics forever, and I was concerned about having him as a third because of his union shenanigans, but he was the best mate I had for that trip. When we were in Manila—at least three days— Richard English was found unfit for duty and couldn't stand watch, so I was standing his watch. One night, in the pouring rain, Holderman came by with a cup of coffee, just to see if I needed any help. Generous—and he continued to do that the whole 127 days.

The other guy was what we call a professional third mate. He'd sailed third mate approximately thirty years, did what was required and nothing more. From Mobile, Alabama, he was a nice enough guy, not that bright, but dependable; he did exactly what I told him. When he fell in love with a passenger, then injured his knee opening a hatch cover, he became a worry.

We had a very good deck gang, including boatswain Eugene Fugate, the best I ever worked with; ABs Isabel Sandoval and Frank McGowan; and Nick Miskulin, OS.

Gene had been on the ship since 1962. If anybody is important to the chief mate, it's the boatswain, because of the ability to do the different types of rigs. You really need a good boatswain to make life easy, and he was well respected by the rest of the deck gang— except Adonis Ard. More about him later. After Gene laid up the *Shirley* about 1989, I had him as AB on the *Lyra,* the last time I saw him before he retired.

And Frank and I went back a while. Frank had worked with Jack on the *Marjorie* a lot, and Jack considered him his "Mafia." If Jack had a problem, Frank would take care of it for him. When Jack was trying to get rid of a drunken chief mate nicknamed "Buddy," for instance, Frank planted a bottle of vodka in his cabin to try to help the process along. Because I knew Nick and Frank from the *Marjorie,* they'd clued in the rest that I was all right. So the first night, when I had problems using a forklift on the dock to move the brow or gangway, the boatswain was right there to help me, and I hadn't even gotten to know him yet. Later I could call him out in the middle of the night and, bingo, he was there. Plus, I learned a lot about rigging from him.

Typically he'd come upon me doing some kind of rigging, watch and say, "You're doing all right, mate. Keep going."

We carried twelve lucky passengers: they traveled four months for a flat rate of $4,000 each.

Among them were Dr. Clifford Moran, a retired pathologist, and his wife, Ginny, from Maui, Hawaii. They were very supportive of the problem I was having with Richard English and the captain, and acted as my sounding board. They were also a lot of fun. At every port they would go ashore and, if I couldn't go, bring me back a T-shirt or some gift. I played bridge with them all the time; our fourth was a single female passenger, a tiny woman.

She was rooming with a seventy-nine-year-old crazy who didn't want anyone to see her passport. She was mean to the other passengers, making it hard to try to arrange things for a group. In Port Louis, this mean woman literally kicked her tiny cabin mate—down a ladder well! Quarters were full, so there was nowhere else to move one of them.

First, we followed a coastwise schedule for several days in the Gulf of Mexico. Then we started around the world heading east from New Orleans. Our first port was Capetown, then East London and Durban, all in South Africa. Next, Mombasa (Kenya), Tamatave (Madagascar), Port Louis (Mauritius Islands), Belawan (Indonesia), Singapore, Palembang (Indonesia), Tanjong Mani (Malaysia), Manila (Philippines), Yokohama, Kobe, Kudamatsu (Japan), through the Panama Canal, and back to Mobile.

Our first memorable stop was Tamatave, a tricky place to get into through and around the reefs, with not the best of docks to tie up to. It is one super-depressed city, and we were docked there for three days. The biggest problem was keeping the local whores off the ship, because we were concerned they would steal from us. They would stand around at the bottom of the gangway twenty-four hours a day. Periodically, the local police would throw them into the paddy wagon, but an hour later they'd all be back.

Early on, at fire and boat drill, as medical officer I gave the crew the obligatory lecture about AIDS. "The condoms," I said, "are in the medicine chest. If you're too embarrassed to ask me for them, ask the mate on watch." They did. So many that at Tamatave we ran out of the condom supply in the medicine chest—and I broke into the cargo for the Philippines to get another case of them for the crew.

We used ABs from our own crew as watchmen. I didn't go ashore, but they told me about streets full of ruts, buildings falling down. Most of the crew went to one of the hotels for a beer, but nobody was interested in spending much time ashore. Jack had been through there on the *Marjorie* several months previously and had arranged with our agent to bring me lobster tails, which he did. It was a pleasant surprise. That was the only time I went to Tamatave.

I spent quite a bit of time walking the passages inside to make sure nothing was being stolen. Captain Smith, unlike Jack, didn't care about helping out the chief mate—no fondness there. He was more interested in drinking his Guinness. This made my job even bigger, especially when extraordinary medical problems came up and I needed help.

That's where I began to have a problem with a Cajun AB, Adonis Ard. One afternoon I came by the gangway when Ard was to have been watchman. I noticed Nick was filling in. He explained that Ard was taking a shower and getting ready to go ashore because he had finagled it, paying Nick to stand his watch. An OS cannot stand gangway watch; he shouldn't have been there. I waited for Ard and confronted him when he came out. I wanted to log him for it, but I knew Captain Smith wouldn't back me up on the logging, so off he went. But that incident set the scene for Ard for the rest of the trip.

On to Port Louis, Mauritius, where we spent two weeks all told— a dream port for a freighter trip, with a dramatic landfall—it has precipitous peaks and Caribbean-like waters. Many fishing boats around; there were Russian whaling factory ships inside the inner harbor. It's a vacation mecca for Europeans, with lovely beaches and hotels, windsurfing, and other water sports. Everybody loved the two weeks there. Shopping is nice. It's easy getting around. The only problem with a port like this is you tend to be quite broke when you leave. I felt really fortunate to get there, and it's one place I'd like to return to.

We were tied up to buoys, where we off-loaded the bagged flour into barges. We only worked eight to five, with launch service to get ashore. After the first week we did have to leave for three days, though—because a cyclone went through the port—and return. I often went ashore with the Morans. Capt. Lindsay Cameron and wife, Lynn, were there from the Lykes office in Durban to expedite cargo operations, and at night I went out with them. I still get a yearly Christmas card from them.

As chief mate, my responsibility included supervising not only loading and unloading cargo but the deck gang as well. Because we were in port so long, the boatswain organized maintenance, and it was a perfect time to get the hull painted. To paint the name on the bow, Gene had rigged a pontoon with runners to lower over the side. He did the same over the stern. Ard had been out painting in flipflops and ended up with swollen, sunburned feet. That's when he started coming to me for medical attention.

From Port Louis it took about a week to get to Belawan, Indonesia, on the eastern shore of Sumatra. Jack warned me about Indonesia, because the longshoremen are tough on mates. The further south you go, the more radical they are. Their reputation was that they would have killed me, stolen, whatever. I never went into a hatch to check securing or for stowaways without a crewman with me. Whenever I had a hatch open, I had a mate on watch and an unlicensed crewman to make sure that the same number of longshoremen climbed out of a hatch as had climbed in. The deck gang was a tremendous help the whole trip, but particularly there.

We were concerned about stowaways, and about avoiding theft of lashing gear. I'd even heard of a longshoreman who had closed a hatch cover on a mate and cut his arm off. I didn't know what to expect, and I wasn't going to get any help from Captain Smith. He couldn't have cared less what I did with the cargo.

From Belawan we went through the Straits of Malacca into Singapore. Like Japan and Hong Kong, Singapore has so much water traffic in such a small area—it was quite fascinating. We were there for three days also, and I didn't even get off the ship; I was vastly disappointed not to be able to see the scenery, especially the Raffles Hotel, and have a Singapore sling. I vowed that when I was master, I would make sure I relieved my chief mate so he got ashore.

Prior to arrival in Singapore, the captain and I warned the crew of the severe penalties for possessing contraband—the vessel would be subject to a $20,000 fine and the guilty crewmen taken ashore by the authorities. A few hours after we docked, the two cadets had gone ashore to buy me a Walkman and speakers, and a dozen Singapore customs inspectors came aboard to search for illegal cigarettes and liquor. Each crew member was allowed only two packs—forty cigarettes. It was up to me to show the inspectors around, answer their questions, find a spot for them to fill out their paperwork, and still work cargo at the same time. The inspectors hit pay dirt. The engineers had several cartons of Marlboros hidden in the engine room. The inspectors also found beer where the cadets had hidden it in the line-throwing apparatus box on top of the after house. We went to the cadets' room, where we found a trash can full of empty beer cans. The captain and I were able to talk customs out of a fine, but the inspectors took all of the beer and cigarettes. It's a good thing the cadets were not on board—I don't think they would have been able to explain away their behavior. But when those cadets returned, they were in trouble with me and with the captain.

After being alongside for three days and working cargo, we went to anchor just to off-load a huge generator for a power plant. It was encased in a wooden box that measured nine feet wide, ten feet high, and fifteen feet long, weighed thirty-nine tons, and was carried on deck. A barge had to come alongside to receive the generator. The manufacturer had sent along a spreader bar specifically for lifting this piece. Because it was so heavy, we had to "marry" a fifteen-ton rig at the forward end of the hatch with a thirty-five-ton boom at the after end to lift it. With the boatswain operating one set of gear and I the other, there was not much room to spare, but it worked fine.

Then we sailed south to Palembang and up the river, where we anchored for three days, discharged cargo, and back-loaded rubber. In spite of locking up as much as we could, we did have lashing gear stolen there by the longshoremen: turnbuckles and shackles, but no chain. It's too hard to throw it over the side.

I never got off the ship there. The Morans hopped in a launch on the Ari Musi river and went to town, bringing back a tie-dyed T-shirt for me.

Next stop, also about three days, was Tanjong Mani on the way up the Rajang River to Sibu, Malaysia. Tanjong Mani was not the concern

Palembang was. The longshoremen lived in a bunkhouse barge along-side the ship and cooked their meals on the fantail of the *Shirley*. They provided their own food and even invited us to share meals with them. The only concern was the depletion of our fresh-water supply. It was the same part of the world, but very different working conditions. There we loaded wood for bowling alley flooring and wooden dowels. Unbelievable. I never knew there were so many sizes.

Just prior to this trip, I had been on the containership *Adabelle Lykes,* where by definition the cargo is pre-stowed in twenty- or forty-foot containers. On a breakbulk freighter, however, planning where to place which cargo is a challenge for the mate, and in Asia the chief mate is responsible for laying out the import cargo for the States. In northern Europe, the Med, and the United States, cargo layout is handled in each region by a central office. The mate has little say in it.

One concern about laying out cargo is preventing a "long hatch." That's when one port's cargo is loaded all in one hatch, instead of spread out in several hatches so it can be discharged or loaded with several gangs working simultaneously. We also had to keep in mind that in Japan we would be loading subway cars, which presented their own special problems.

When the *Shirley* was built in 1962, it was a Pride class ship like the *Aimee,* with only five hatches. In 1967, the ship was cut in half and a container hatch with thirty-five-ton cargo booms was added, which turned it into a Pacer class. First we loaded the rubber from Palembang, maybe twenty feet high, in number four hatch, which was wide open top to bottom. To protect the rubber from the accumulated weight atop it, we had to build a floor out of dunnage or throwaway lumber. Then in Tanjong Mani we loaded the wood on top. This particular hatch is divided into three equal sections, port, center, and starboard, each covered separately by an eighty- by twenty-two-foot heavy steel cover, each of which weighs somewhere between seven and ten tons. Their weight means the thirty-five-ton gear is needed to open this hatch, to stack the covers on each other as the hatch goes skin to skin, or on the dock if we are docked.

In rain we always had to cover up the hatches so that the break-bulk cargo such as flour or lumber didn't get wet, and we had to do it in a hurry. It took maybe twenty minutes to do this. I couldn't always cover the number four hatch by myself, but the boatswain was usually there to help. As you would think, it's not as easy to move these covers as it is the hydraulic lids on the other five hatches. To lift one of these, I had to switch the running cargo gear from the single whip (three-and-a-half-ton capacity), used to load lighter cargo, to the thirty-five-ton—a two-minute operation. Then we had to hook into the forty-foot container spreader bar, lock it in place on top of the hatch cover, and move the hatch cover into place. That's the hard part to do alone, because when the hatch cover is suspended it starts to swing, and you need a hand on deck to guide it into place.

I was working cargo in Tanjong Mani in the middle of one night with everyone from the deck gang sound asleep, and it began to rain. It was up to me to cover the hatch and protect the cargo. I remember running into the house as the rain started, banging on the boatswain's door to wake him and telling him I needed him as soon as possible, then running back out to start covering up.

Gene came right out and said, "Keep it going. You're doing fine," as he helped guide the cover into place.

When it came time to open back up after the shower, the moon was rising. As I stood at the controls on the winch platform at the forward end of the hatch, moving that big cover, no one else around, the captain long gone in his Guinness, I thought I couldn't ask for better working conditions.

From Tanjong Mani we were off to Manila, a good liberty port with good shopping. I did get ashore with the Morans to see MacArthur's bar at the Manila Hotel and had a nice meal at the yacht club. I'd never been there before, but I'd heard about the Manila Hotel because my parents had stayed there before joining the ship in Subic Bay when they rode with Jack in 1985 on the *Ruth Lykes*. The biggest help was Arthur Holderman, the third mate who offered repeatedly. He even covered for me on the ship so I could sneak ashore.

Prior to arriving in Manila, we had a run of conjunctivitis through the ship. Dr. Moran helped me by telling the men not to share towels, and to wipe the binoculars with alcohol after they used them; he did whatever he could do. The conjunctivitis started with Richard English, and moved to Adonis Ard—both were on the four-to-eight watch. English went to the doctor in Manila, and got an unfit-for-duty for the few days there. I had to stand all of his watches in addition to my normal duties—which turned into more than just normal duties because we had incessant rain, requiring repeated covering and uncovering of the hatches. I accused him of spending $20 to get the unfit medical report; subsequently, he went ashore and drank, then came back and ridiculed me daily. Ard went to the doctor in every port after that.

Next call was Yokohama. Ard went to the doctor, he said, for venereal disease he claimed he got off a dirty toilet seat. His medical record was getting thicker and thicker and thicker. In fact, the medical log for the whole crew was the biggest I ever accumulated.

After Yokohama and Kobe, where we discharged and loaded containers, Kudamatsu presented a most interesting challenge. There we loaded maybe a dozen subway cars, along with their wheel assemblies. Most had to go in fore and aft positions in the well between the outside edge (or coamings) of two forty-foot hatches and the skin of the ship. The trouble was the cars were eighty feet long, and two vang guys, which help to position the cargo booms for each hatch, were smack in the middle of that well area. So we had to disconnect the vang guys. That was a several-hour job for the deck gang, using sledge hammers and hydraulic jacks to get the pins out of the blocks. Except for periodic inspection, it was probably the first time they'd been disconnected since the ship was built. Then we had to reconnect them after the cars were in place, not as difficult after we greased all of the pieces.

We placed the remaining two cars on top of the number five hatch, athwartships as opposed to fore and aft, a last resort because the ship rolls side to side more than it pitches fore and aft. Because the *Shirley* was only sixty-nine feet wide and each car eighty feet long, they overhung. We made sure they overhung only on one side to get through the Panama Canal; in case we had to tie up to a lock wall, we had to have one side completely clear.

As I said, I rarely went ashore as chief mate; if we were loading cargo—the object of being in port—*I* had to be there. If we weren't working cargo and I could get away, I usually went with the deck gang, if not with the passengers. I remember I took the gang to dinner in Japan, a gesture that was most appreciated. But taking an unrefined crew out for a meal in a country that is the epitome of etiquette . . . just picturing them removing their shoes, sitting on the floor Japanese style, brings a smile.

On the return trip, crew problems arose between Carl Stayton and the rest of his officers on the engineering side. I knew Carl as first assistant engineer on the *Sheldon* when I made my first trip foreign, and he took me to the Crazy Horse Saloon in Durban on a date. On the *Shirley* this trip, he was the chief engineer, and he was acting nuts. He was in charge of the movies. He had a VCR in his room and he had wired the ship at his own expense, so what he showed could be seen on the television sets everywhere—including the VCR in the passengers' lounge. He offered three showings a night, and the third tended to be X-rated. His first assistant engineer and one of the third mates didn't get along, and when we reached the Panama Canal, the first assistant left with chest pains.

At Mobile, our first U.S. port, the twelve-to-four third mate who had had the shipboard romance had to say good-bye to the passenger on board, because his wife was on the dock. A shipboard romance is usually only good for the length of the voyage.

That third mate had also been injured, trying to open the cover for number three hatch. It happened in Port Louis, early in the trip. When the hydraulic system that normally moved the hatch cover failed, we had to open the cover by using the cargo runners. They were attached to a pad eye on the hatch covers with shackles. Just as we were taking the weight of the cover onto the runner, the third mate appeared out of nowhere and stepped up on the hatch. One of the shackles parted and hit him full force on the knee. He'd been going to the doctor every port thereafter to have the knee checked out.

Halfway across the Pacific, one oiler had a boil in the groin area; Dr. Moran said he'd look at it. We just wondered what would be next. On the way home, the crew had a union meeting where Ard claimed I had made advances toward him! My buddies' reply to him: "And you turned her down, you fool?"

He was just trying to get things stirred up, but Jack caught wind of Ard's claim and was ready to beat him up in Mobile if he found an opportunity. He didn't, and he didn't. At Mobile, half the crew went to the doctor; Ard got an unfit-for-duty and finally got off the ship.

About two years later, though, Ard did file suit against Lykes for permanent eye damage, and I had to go to the office long after the fact and tell my side. Lykes settled with the guy for about $3,000 in damages resulting from the pinkeye. It was cheaper than fighting the claim, even if it had no merit. Medical claims pick up when shipping is on a downslide—seamen are not working, and medical claims earn easy money. The men leave the ship on a medical because they know they're going to be on the beach for a while.

Despite the problems, that trip—my last on a breakbulk freighter—represented the ultimate in breakbulk shipping. With four mates I didn't have to stand watch. We were loading overseas. The cargo was varied and interesting. The ports were fascinating. Passengers were on board for company for four months. It was the best in shipping.

I felt very lucky to make a trip around the world. As chief mate, my trips usually were only forty-five to ninety days, and whenever I could I would catch a job with Jack on his ship, which was the most fun for both of us. We were doing what we loved and could still be together. But we knew that if I sailed master, we would be apart. A ship needs only one master.

Landlubber's Log
22–23 February 1994

Tuesday, 22 February

At 0200 Deb sticks her head in my dark room. "We're almost there—we've been flying all night."

The rain we went through before midnight has left the sky bright and clear. It's quiet on the bridge. Outside are many fishing boats, both sides, some with blindingly bright lights. When they have their bright lights on, they're not moving, so that's good. On the other hand, their lights ruin your night vision and make it very difficult to spot the other fishing boats with tiny white lights and no red or green, so you have no clue what they're doing. We weave through them, seeing a rock to starboard with a light that flashes every four seconds. Five more fishing boats are lined up on that side as we're coming up on the next starboard island.

"You can see the boat lights reflecting off the water, it's so flat," the captain remarks. "This is beautiful." She's totally confident navigating; it's not knowing whether we're anchoring or can berth immediately, or when we'll get a pilot so we know how fast or slow to go, that causes her some trepidation. She stays a mile and a half off the islands as we go between them.

The captain tries to raise Izmir pilots on the radio as we pass a spot where she's been able to reach them on previous voyages. No answer. She remarks that besides enjoying the challenge of running the Khios Straits, she finds going through them instead of taking a course west of the island of Khios saves thirty-three and a half miles, maybe two hours.

To port, periodically a light flashes twice at intervals, then is dark. Nothing marks the dark island to starboard. We change course again at a point some two and a half hours from the pilot station. "When the lighthouse to the right bears east, we haul," she notes, referring to our next course change. The tightest spot at this turn is 1.6 miles.

Debbie explains that changing course must be anticipated. It can take two minutes to make a major course change, and if you wait until you're at the way point to turn, you miss the new course line.

The *Charlotte* makes the last big turn southeast into what sailors call the black hole—nothing to pick up forward, so it's necessary to navigate backward. As the 0400 watch change approaches, a slew of fishing boats appear in the distance. Amy remarks she's glad they won't be on her watch. Through the fishing boats, we arrive at the way point. It's three miles from this turn to Pelican Bank. The water is very flat now, with deep reflections and an almost eerie phosphorescent display. At 0524 we take arrival at Izmir, 638 miles and twenty-four minutes shy of a day and a half sailing time from Haifa.

We pick up the sea pilot at Pelican Spit, a tiny bit of land that sticks out into the channel eleven miles from the harbor. Having a pilot is the ship's choice here, but the captain says at a few hundred dollars, it's cheap insurance. Capt. Jim Cullen on the *Sue Lykes* elected not to take a sea pilot when departing a few years previously and, trying to avoid a fishing vessel, he ran aground on Pelican Bank. The ship was delayed three days while they off-loaded fuel oil in order to refloat her.

In the late 1960s a former Lykes master, Capt. Hans Beck, collided with a ferry in Izmir harbor despite having a harbor pilot aboard, and had to push the ferry to land to keep her from capsizing. Even so, some deaths resulted from the accident, and Captain Beck was under house arrest for five years, living with Lykes's agent in Izmir and allowed to return to the States only for his mother's funeral.

As we come into the harbor, garbage floats in the water. The air smells of smoke. Lots of big seaside houses, out a ways in an area of nurseries where the captain says she had dinner the last time ashore here; in the city are big blocks along the waterfront as we come in. After about forty minutes, the sea pilot is replaced by a harbor pilot. He is very slow and deliberate, moving at a snail's pace to the dock, but he does a good job; it's the first port where we haven't had to use lines to help position the ship before we can tie up. Paperwork is amazing—the routine is in marked contrast to Haifa.

There are enough officials to fill every chair around the passenger table on the first superdeck—in Turkey the captain doesn't allow them up to her office. Every page of the cargo manifest has to be initialed by the captain. Each official brings a briefcase empty of papers, but just the right size to hold four cartons of Marlboros.

Alexandria cost sixty-four cartons; Izmir, about the same.

It's a little like living in fast forward, trying to cram so much into so little time. After a quick bite of breakfast with one of our agents, Ali Riza Zeybekoglu, about 0830 his driver, Mustafa, arrives with the Arkas agency's car. Mustafa, looking warm in his wool overcoat and sweater, a bit of a mustache decorating his pockmarked face, drives us downtown a little after nine. We stop at the PX to leave a crew list so everyone can get credentials to get in, discover it isn't open until 1100; buy a tin of Turkish olives and two kinds of halvah with our funny money (17,850 lira to a dollar) in a great grocery store, and head for Ephesus.

The captain sleeps in the back seat while I watch from the front. Last trip, when Jack was with Debbie and they made the same trip in darkness and pouring rain, the windshield wiper on the passenger side stopped working. It was, the captain says, a hairy ride. Today is sunny and warm.

Driving here is very reminiscent of Egypt, except Turkish drivers do use headlights after dark. On the highway the speed limit is 100 kilometers, but the speedometer says 110 most of the time. Lanes are marked, but people drive right down the middle of the road, moving over to the shoulder of a two-lane road to let someone pass in the middle. Lots of honking. Flat carts here, too, and unled donkeys bearing loads, women carrying bundles on their heads. Here sheep, there goats or cattle graze in small groups along the side of the road, any little spot where there's grass, always tended by a picture-book shepherd or shepherdess. Even where the countryside or village looks poor, a mosque dominates with its rounded dome and pointed spire.

Passing through the countryside we see lots of cypress trees, with their twisty trunks and tall greenery; knobby peach trees (many peaches are shipped to Germany), trimmed but not yet leafed out; orange groves; olive trees with their grayish, bushy foliage; and a light-barked tree Mustafa can't name, but it grows in rows and is cut to make scaffolding for construction. A big Marlboro plant is on the left, then a huge lumberyard, nurseries, plastics factories, and a modern-looking international airport a short distance from the heart of Izmir.

First stop is Selcuk and inside a compound, the rug-making school. You think you're out in the middle of nowhere, but posted on the wall of the courtyard outside the showroom is a board with the latest exchange rates. And an English-speaking salesman. And they do take Visa! Apologetic that the captain's rugs, ordered last trip, are not ready, they give her a saddlebag and drop the price for me on a West Anatolian rug with an irresistible pattern. With both wrapped and packed away in a canvas carry bag, we head for Ephesus only minutes away.

Even having seen pictures of the city, one is unprepared. We buy tickets and a guidebook, then wander streets paved with huge stones, skipping the available guided tour. Very few tourists are there off-season. No guards either. Unlike Pompeii, destroyed by a volcano that buried it, Ephesus was toppled by an earthquake. Hardly anything is whole, except a capital here or a column there, maybe a staircase or an arch. Each piece is numbered and it's being restored, so drawings are posted that approximate this version of the original. The last incarnation was the sixth, starting with the Romans, then the Byzantines. After this tour, it would be impossible not to recognize Corinthian columns ever again!

Reluctantly we head back to Izmir. Next stop: Alexander's Castle. The stone wall around the compound seems intact; today children are playing on it, although the signs warn of the danger. We take a new walkway, freshly planted, up stone stairs to the top of the wall. Mustafa points out the older part of the city; it looks yellow, with colored roofs everywhere. Small houses cover the hillside right to the water, where the *Charlotte Lykes* stands out. The house that Alexander the Great occupied for a short time is gone; only the foundation for the three-story building is visible, and the openings to long, elaborate tunnels.

The ride up and down the hill from the castle is fascinating, with cheek-by-jowl houses right on the sidewalk . . . shops selling breadstuffs, or fruit and vegetables . . . butcher shops with whole lambs, brains, and big pieces of tripe hanging in the window . . . a woman carrying home a chicken that's dead but still has all of its feathers. A flight of stairs rises steeply for several blocks to hundreds more houses along the way. Lining the road are huge piles of coal for sale as fuel. As we stop for a traffic light, we glance inside a dusky building where old Turkish men wearing their distinctive caps are drinking cognac or raki and playing Rummikub.

Mustafa points out a tiny yellow house; he was born there, and there his unmarried sister still lives, at seventy-five. Further down the hill he points proudly to a mosque on our left. He explains that he was an unpaid muezzin or singer there for two years when he was high-school age, before he went into the army.

At the bottom of the hill, we head downtown . . . past second-floor dress shops with flashy outfits for belly dancers in bay windows . . . small furniture factories, with couches and chairs in gaudy floral prints sitting on the sidewalk . . . an awning made of tree branches, old style, then covered with newfangled plastic, and residents sitting outside on cheap molded plastic furniture. Turks are lined up at bakeries to buy bread for the evening meal.

Downtown, we pay a man a few lira to watch the car as we head for the gold street in the bazaar. Mustafa's brother's store is among the two hundred lining the narrow covered walkway. While Mustafa hurries to the mosque, we have apple tea sweetened with lump sugar, served in tiny glasses on saucers, and then we make our purchases—no bargaining here. The last bit of business for the afternoon is a stop at the PX to buy tapes, and a camera the captain has promised to a friend in Italy. Then we head for the waterfront again, and Mustafa drops us at Deb's favorite Izmir restaurant, the Deniz, in a fashionable waterfront section.

We face the harbor and a full, beautiful orange sunset. This is a fish restaurant, and again we've ordered before sitting down: a big salad, a piece of feta, grilled prawns, three barboni each with garnish, a bottle of dry white wine, a baklava between us, Turkish coffee (in tiny flowered cups, sort of chewy and Clorox-y), and raki. We relax as we sip the clear, anise-flavored liquor, milky when it's mixed with ice and water, before Mustafa and work call.

He brings us back through the checkpoint to the ship just after 2000. Metin is waiting with three decoratively wrapped red roses for each of us. He'd been there since 1815, as he'd hoped to take us to dinner. He had worked for Arkas, the agency that handles Lykes ships in Izmir, but with no future there he left to start his own trucking company. Not too long ago his driver had a wreck and lost twelve thousand pounds of pickles! Metin had been several hours away, where the trucks are being repaired, and drove back only to see Debbie; he has to return north about 0400. There's also a tin of Turkish olive oil for each of us, from the agency.

Falling on my face, I climb the ladder for bed with promise of a wake-up call from the captain thirty minutes before sailing.

Wednesday, 23 February

It's a case of too much too fast, and it's hard to keep track of day and date. I awaken at 0430, but I can hear the stevedores still working cargo and assume we're not going to make the sailing board that had been posted for 0500. Finally at 0600 I shower and dress. Breakfast on the run is Israeli pastry, gourmet coffee, and Jaffa oranges—it is definitely possible to make do! By about 0715 the tug *Söndüren* is pulling us forward a short distance from the yellow gantries and booms, leaving Izmir in a haze. Slow for seven minutes, half ahead for five minutes or about a mile. We pass the Turkish Maritime Lines ferry (white with distinctive blue writing), which comes to Izmir from Italy once a week.

There is a reluctance to leave—Izmir gets the crew's vote for favorite port on the Med run. It has a European feeling, it's inviting, everything is available and not as expensive as other ports, the people are pleasant to deal with. The PX gets its share of the crew's money—most everyone seems to want a draw before Izmir—but so do the rug shops, gold shops, leather shops. Some crew fritter it away, but others buy nice gifts to take home for family and friends. In some ports, crew members don't get off the ship longer than to use the telephone or buy groceries. Not Izmir.

"Hope the visibility improves," the captain says as we begin the forty-eight-hour run to Naples.

A Greek containership is gliding toward the terminal as we leave; many more are anchored to our port side. Large, fancy buildings line the starboard waterfront, where, Mustafa said, rich people live. It's possible to pick out the two spires through which we can see Alexander's Castle on the hill. A car ferry, with a bus on her stern, crosses our bow going toward the fancy side. The green and white Turkish containership *Bolu,* a crest on either side of her stack, is still moored off the waterfront where we saw her last night when we went to dinner.

Ducks fly in formation around the *Charlotte* as the pilot speaks proudly of Ephesus, the best maintained of the Turkish antiquities. He stands about six feet, his handsome mustache and graying, softly curled short hair contrasting with his navy parka. We agree we're lucky we saw Ephesus without blazing sun, without rain, and without the huge crush of summer tourists.

We pass the Sea-Land containership *Sea Leader* on our port side as she steams toward Izmir. The second mate remarks that she's a good size, with a stern bay. A foreign-flagger, she's registered in Nassau.

"That's our competition," the captain returns.

As we pass between the buoys at Pelican Spit, the captain asks if we should slow down for the extremely shallow water. The pilot says no.

As we change course to 254, many low beach houses with red tile roofs pass by. Just outside the light, the pilot says, "Bye bye, have a nice trip," and he climbs down the outside ladders to the main deck. The red pilot boat with her green deck comes port side, and shortly Amy calls, "The pilot's away." We're on our own, heading back to sea.

"253's okay, Ben," the captain tells the AB who's steering. Tall, with a beard and mustache against his mottled skin, Ben looks like he's too big for his paint-stained flannel shirt, outgrowing his clothes like a twelve-year-old boy.

The call is "slow ahead" as there are tiny fishing boats to contend with, a pretty good one working with nets to port. The pilot has marked on the chart where a barge sank in last week's storm; help is coming all the way from Germany to try to raise her, but it's not there yet. We see no evidence of her.

At "half ahead" the buildings become more sparse against the mountains to port. Starboard it's too hazy to see anything. It's barely possible to make out the breakwater as we glide forward. On deck, two center cargo bays are empty; there are holes scattered among the containers elsewhere. Around us we see garbage floating in the harbor, along with clusters of seagulls.

As we pass a buoy, the captain tells the chief mate, "Okay, Bob, let's go full ahead."

In turn, Bob calls the chief engineer on the phone from the bridge with this message: "Departure was at 0806—sea speed at your convenience."

We maneuver to miss little white fishing boats with their pointed bows. One containership is coming in, another going out. A cool breeze blows through the bridge. There's still low haze as a red-hulled tanker crosses our bow to starboard. We pass a Greek containership heading into port.

In open water, it's time to try navigating, try out the radar, take bearings using the gyro repeater on the bridge wing, and, using triangles and a compass, mark them on the chart. Luckily, time is not of the essence.

Responding to its program, the GPS beeps to tell us we're at a way point to change course, and a cool breeze comes through the bridge once more as the second mate goes up to the flying bridge to take down the flags that flew over the house in port. There's a light chop with a few whitecaps as we overtake a tanker, and I remember the captain's comment that it's always a relief to be under way again. As the ship navigates through white fishing buoys, the boatswain makes his way across the empty deck in the sunshine, tossing unused turnbuckles and twist locks aft to an unseen spot.

At 0940 the visibility is five miles as we pass 1.2 miles off the rocky island to our left. More freighters, one each side of us, head in as we start our ninety-degree turn at the light at Kara Burun. Only land to the left here.

Momentarily the captain and second mate clash when she discovers we're two-tenths of a mile inside where she intended us to be—less than a mile off the next island—then notices that sightings haven't been taken every ten or fifteen minutes and noted on the chart. The second mate is using the GPS, good for latitude and longitude. Running the coast, the captain wants visual sightings and radar, much more precise in close quarters. He calls a heading, she disagrees with his timing.

"No, I've got it," she states, taking the conn or control back momentarily. Inexperienced, he hasn't got an overall perspective, and isn't nearly concerned enough about running aground, she says. She's not as impressed with him as last trip, she admits.

"I guess I should have expected to get chewed out once before the trip is out," he remarks. After the crisis has passed, the captain asks, "May I share something with you?" She explains why it has to be done her way, and he agrees: the GPS only tells you where you are when it beeps, but the radar shows how far off the landmarks you are and exactly where you are going.

At 1115 the island of Khios is to the right, and we're at the last tight spot through the Khios Straits. We must stay nine-tenths of a mile off the island with the lighthouse to avoid two shallow spots, one of ten meters to starboard, another of eleven meters to port. At the city of Khios we can see huge beautiful white houses with red tile roofs and curving arches over big windows or balconies—we decide it's another place we must have a closer look at from the French barge we've spotted in a yachting magazine. We think this barge is the one to buy for our dream trip.

With Khios falling behind, it's lunch and some work before other Greek islands need our attention. After lunch I get another lesson in taking visual sightings and plotting them, using radar to determine how far a landmark is, and steering—Juan is very patient and very helpful. More sights to see—this time Mykonos—then the usual cribbage (another loss: in the stinkhole) and cocktails, dinner, and a movie before it's time to watch the Peloponnesus go by in the dark.

Lots of freighter traffic as we head for the bridge about 2130. It's a clear moonlight night, good for sightseeing, but with a strong wind on our bow. Dead ahead is a lighthouse marking Cape Sparta, flashing three times in thirty seconds. Unmistakable. Finally a course change puts the lighthouse to our port side; the island itself seems long and low, unlike others we've passed. Also, no other lights surround the blinker, but some are farther back on the island.

Cape Sparta is long gone by midnight. Retard clocks tonight, because tomorrow night we'll be busy threading the Straits of Messina.

Joanne Foster and Captain Dempsey posing with Gibraltar in the background.

The captain in her office aboard the Charlotte.

Chief Mate Bob Strobel sells Marlboros from the slop chest.

Second Mate Don Josberger shares a light moment with the captain on the bridge wing.

Third Mate Amy La Cost and the captain confer at the chart table on the bridge.

The stern view of the Charlotte, framed by gantries used to work cargo at Port Elizabeth. Photo by Albert F. House

A panoramic view from the bridge over the bow of the Charlotte.

*Taking a position on the bridge wing the old-fashioned way,
with a sextant.*

Through a ham operator, the captain calls home from aboard the Charlotte.

8. *It's More Fun When You're the Captain*

*T*he biggest difference between being a chief mate and a master is that when you are the master, instead of asking the questions, you must have the answers. That's sobering.

As I prepared for my first voyage as captain in the summer of 1989, I reflected on just how long it had been in coming.

The scenario went like this:

I had sat for my master's license at MITAGS in Linthicum Heights, Maryland, just outside Baltimore in November 1984. It was what you could call a rigid Coast Guard exam. It's four and a half days, and follows the same format as the ones I had taken previously, but the material increases in difficulty as you go up the ladder. And there are sections directed toward the captain's responsibilities—ship's stability, more ship-handling and seamanship, fuel consumption, more admiralty law. Although I knew I'd passed, on Friday afternoon after the final half day of the exam I went with a friend at MITAGS to the Coast Guard office in Baltimore to find out my scores.

That night Jack and I celebrated at a Spanish restaurant in Baltimore with two friends who also had been at MITAGS, Mark Robinson and Joan Urban. Mark was captain of the *Sue Lykes,* which was scrapped in 1995, and he retired; Joan managed the passenger department for Lykes until she retired in 1993. They have been married since January 1991. It was a bittersweet night. Jack had planned to present me with shoulder boards, but at dinner Mark and Joan gave me a set, and Jack just sat there, saying nothing. When his plan finally came out of him, I felt awful. He did give me his after all, and I use them for having my picture taken or on official occasions.

At last, I was sworn in on a blowing, cold 7 December 1984, in ceremonies at the Coast Guard base in Boston. Nice that the honors were done by Lt. Cdr. Phillip Chase, U.S. Coast Guard, also a Maine Maritime grad. I had run into Phil at MITAGS, and he had asked me to transfer my records to Boston so he could perform the ceremony. My parents came, as well as my brother John and his wife, Wendy, from Manchester, Massachusetts, and, of course, Jack. You'd never know it from the pictures, though. He was taking them and isn't in any—as usual.

At the time, Commander Chase called receiving my license "almost an impossible feat. It's just incredible."

The article in the *Hartford Courant* quotes Commander Chase as saying he was impressed. "Those are not easy tests," he said. "She did unusually well."

I did score two 100s (in rules-of-the-road and celestial navigation), two 95s, in safety and deck general, and a 93 in navigation general, among other scores. To pass, you have to get 90 percent right on rules-of-the-road and celestial navigation; the others, 70 percent.

Although I'd been the first American female to earn, in turn, a third mate's, second mate's, and chief mate's license, my becoming the first female seagoing master created quite a stir in the press. My picture was in many newspapers, from the *Boston Globe* to the *Cape Cod Times,* and even as far away as the *Japan Times.* Jack had been in my corner all the way, and, along with my parents and friends, he was ecstatic. Naturally I was excited. Some particularly nice recognition came my way.

Rear Adm. R. A. Bauman, commander of the First Coast Guard District, wrote as a trustee of the prestigious Boston Marine Society, inviting me to apply for membership. The Society is made up of master mariners who have held command of ocean service vessels for at least one year.

"Your achievement is a famous and highly deserved first," he wrote. "To be the first female to hold an unlimited master's license in the U.S. Merchant Marine is a great accomplishment. As a graduate of Massachusetts Maritime Academy, I wish our school would follow your distinguished lead."

Julie A. Berke of New York, who is married to a Kings Point graduate, put up $10,000 each for the first women from Kings Point to get a master's license and a chief engineer's license. Although I didn't qualify, she sent me a congratulatory note saying, "How lucky those fellow shipmates are to have a fresh, beautiful face to guide them on their journey and to help ensure their safety. . . . A guiding Angel!"

After the hoopla, normalcy returned. I continued to work as chief mate, never returning to work on the same ship after vacation. Sometimes I worked with Jack, which was more than okay with me.

I know I'm prejudiced by marriage, but Jack was the fairest, ablest of all captains. I learned more from him about how to be a captain than any school could teach me. He was total experience. He did more with a ship than anyone, and far more than all of us academy graduates. He took care of the whole crew, and he was always willing to help any mate, able seaman, ordinary seaman, or cadet if the inclination to learn was there. Even the engineers and messmen went on vacation when Jack did. As Mr. Green, the saloon messman on the *Howell Lykes,* Jack's ship, always said, "No matter how bad the weather or how difficult the port, there is no reason to be concerned, because Captain Dempsey is in control."

He never forgot what it was like to sail chief mate and he helped the mate more than any other captain. Working with Jack as chief mate was fun for both of us. So I bided my time.

Then, in April 1988, I saw where David Boatner, who had had his master's license only about four months, had been given a Lykes ship. And I'd had my license four years! Dave, a 1978 California Maritime grad, had been second mate when I was chief mate on the containership *Adabelle Lykes* in 1985, running from the West Coast to the Far East. His promotion was a matter of being at the right place at the right time—he had been the only one available to relieve an ill captain. But, stating the obvious, I was a bit jealous. I went to my boss, Capt. Richard E. Manchester, then vice president of the marine division, to ask why Dave and not me.

"I've just been waiting for you to ask," he said.

Grrr!

It's not for everybody. It's not for all women or men, either, going to sea for months at a time. Just picture a man with a wife and three kids, who leaves all of the responsibility at home. I think that's awful—a very selfish existence.

There are only a handful of American female skippers in the merchant marine with unlimited master's licenses, which say we can command any "U.S. steam or motor vessels of any gross tons upon oceans." Not all have sailed on our licenses. We are all products of one of the seven maritime academies (Kings Point, which is federal; state schools in New York, Texas, California, Massachusetts, and

Maine, and the Great Lakes Training School in Michigan). Among the others:

Ann Sanborn, a Texas Maritime grad. She was the first to sail master, on the Texas maritime school ship, *Texas Clipper,* in 1987.

Lynn Korwatch, who graduated from California Maritime Academy in 1976, about a week after my graduation. She got her master's license after I did, but sailed on it before I did, in June 1988. She's now manager of the marine division for Matson.

Nancy Wagner, a graduate of Kings Point in 1978, the first class there that included women. She received her master's license in January 1986 and sailed chief mate for Exxon; she's now a San Francisco Bay pilot. She did not sail master.

Ellen Warner, who sailed master on coastwise tankers for American Heavy Lift Co. She is now a Sabine River pilot.

Numbers are increasing. As of the summer of 1992, female enrollment at Maine Maritime, for example, was 6 percent and, according to their alum magazine, "certain to go higher." After eighteen years of coeducation, my alma mater had graduated forty-seven women, among some seven hundred women graduates from maritime academies nationwide. Its class of 1999 alone includes thirty women. Where twenty years earlier the merchant marine academies had graduated no women, the proportions of women in the 1995 graduating classes ranged from 6 percent at Mass Maritime to 30 percent at Great Lakes.

When I was named captain of the *Lyra* in 1989, seventy-two masters were on Lykes's roster, a third of them Maine Maritime graduates. As of July 1992, Lykes was down to forty-seven active permanent masters (sixty-two masters including relief masters) for twenty-three U.S.-operated ships. One woman. Me. By July 1995, Lykes's fleet was fourteen, its roster similarly pared.

Due to union regulations, each captain is paid the same for the same work, regardless of ability or effort, depending on the class of ship—from Pride and Pacer at the bottom to Seamaster at the top. A RO/RO ship is the next class down from Seamaster, ranking with the Clipper and Express classes. A full-time captain earns from $80,000 to $100,000 a year.

Although I no longer captain the *Lyra,* I still think of her in the present tense.

For 180 days at a time, home is the master's stateroom, with a view and a private bath, on E Deck (the captain's deck). Deck layouts are variations on a theme; to reach my stateroom on the *Lyra,* for instance, you have to walk a few steps from the elevator and turn left.

Posted on the wall behind glass, under lock and key, for all to see along with all of her other vital papers, is the certificate of the ship's insurance with the Frank B. Hall Company of New Orleans. We had $500 million liability, with a $50,000 deductible, except for seepage or pollution. That's payable in full. We also have separate insurance policies for hull and cargo. Those are sobering reminders of the responsibility the captain alone holds. Also posted there is the certificate of inspection from the Coast Guard, which regulates the crew requirement and safety equipment on board, along with life raft and lifeboat certificates, all of the Federal Communications Commission (FCC) certificates, and our safety construction and equipment and load line certificates issued by the American Bureau of Standards (ABS).

The crew list is another reminder of the captain's responsibility. The Coast Guard certificate indicates the crew requirement at one each: master, chief mate, second mate, third mate, radio officer, chief engineer, first assistant engineer, second assistant engineer, third assistant engineer, two engine maintenance personnel, and six able seamen. In addition, we may carry eleven other crew members and twelve passengers (no passengers when we are under military charter), for a total of forty. We operate with a crew of twenty-two.

Bulletin board notices address everything from social diseases and smuggling to drugs and alcohol. There's even one warning crew members not to trade video films with another vessel, or the rental fee will be charged—the company supplies movies, usually about twenty for a forty-five-day voyage. One notice contains rules on dumping trash, another on drug-testing regulations. A Lykes safety notice states: "Boarding vessels should only be accomplished by climbing a safe accommodation ladder, gangway, or approved vertical boarding ladder."

Then you go past the chief mate's office on the right and racks on the left that hold licenses for the master, chief mate, second and third mates, and radio operator; through the outer door with its overhead sign lettered in black on silver, MASTER; and into the little lobby (complete with mirror, shelf for gloves, three white coat-and-hat racks) and through the inner door into what is designated Room 23, the captain's office.

It's not fancy. Linoleum on the floor is brown. Wallpaper is brown in a herringbone pattern. The furniture is fake dark wood, with gray vinyl upholstery. Brown curtains frame the ports on two sides of the office.

Straight ahead is my desk, to the left a bookshelf, to the right the upholstered couch, loveseat, and chair around a coffee table, all secured to the deck. There's a cupboard, sideboard (complete with coffee pot and packets of powdered orange juice), paper cutter, and all of those things that make an office an office, in a space about thirteen feet by seventeen feet. Above the bookshelf hangs notice of the ship's mortgages. There are a couple of nautical clocks, a thermometer, an electric fan. I have an internal telephone, number thirteen. I have an STX radio, which allows me to communicate with the office in port, and a walkie-talkie that lets me keep in constant touch with the chief mate, boatswain, chief engineer, engine control room, electrician, and bridge. Sometimes in port I also have a cellular phone so I can talk with our agent there or make other infrequent calls. Once I used it for a long-distance phone call, and the next trip I had to pay the bill—$80!

I also have a safe, which contains the valuables. By law, narcotics for medical use must be secured in the safe. Usually it holds about $20,000 in cash, available to the crew for advances against wages. The *Lyra's* safe contains six pairs each of handcuffs and leg irons, unused, and a .38-caliber Smith & Wesson with a hundred rounds that belongs to the ship and probably has never been fired. (Some guns have been—including the one on the *Louise Lykes,* which the captain used to commit suicide in his stateroom. A subsequent captain, bugged by signing for ninety-nine rounds each voyage, finally traded them for a new allotment of one hundred.) Before crews on merchant vessels were unionized, it was up to the master to keep order. Jack, whose experience dated back farther than mine, remembered seeing a master use a gun during World War II. Lykes's view is if you have to use a gun, "it's better if the guy you use it on can't testify."

Some captains, like Jack, also carry their own guns. I don't. I keep my wallet, passport, and jewelry in the safe. We also keep passengers' money or jewelry in the safe, but souvenirs are locked up in the ship's slop chest.

The most notable items in the safe are the naval publications to be used in time of national emergency when, theoretically, all American commercial vessels could be taken over by the military. They consist of two sealed envelopes, Alpha and Bravo. They've never been opened, so their contents are a mystery, but I know they are checked each time a group of naval reservists boards.

My bedroom, identified by a sign above the door that says "bedroom," is about ten feet by thirteen feet. It's furnished with a single bunk, light-brown dressing table and chair, a three-drawer dresser, and a brown-striped couch, covered with a blue throw. The floor is the same brown linoleum, the wallpaper there is green. I hate that wallpaper. In fact, I tried to tear it off once, then glued it back. Two corners are taken up with hanging lockers, one with a life jacket cabinet above it. *The Best Years of Your Life* and *One Watch at a Time* are on the bookshelf. A still life of a woman with a wine glass decorates one wall. I usually hang something over it, like a picture of Maine. I was going to hang a dart board over it, but decided I would do too much damage. Compared with military quarters, they are spacious. In fact, I compared notes with my nephew, Mark, who was on the newest nuclear aircraft carrier USS *George Washington,* commissioned 4 July 1992. As an ensign and a boatswain on the flight deck, he still had to share quarters with one bunk mate, and bathroom facilities with numerous officers.

The bathroom is not what you'd call luxurious. Red tile squares cover the floor, and blue wallpaper is pretty well covered by a wall cabinet. It has a shower but no tub, pipes up one wall, a pink john brush in one corner, and towels hanging on anything.

Everywhere are reminders that this is not a motel, but a ship. A double book rack over the bunk is built into the wall, to keep books from being tossed about. Furniture is all hooked to the walls or floor. Pictures—here a ship, there a pastoral scene—are screwed to the walls. Everywhere in the passageways are handrails. There are locks on every door, numbers above every office. There are constant reminders of the dangers—lifesaving equipment here, a lifeline for emergency escape there. Here a hardhat, or a red-headed Indian Chief ax, or a fire station, there a fire and emergency station list, or a lifeboat. The infirmary has a gimballed bed, a must on a ship, and a large medicine chest equipped to handle almost any medical emergency we might have (we once were set to perform an appendectomy on a cadet, but he was taken off by helicopter about one hundred miles southeast of Sable Island in the Atlantic). Other "musts" include laundry facilities (we each do our own, although beds are changed weekly and clean towels provided), and separate coffee rooms and dining saloons for officers and seamen.

Because the ship must be provisioned for ninety days, there are large lockers for frozen food, dairy products, and dry stores. The ship has archives, an office complete with computer and copier, and storage space for everything from paint and parts to official stationery, ship's flags, and spare carafes for the captain's coffee pot.

There are recreational facilities. The swimming pool, when not filled with salt water, is covered with a safety net so no seaman accidentally falls in. Overlooking it is an old-fashioned white fiberglass porch swing, a mottled green four-person plastic bench, a plywood plank good for sunbathing, a twelve-foot picnic table, and a barbecue. There's also a gymnasium with workout equipment, from barbells and a stationary ladder to a stationary bike and other machines. And the view from the bridge is spectacular.

My day goes like this:

I always leave night orders: If there is any doubt or there are any problems, call me. I'd rather be called and not needed than needed and not called. Otherwise, I leave a wake-up call for 0600.

The first voice I hear at that hour is the second mate's, as he or she fills me in with the ship's speed, weather, and so on. Next I exercise for thirty minutes, swim if the pool's filled, shower, and dress. Typically it's a blue polo shirt with the company's blue and white emblem, khakis, and tennis shoes. I always wear a watch. Then I head for the bridge and a cup of coffee. Back down one deck to my office and paperwork—it's quietest before breakfast, which is at 0745. After breakfast I usually talk to the steward in the galley. I check the sanitary conditions (see what's dirty, see how many roaches are around), see what's cooking, and listen to his problems.

Typical steward's department problem (with a high priority among the master's responsibilities): The oiler, Isaac Laboard, and wiper, Roosevelt Johnson, complained about the crew mess person, Neva Wood, taking pornographic magazines from the crew's recreation room adjoining their mess and throwing them over the side. Neva did not think she should have to look at such filth. It's all you can do not to laugh.

Then it's back to the office to send the required 0800 messages, followed by a check with the chief mate to see if he wants to be relieved on the bridge during his watch to meet with the boatswain. Because the chief mate is the department head for the deck department and the boatswain runs the deck gang, they need to coordinate.

Maybe every other day I check the steering gear. Then I'll wander the other decks. I check the engine room now and then, see what the deck gang's doing for maintenance, stroke the boatswain to tell him what a good job he's doing, check the rooms for cleaning to see if the steward's doing his job. More paperwork, more messages, up to 1145 and lunch.

After lunch I head for the bridge again and about 1210 I check the third mate's noon slip. It shows the past day's run, our latitude and longitude, speed made good, course made good, total distance, distance to go, number of hours in the day (crossing datelines and time zones, it's not always twenty-four). Warnings about weather, or whether clocks will need to be advanced or retarded, are shown under "Remarks." About 1230 I head for my quarters, read for a half hour or so, and nap until 1400. Then—you guessed it—more paperwork. I send a daily message to Lykes of our noon position, and our ETA, which is figured daily. At 1500 I take a coffee break either on the bridge or with the engineers. Another quick round of the ship follows, up to the bow this time. I have a beer, maybe two, at 1700, followed by supper at 1730.

At 1800 I send messages again and check the bridge, and at 1830 head for the office of the chief engineer (Brian Norton) and movie time. When we're under military charter I send the last messages to MSC (Military Sealift Command) at 1930, watch the rest of the movie until about 2030, check the bridge at 2200, and fall into bed about 2300.

That's on a calm, cool, collected day. They seldom are.

On 6 June 1989, I took command as master of the *Lyra*. I'd arrived in New Orleans the night before, and I got to the ship about 0930 Tuesday morning. She'd been at Lykes's Andry Street lay berth since 12 May for repairs, because there was no work for her. I relieved a sweating, undershirt-clad captain, Ed Batcho. A former Panama Canal pilot, he had been captain of the *Lyra* during hurricane Keith in November 1988, when the ship did a fifty-two-degree roll. In the June heat, without air conditioning, he was anxious to leave. I had to sign a change-of-command form and certificates acknowledging receipt of the gun, narcotics, sextant, binoculars, Breathalyzer, computer. Usually the master also signs a receipt for money aboard; because she'd been laid up, there was none. Since it was my first go-round, transfer was a little more involved than usual.

Usually the master hands you the radios and the keys—the grand master—and combination to the safe. Radios: plural, because you need the walkie-talkie to communicate aboard ship and the STX to communicate with the office. You can always tell who the captain is—the one with the most radios.

It took a while for me to get used to answering when the office called "*Lyra.*" Sometimes it was Elroy Hartman, a good, loyal friend and manager of the purser's office in Lykes's headquarters in New Orleans, on the other end. He'd sign off with "*Lyra,* Captain Dempsey, okay sweetheart, thank you." Anyone and everyone within earshot of either end of the conversation could hear it. After three days of this, I called him on a land line—so no one else could hear—and asked him please to do without the "sweetheart."

His response? "Okay, honey."

For most of those three days, only chief engineer Brian Norton and I were aboard, going through a Coast Guard inspection. Finally on Friday we recrewed, and I visited the head office at Lykes Center, 300 Poydras Street, a few blocks from the Mississippi River. First I exchanged my usual khakis for a skirt. When I went into the office, I always wore a skirt. The men all wore ties.

When I earned my master's license, Jack gave me the shoulder boards. To go with them, when I got the *Lyra,* he presented me with a wool Lykes Lines baseball cap with the "scrambled eggs" on the front, part of my usual "uniform"—L.L. Bean khaki pants and a Lykes shirt from the ship's slop chest. Normal routine does not require a uniform, and deck officers usually wear khakis in port for identification. If you feel you need to wear the four stripes to identify yourself as captain, then I guess you shouldn't be captain.

First I saw my number one boss, Captain Manchester, for the initial master's briefing. He was in the process of sending a telegram to my old training ship, the TV *State of Maine.* The message: "Master. FYIG Deborah Dempsey MMA Class of 76 assigned master *MV Lyra* on June 6th 1989. Regards to all aboard for successful voyage. Manchester/Lykes (68D)."

Their reply: "Captain Manchester. Please convey congratulations to

Captain Deborah Dempsey. All hands wish her great success. State of Maine en route Leningrad to Copenhagen. Cummings Master."

I also received a congratulatory telegram from Lykes's Charleston office, which read: "Congratulations on your becoming master of the Lyra. We just heard the good news." It was signed by John Perez, the terminal coordinator. A nice guy.

Captain Manchester put "68D" after his name to indicate he was a 1968 Maine Maritime grad; the "D" was for deck (as opposed to engine). He was very good at what he did, and very overambitious. He told me to use the telephone to call him while in port or at sea anywhere in the world, twenty-four hours a day, because he was more experienced at making decisions than I—his job was to handle shipboard operations for twenty-eight vessels, making sure they were always in a seaworthy condition. The *Lyra* would be my baby when I got off the coast, when I'd really be doing my thing—maneuvering to take on harbor pilots and so on. In 1988 I had been chief mate on the *Cygnus,* the sister ship of the *Lyra* (one of the reasons I was put on the *Lyra*), and Captain Manchester, having seen the public reaction then, let me know he was aware of the publicity that would come with my new status.

Next stop was the manager of the marine division and my number two boss, Capt. Clark Seelig. I reminded him that the first time we had met was when I was a young cadet in 1975 and he was the port captain assigned by Captain Hendrix to carry my luggage and see that I got to my assigned ship, the *Velma Lykes,* safely.

"I won't tolerate any mistakes," were his first words.

"I might as well hang it up now," I replied.

"I mean *stupid* mistakes," he returned, reminding me to check in before leaving the coast and upon returning. His farewell comment was always, "Keep her in deep water."

I made the rest of the rounds, stopping to see Tom Huggett, in charge of Line B or Operations Northern Europe. That's where I was going, for thirty-five days: After Galveston and Norfolk, Virginia, we were sailing to Rotterdam, Bremerhaven, and Felixstowe, then back to Norfolk.

But before that, in order to load, we had to shift the ship to the France Road Container Terminal on the other side of the industrial canal. That meant having to go down the Mississippi River to the mouth, around the delta to the Mississippi River Gulf Outlet (or Mr. Go, as it's affectionately known) and back up to the terminal. It's a trip of about eight hours to the mouth, maybe four hours outside, and another six back up to the terminal. My concern was the 140-foot height clearance under the Paris Avenue Bridge. Without cargo, we were riding high. By lowering the radio direction-finder antenna, the highest point on the vessel, we cleared the bridge by four feet. I also was concerned about the possibility that TV crews wanted to ride with me. Despite the fact that Lykes's public relations people were in favor of the idea, I told Captain Manchester I didn't feel good about company because it was my first time on the *Lyra.*

We made it, without the press aboard. When they met me at the France Road terminal for interviews on the bridge, I literally fell on my face! It was wet on the captain's deck, I had run down to my office to get some information, and my feet went out from under me. The interviews were successful, though.

That was Sunday, and at 0800 Monday we started working—loading, taking stores, finishing the Coast Guard inspection, doing fire and boat drill, stretching hoses. About 1000 Miss Nell, secretary to Captain Manchester, called from the office to say they were sending me a body.

"More help?" I asked.

"No, a dead body." It was a former seagoing employee of Lykes, for burial at sea.

Taking a break at coffee time, I eased down to check with the chief mate, Eric Wilcox. Also there was a cadet, Jason Bright—a terrific kid, eager and helpful. After I left, the cadet asked Eric, "Who's that?"

Eric told him, and afterward told me about the cadet's surprised response: "The captain's a woman?"

I told Eric, "Ask him if his mother's a woman."

Before Jason left the ship, he sent me a very nice letter. It read, in part:

I would like to thank you for everything. I have had a great time aboard the *Lyra,* and have learned a lot too. I almost think it is a shame to leave such a great ship, crew, and captain, but I suppose, as you said, I should not get attached to any one ship or person. The next cadets do not know how lucky they are. It seems like only last week I got on this ship, and already I am leaving.

Anyway—I just wanted to thank you for everything. Thanks again, and as our waterfront director at school says—Warm, fair winds and following seas! Good luck to you and the *Lyra.* Adios.

We finally left New Orleans for Galveston, twenty-five hours dock to dock, on Monday evening.

I could not have asked for a better chief mate than Eric Wilcox. In addition to being a workaholic, he was very experienced with RO/ROs and the *Lyra* in particular. And—after struggling for the first three days in New Orleans to make sure we had the right charts and publications for northern Europe—boy, was it a tremendous relief to go up on the bridge early Friday morning and discover that the navigator would be Bill Mago (who eventually became chief mate on the *Lyra*). He had been the second mate on the ship before, and he was well familiar with the bridge and the run. Only the first assistant engineer, Peter Smith, who is six years younger than I, had a tough time with a woman on board, especially as the captain. He finally got used to my presence, and it was no longer an issue.

I had no crew problems. They were all rooting for me. In fact, they presented me with the house flag and life ring. We were in Rotterdam when I celebrated my fortieth birthday, and the whole crew signed a card to me. As Eric—who coincidentally shares my birthday—so nicely put it, "Your being captain is just as much a first-time thing for us as it is for you. Let us be a part of it."

One birthday letter that really meant a lot to me was from my old seamanship-meteorology instructor, Capt. Louis Hathaway, by then living in Yankeetown, Florida. "You have worked hard and put up with a lot and really deserve the recognition you have finally received."

A card from my sister Timotha described her frustration in sending me a birthday telegram:

Timotha to the operator: "I want to make a call to the captain of the MV *Lyra*."

Operator: "Do you know the call number?"

"No."

Operator: "Who are you calling?"

"Deborah Dempsey."

Operator: "I thought you said you wanted to call the captain!"

"I do, and she is."

Operator: "Oh."

I definitely had first-time jitters going into Norfolk, loading outbound, and going into Cherbourg, where we picked up the North Sea pilot. My first port docking overseas was Bremerhaven, but I wasn't nervous about that one. I had been there before as chief mate, I had the North Sea pilot aboard, and the German tugs are very good. Rotterdam was something else. Except in theory, I didn't know anything about that port.

My biggest concern was doing the messages right, because as chief mate you never have to do that. Once you get the messages into a routine, that also settles down. And the female aspect was not as big as you'd think. I'd been with Lykes Lines since 1977, and been associated with the company since I was a cadet in 1975, so everyone knew me. Still it was nice, for instance, when Hans Poll, the managing director of Kersten Hunik, our agency in Rotterdam, sent me a huge bouquet of flowers.

Bas, the North Sea pilot we picked up in Cherbourg, also sent me flowers. Bas Vliegenthart is a character. He's the only North Sea pilot who doesn't come aboard in uniform. He always brings cheese and French bread, papers and magazines, prepared to stay on the whole North Sea run. Most shipping lines keep a pilot aboard for that run because the North Sea is so busy; it's cheap insurance. Bas usually handles Express class containerships and, with four on that run, he's very busy. I had met him briefly the previous year, so the captain of the *Charlotte Lykes,* Jim Brasier (Maine Maritime '70), kidded him, "You're only going on the *Lyra* to see what Debbie looks like now." It's the only time he'd been on the *Lyra.*

As in any field, being a woman among many men can be a problem. It depends on how you handle yourself. For instance, we had a situation on the *Lyra*'s first trip to Ad Dammam during the Persian Gulf War, where the third assistant engineer, Sue Kealey, was working with two young men, Scott Sillery and John Kinane, as first and second assistants, respectively. She was a graduate of the Marine Engineers Beneficial Association (MEBA) three-year union school in Baltimore, and she had a tough time handling their resentment. Their first comment: It was okay to have women on the ship, but not as officers (maybe in the galley?). Our electrician that trip was a woman, too, but a go-getter; she had no problem.

Sue still had much to learn about the evolving dynamics of women in this previously all-male world. She would show up in the saloon in a skirt and pumps, then cross her legs exposing more than was prudent in this situation. I will admit it is harder for a woman to "go engine" than "go deck," as I did. As an engineer, you're dealing with people in a situation that requires physical strength and mechanical ability in close quarters under the fluorescent lights, day in and day out.

Toward the end of that trip, both Scott and John threatened to quit, saying they wouldn't take another trip. Finally, at the last barbecue before we returned stateside, I commented to Scott, "Just think. On your next ship the chief engineer could be a woman."

His reply: "Over my dead body."

I'm always aware of potential problems associated with my being a female captain. For example, when I took over the *Lyra,* Brian Norton was soon relieved by Charlie Kyle, who was new to the chief engineer's job. I was concerned that he was feeling anxious because he had to work with a female captain, and I asked Captain Manchester about it. He, in turn, called Louis Castro, manager of MNR for Lykes, into his office to inquire if there was a problem.

"Absolutely not," Mr. Castro said.

And there wasn't. I never did have a problem, and Charlie and I had a wonderful working relationship. Charlie is a perfectionist and a problem solver, and he handled his department with quiet efficiency. Each of us respects the other's expertise.

My being a woman had one amusing consequence in Rotterdam. It was my first trip there; I didn't know the port or where we were going to dock. The docking master, Mr. Houthvot-Hase, had asked in advance how many tugs I wanted.

"One," I replied. "With two bow thrusters, we do not need a second tug on the bow."

We had to back the ship down a narrow two-thousand-foot slipway, with working vessels on either side. Docking became a bit hairy because the twelve-thousand-horsepower bow thrusters used for maneuvering the *Lyra* kept overheating and kicking out.

Despite that problem, we managed to dock safely. I'd worn a sweatshirt to ward off damp and cold while we docked. Afterward I took Mr. Houthvot-Hase to my office and, pulling back the hood on my sweatshirt, I remarked that if I'd anticipated the difficulties, I'd have had a second tug standing by.

"It's no problem," he said. "You handle a ship just like you would a woman. Coax her a little, back off, coax her a little more, back off."

He left my office never realizing I was a woman!

I don't know what it is about Rotterdam, but that was only the first of three memorable incidents there.

On my second trip to Rotterdam aboard the *Lyra,* Teresa Kyle, the wife of chief engineer Charlie Kyle, was riding under a spousal agreement. As we were docking, she was outside on the bridge wing with me and blocking the remote console where I needed to work. I very nicely turned her around and gently moved her out of the way. The docking master turned to me and asked, "Your wife?"

"No, the chief engineer's," I said, and started to tell him about my husband.

"You had a sex change?" he asked.

The cadets got a big roar out of that.

Even the last time I went into Rotterdam—after I'd had my finger-nails and toenails painted—the docking master still wasn't sure if I was a man or a woman.

The British are very strict about bringing in pornographic material, and before we called at Felixstowe, as before any port, the chief mate collected all of the pornographic videos and magazines. One day at lunch the men were going on and on about the quantity of magazines that had been turned in. Eric was kidding that if I ever needed one, he could get it for me.

I piped up with, "I wish I had a *Playgirl.*"

That was the end of it until the next trip when Eric's wife, Donna, rode with us. Three days out I returned to my office to find on my desk, what else, a *Playgirl.*

It was three trips before I was relieved by Joe Bridges, a 1976 California Maritime grad. He was later manager of Lykes Charleston, Lykes New Orleans, and last, Lykes Houston.

Previously, whenever I relieved another chief mate, I had center-folds in my face wherever I turned in my stateroom—on the bulk-head, on the overhead, inside the hanging locker. This time, I took a centerfold from *Playgirl,* wrote "Welcome Aboard" across the private parts, and taped it inside the medicine chest. Charlie Kyle, my chief engineer at that point, knew, but I never heard a word about it from Captain Bridges. Another captain, Brian McNamara, told me he'd heard about it when he, in turn, relieved Joe Bridges.

"Really, Debbie," was all he said.

• • •

When you go master, it is an incredible high. You've finally made it. It's exciting. And the job is fun, after you get over the "firsts"—the first message, the first time you move the ship, the first time you dock her, the first fender bender.

It makes you feel good, but you go from being able to ask the captain to *being* captain and having to answer questions. Some people don't want the responsibility. They're afraid of it. They still want to have somebody to ask. But you've been trained for the job, so it's not an all-of-a-sudden thing. And you want to do it right, better than anybody else has done it before you.

Being captain can be very lonely at times. Your ultimate responsibility for that ship means that in pea-soup fog—with the ship's whistle blasting in your ears every two minutes, getting bleary-eyed watching the radars—you're the one who stays on the bridge watch after watch, those long hours, days, nights, avoiding the Grand Banks fishing fleet off Newfoundland or maneuvering through the Nantucket fairway approaching Ambrose light tower entering New York, until the visibility is clear again. Heavy weather or a third mate whose navigating skills you don't entirely trust means you're on the bridge continuously. A fast turnaround in port after port, where you are required to be on the bridge for long stretches as you enter and leave, as well as handling your duties in port, never allows the master enough rest. Three trips through the North Atlantic in winter, and you come home looking like a zombie. Through trying times, you try not to show anybody your emotions. At times you have to go to your quarters, shut the door, and let loose.

Help makes the difference. If you have good help, it's fun. It's fun to be the boss. You want to make it easy for the crew to do their jobs, not be a hard-ass and make unnecessary demands. You don't want to make captain, then forget what it was like to be the mate and think everybody's there to wait on you. If you don't act spoiled, they'll go out of their way to help you.

Case in point: The last captain I sailed for as chief mate, on the *Cygnus* in the fall of 1988. I got stuck with things he should have done, especially paperwork, while he watched movies in his office. I was going to have the boatswain in Charleston turn his TV on its side so he wouldn't have to hold his head up! Once when we were tied up at the army's dock in North Charleston, his wife was flying in to meet him and it was pouring rain. He wanted me to get his keys, walk onto the dock and get his rental car and drive it up the stern ramp onto the ship so he could get in without getting wet. I didn't do it. But the second mate did.

When you don't sail, you miss the glory. You miss the adventure and the challenge. You miss all of the different countries, and the people you meet overseas. By the end of a three-month vacation period, you're ready to go back.

The toughest thing you do is discipline, which is always distasteful—firing someone; chewing out the third mate for coming back drunk, as I did when we were in drydock in Bremerhaven; lecturing the mate, who thinks you're treating him like a cadet. It's not an attractive side of the job, but as boss you have to do it.

Dealing with contraband is another of the captain's jobs. Contraband includes not only drugs but excess cigarettes and undeclared souvenirs, all subject to a fine by customs officials. Lykes requires masters to do frequent contraband searches, always after leaving one country and prior to arriving in the next, and as the captain I'd delegate this responsibility to the three department heads—chief mate, chief engineer, and chief steward. If drugs are found aboard, you are guilty and fined, and the company must prove that as carrier, it was not responsible. Stops at South American and East African ports are notorious for prompting drug problems aboard freighters.

Stowaway searches are handled the same way. Luckily, I never had stowaways aboard after I became captain. If found, they require a twenty-four-hour guard and they must be handcuffed in a vacant room and locked up to prevent escape. On a 634-foot ship with four cargo decks and seven levels in the living quarters, there are an infinite number of spots to hide.

The most fun? Maneuvering the ship, bringing her into a harbor or pilot station. Going into Port Suez to await convoy for canal transit, for instance, I maneuvered up to the head of the line, through numerous anchored ships and around the pilot cutter, and dropped the hook. Their reaction of, "That's far enough, *Lyra.* That's very nice," makes you feel good. It's fun to run the North African coast, from the Straits of Gibraltar to the Suez Canal, taking the shortcuts and saving twenty minutes with favorable currents, two to five miles off the coast.

Most captains go the easy routes. But in striving to help the company, Jack and I went out of our way to get the ship from A to B as quickly as possible by taking the tougher route. We never put our ships in any danger by doing so, but it does require more diligence and the captain's presence on the bridge. It's definitely appreciated by the Mediterranean offices, and they looked forward to seeing ships we commanded. We went the extra mile to save a mile. It's passing through the Khios Straits en route to Izmir, Turkey, rather than passing west of the island of Khios, to save thirty-three miles. It's passing through the Piombino Straits between the island of Elba and Italy en route to Livorno from Naples, which saves fifteen miles. It's cutting across the shoals heading into Norfolk to save Lykes paying the longshoremen for twenty minutes of stand-by time. It's taking the ship into the port of Livorno without tug assistance during a four-day tug strike—when normally it requires three or four tugs.

The route from Livorno to Alexandria passes between Sicily and the boot of Italy, where, due to vessel size, we must embark and disembark the Straits of Messina pilot. Jack and I both picked up the pilot at our sea speed of sixteen knots rather than on a slow bell as conservative captains do. We did compete, though. A copy of the bell-book entry from his transit on the *Mason Lykes,* which he stuck in my forty-fourth birthday card, said, "Beat this, Wonder Woman." I had picked up the card in Livorno two days before—he had left it two months before, when he went through. But I had waited to open it on my birthday, and coincidentally, I had just transited the straits. I was proud I'd just done my best time: twenty-three minutes.

His entry showed, "Pilot aboard: 1522. Pilot away: 1540." Only eighteen minutes!

Still, the most enjoyable work—more even than being captain—was working chief mate for Jack. I didn't have to worry about anything because I knew he'd always come up with an answer.

If I have a fault, it's that I try to be too much of a perfectionist. If I cost the company twenty minutes, I worried about it. Even when we were under military charter, and there was no pressure for a schedule, I didn't slack off. I enjoy it when I'm pushing it.

The biggest downfall for any captain is becoming too complacent. That's probably when the most accidents happen. Just before my second trip as captain on the *Lyra,* I commented to Captain Manchester that I was feeling more relaxed. He advised me not to become *too* relaxed. The captain's most important asset is good judgment—never putting the ship in harm's way unless you *know* you can pull it off.

• • •

The most anxious I've ever been during an approach was going into Ad Dammam, double-checking the chart to make sure of the ship's position due to the mine threat, and the most nervewracking sail I've ever had was out of there on 17 May 1991. Both were at night.

We left there with a northerly wind; the visibility was less than a half mile because of the oil fires. We had had a wind of more than Beaufort force five, averaging nineteen knots, and the pilots would not sail us until the wind slackened. The sailing board had been posted for 2200, and by 2300, when the wind dropped to force four—a mean of thirteen knots—I wanted to go. First we had trouble finding a tugboat to take us out, then we went slower than normal because of the visibility. It's one of those situations where you do it if you feel you can, and we had good radar to help guide us. The second mate stayed on the bow for the full six miles of the buoyed channel, watching carefully. The next morning he said, "Captain, why'd you go? Why couldn't we all have gotten a good night's sleep?"

The "why" was that we may have saved a day in Port Suez eight days hence. You have to drop the hook by 0300 on the Port Suez side to transit the canal that day with the northbound convoy. One trip I missed it by twenty minutes and I felt bad. It may have cost the company. Under government charter, money is no concern and nobody—including the company—really gives a damn whether you save or lose a day. My professional pride makes me care.

I have had an accident. One. We were going into Bremerhaven in August 1989, my second trip as master on the *Lyra*. We were coming up the Weser River in a force seven wind, more than thirty knots. We would have been okay except a force eight gust came up unexpectedly, just as we were maneuvering to enter the lock, stern first. Even though our engines were operating and we had two tugs helping, one each on the bow and stern, we couldn't hold the ship. We were helpless to do anything but drift. On hindsight, we probably should have waited for a second tug on our stern. Luckily we missed a smaller RO/RO ship that was already docked, but we hit the seawall. And because our ship has so much flair on the quarter, we also hit a fixed vertical green navigation light along the channel, placed right at the elbow of the dock where we were maneuvering into the lock. It has not the first time a ship hit that light, which ended up horizontal. It has since been reinforced. The *Lyra* ended up with a five-foot crease eighteen inches wide on the port side of the hull. I had to go to my quarters and change my pants.

It took three hours to fill out all of the paperwork. Our agent in Bremerhaven, Rolff Zeichner, a tall young man and former German merchant captain, called a surveyor. Fortunately, there was no structural damage, just a big indentation about eight feet above the water line. The water police informed me that the Japanese car carrier that had wiped out the light just over a month before had had to pay about $5,000 to replace it. When I called Captain Manchester to tell him what happened, he just said, "That's what insurance is for."

Landlubber's Log
24–26 February 1994

Thursday, 24 February

Early sun turns into clouds, but the slightly bigger seas remain. The second mate, coming off watch at 0800, says at breakfast it's a little cooler—fifty-eight degrees. We're doing well with our speed, and the captain has sent a message saying we expect to arrive in Naples at 0430 tomorrow, depending on how the weather holds. If we get wind from the northwest after we transit the Straits of Messina, we'll be okay, but we're competing for a berth with a containership coming from Livorno whose ETA is thirty minutes before ours.

At 1030 it's boat and fire drill (the order reversed this time to catch the complacent) on the bridge. Fire drill, signaled by one long blast on the general alarm and ship's whistle, usually comes first. This time, the abandon-ship signal—five or more short blasts followed by one long—was sounded first. Back to work before the straits, expected at dinner time. The good news is that the mid-afternoon sun is burning off the haze and it may be possible to see Mt. Etna. The bad news is that we'll probably have to anchor when we reach Naples, not able to dock until 2100, then work all night, and sail. The good news is that puts us in Livorno on Sunday, and longshoremen do not work cargo Sunday afternoon and evening, so we'll get an extra day there and may be able to go to Florence.

At 1500 a U.S. Navy warship on our starboard calls to say she's practicing maneuvers and would we alter course to give them three miles. The captain of the *Charlotte* replies: "We'll obey the rules of the road." Back at us comes a curt "Have a nice day," as we hold our course.

About 1700 the captain says it's time for the passenger to have cocktails on the bridge, with a view of Mt. Etna off our port side. It's there, in cloud cover, but the clouds lift momentarily to permit a picture with a clear outline.

As we're running four miles off the coast of southern Italy—sufficiently refreshed, feet up—we see some of the trip's most beautiful green high country, a rocky layer below it. Many spots to come back to with our as-yet-unsecured yacht. Just before we make the turn north to the call of "322," we spot a huge chimney marked on the chart. Unforgettable—a full moon is just rising behind us, the bright sun is beginning to set over Mt. Etna in front of us. Two boats under sail, one heading south along Sicily, one heading north along the mainland, complete the picture-postcard setting.

At 1800 the captain calls the boatswain to rig the pilot ladder starboard side, three feet from the water. Without our slowing down, Captain Scotugno (his brother took us through the straits southbound) is aboard at 1830. He whistles and sings "Greensleeves" and "Over the Rainbow." The sky is clouding over one minute, then suddenly it's clear and the full moon shines on the ferries crossing everywhere. Twenty-minute passage—not a record. The engineers have had a cookout on the second afterdeck of the house, to which we are invited, but Messina keeps us from it. So first assistant engineer John Catanzaro brings it to us—burgers with avocado and onion and even potato chips, our first since leaving home.

"Would the passenger like cocktail hour like this every night?"

"You bet!"

The swells have come up; the ship shakes and shimmies. After an unproductive look at Stromboli (too cloudy to see sparks fly from the volcano) and a productive cribbage game (for the record, the passenger skunks the captain again), to sleep, early.

Friday, 25 February

Once again, the scenery won't wait. At 0345, Debbie says, "We're almost to Capri." We watch from the bridge as three small rocky shapes appear off the port side, then a tall irregular island with a light at the northeast corner. It's the Isle of Capri. In fact, it's possible to count only seven lights on this grotto side of Capri—on the mainland to starboard are many lights.

"001."

As we sail farther north, the island becomes wide east to west, and we see all the lights of a city in the center on the north side. On the mainland are the widely spaced lights of Sorrento, farther ahead is Mt. Vesuvius in the clouds, southeast of Naples.

At 0400 we change course—350—and we're past Capri. Two objects appear under spotlights along Sorrento, but it's impossible to make them out. At 0424 we take arrival at Naples. A long string of lights is dead ahead across the bow; we head for the break in it. Pedro hand-steers. There's no traffic other than a tiny boat to starboard, and we have deep water all the way.

"Slow ahead." We have less than three miles now. "355 . . . stop her . . . dead slow ahead . . . 357 . . . slow ahead . . . okay, mate, walk out your starboard anchor to one in the water . . . 359."

"Do you need lights up there on the bow?" the captain asks the chief mate.

"No, we've got enough from the moon." Then, after a silence, "We've got one in the water and it's back on the brake."

"Hard left," then "dead slow ahead." There's a full moon over Naples as we turn to anchor. "Slow ahead."

Then "We're smack in the middle now," the second mate says, navigating.

"Midships . . . stop engine."

The break in the lights turns out to be a huge castle. A sign that's flashed at us from way out, then turned blue and red, now reads Cariplo. Too bad we don't understand Italian.

"142 . . . dead slow astern . . . let your anchor go, mate." Silence again, then, "We want seven on deck." The chief mate replies: "Three in the hawse right now." When Bob reports four ninety-foot lengths in the water, the captain calls slow astern, then tells him to hold it for a second until it takes a lead. Lights are lit on the beam, then the stack. "Five in the water now, broad on starboard . . . she's holding good now . . . seven on deck, putting the brake on."

Twice the captain calls, "Naples Port Control, *Charlotte Lykes*." No reply.

"Naples pilots, the *Charlotte Lykes*—we're at anchor now." This time the captain is told nobody knows when we'll berth. For two months now, with only one gantry working, and no idea when the others will be back in working order, every ship has been delayed. And the Mediterranean line gets preference for the berth over Lykes. Stand by on channel eleven or sixteen, she is instructed.

"Okay, mate, if you're satisfied, come on back and we'll put up the anchor notices," the captain calls on the radio.

The sun is up now. In the harbor, coming from a yacht club

marked by many tall masts, are racing sailboats; orange buoys dot the water between the ship and the land.

Talking with the local agent, Francesco Boccanera, leads to a plan. Anchored one-half mile from the castle, we have to wait for a couple of containerships to off-load and load (one arrived only ten minutes before we did), and at 0730 we will know more. The captain wins three games of cribbage, we eat Jaffa oranges and biscotti for breakfast, then we wait. Lunchtime, and we wait. Finally, when we find we cannot berth until midday Saturday, the captain arranges launch service at $70 a trip (it's $250 in Livorno), and at 1630 six of us—Debbie, Amy, Steve Ballor, third assistant engineer Stu Negoescu, John Catanzaro, and I—await the first launch.

Getting onto the launch makes riding a camel look easy. Those swells that look tiny from five decks up look mighty big at water level. The driver is very good, never touching the gangway that is being lowered even as we make our way down the thirty-seven grubby, slick, thin, grooved metal rungs to the platform. The launch bobs up and down, making the gap between launch and platform grow and close, grow and close, two feet sometimes, sometimes more, sometimes less. When it closes, it's time to jump, and land, hard. "Now!"

And we're aboard. With an up- and down-floating ride, in ten minutes we've covered the mile and a half from the *Charlotte* to the breakwater, and we're off at the dock. The driver takes us through crowded streets and past many Italian marble statues surrounding a waterfront park, up winding narrow roads to a lovely spot halfway up the hill facing Naples harbor—to the apartment of Francesco and his wife, Valaria. The apartment, a large one-bedroom, has been divided into two, redecorated magnificently by Vale's brother; her parents live in the other half. Son Pierpaulo, at ten months, shares their one bedroom. With a population of 2.5 million, Naples has too many people and too many problems, Vale says. Maybe Genoa, a possibility, would be better? No, although she has friends there. Paris, where she lived eight years? Yes. We see pictures of a condo that they shared before the baby came. It's in Sorrento, where they fell in love. The view? Capri.

After a visit, we're driven back down to the shopping district. A few beggars approach us, but mostly we wander and gape. Ferragamo, Armani, Perugina, every Italian name you've ever heard of, with beautiful stores and beautiful wares, many antique shops, many others. Finally, we stop in the square for cappuccino, and watch what could only be happening in Italy. Four gentlemen are sipping something clear in tall glasses, then begin to sing. Into the picture comes a typically well-dressed lady, walking her dog. She visits with the oldest of the men.

We start to walk again, a horn honks, and it's Francesco and Vale. To dinner, up winding roads again with old walls, to a wide spot and a pizzeria—Al Poeta. Terrific homey place. First, thin crispy bread sticks and, of course, dry white wine and bottled effervescent water. We have appetizers—cold shrimp, tiny deep-fried fish, smoked salmon, cold shrimp in a Thousand Island sauce inside pastry. Then soft, white mozzarella with cherry tomatoes and thin green leaves. Next, seafood pizza—red sauce and octopus, squid, shrimp, mussels in their shells, but no cheese. It is customary, Vale says, to offer to share, and if you don't offer, others are expected to ask to try yours. Dessert is followed by espresso. We stop for one second at an overlook, where lovers park now, but Vale walks with the baby during the day, to see the view of the harbor. It is a funny feeling to see the *Charlotte* there, Debbie says—she's never left the ship at anchor before. Then it's a mad race to the dock and we have only a minute or two to wait for the last launch back to the ship, at 2300. The driver had asked that the pilot ladders be rigged for the return trips, but the swell has dropped some and we're able to climb the gangway after all. Not quite as scary embarking as it was disembarking.

After one game of cribbage, which I win—again—it's off to sleep. This grueling pace is really catching up with me.

Saturday, 26 February

Another magnificent day, too warm for more than a shirt. How lucky can you get? We watch the sailboats racing back and forth in the harbor, a pretty spinnaker here, a rowing shell there, tiny power boats at anchor, rocking. Write a little and do laundry; at 1115 the captain gets word we can shift the ship to the container berth. Very little distance to go, but it's interminably slow. First, a pilot asks to come aboard more than a mile outside the breakwater, and when four shots of anchor are still in the water. Previously, Francesco has told Debbie not to let him board outside a mile or before the anchor is picked up.

"I won't sign for him," the captain says, so he leaves (if she does-n't sign, he doesn't get paid). And he doesn't return. Slowly the ship maneuvers into position a mile from the breakwater, stops and waits. In the meantime, glitches develop. The light for the bow thruster, which the captain counts on to dock in tight quarters, indi-cates it's not working. "Reset it, second," the captain says urgently, repeatedly, until finally it seems to be okay. Then there's a call on the two-way radio from the stern: two of the winches needed to pay out docking lines don't work, and the electrician can't fix them. "Call the chief and ask for help," the captain responds.

Finally a pilot, Captain Gorregon, is on the bridge, and the tugs *Mastino* and *Sant' Elmo* make up. With a right at the breakwater and a hard right to put the ship at the best angle, the pilot backs her to the dock, but it's nearly 1330 before the shift is completed. Ask-ing for four and two at each end, the captain settles for two spring lines fore and aft, but only three bow and three stern lines on the bollards.

The polizia come to the captain's office again; they cleared the ship at anchor yesterday, but come back for more crew lists, more passenger lists, more cigarettes. The line handlers come up for cig-arettes. More paperwork. More cigarettes. The second assistant comes to bring the captain the two-way radio—"our lifeline to civi-lization," he says—and to ask Francesco where to buy cameos. The watchman is due at 1430. Pastries, $60 worth the captain has ordered for the engineers and herself, are delivered. She sees the manifest for Naples, and needs to call the office in Genoa to speak to Franco Cozzolino about the problems with the stability printout. It is not possible to deballast in port, so it is essential to achieve the ballast condition needed for sailing from Livorno prior to arrival there. The captain promises him a tank report tomorrow, and, in return, he will let her know about the required ballast. The harbor-master asks for his cigarettes. A very agitated chief mate bursts in to say the four elephant feet—devices needed to lift the hatch covers—were left in Izmir. He's responsible for seeing that they're on board after the gangs are finished working cargo.

"He screwed up big time," the captain says, setting about to fig-ure out a way around this. Attaching wires is the preferable solution. She'll have to send a report to the office and order new ones, with-out making the crew on the ship look like a bunch of idiots. Another annoyance—but New Orleans isn't keeping score, she says.

26 February 1994   **189**

She turns her attention to deciding when to post the sailing board. Because 197 containers are to be moved at some 20 an hour, it's agreed to post 0100, meaning the crew will be on board an hour earlier; if we're finished earlier, we'll go earlier, she says. Not all captains would do that. Why not? is her attitude. The alternative is to post an earlier sailing board, only to have to change it. On weekends, according to the union contract, she gets one free change; after that it costs the company more money for each member of the crew if she has to change it.

Business settled, it's time to play. We ride with Francesco to the ferry terminal and, with only minutes to spare, we buy tickets and board a hydrofoil for the smooth forty-minute ride (the ferry doubles the time, and we're always short) to Capri.

Reaching the tiny picturesque harbor on the north side, we climb, and climb, and climb. A flat walk, then stairs; at each landing is an entry to a yard, always with an Italian tile number, maybe a name. Inside sometimes is a shrine, then a turn so you can't see further. Gardens cover every inch houses don't, with many orange and lemon trees, palms, fuchsia-colored bougainvillea. Finally, we turn onto a street, head across and back down another walkway, past a beautiful yellow hotel. It's hard to tell if the stucco houses are a year old or a hundred years old. No one smiles when we pass them. No other Americans.

Coming full circle, we discover the funicular isn't running, but buses substitute and we climb aboard for the ride back up to where we were, higher, to a promenade. We find the Venetian beads we'd planned to buy in Florence, just in case we don't get there. The most intriguing parts of the architecture are the portals, which reveal whole other worlds. At the square we enter one, and find a school, bookstore, jewelry stores with beautiful things, restaurants, a tiny grocery, and more stairways and little alleyways leading to houses and who knows what. We stop for gelato—green pistachio is divine. That's lunch. Back down the hill, we buy lemon liqueur—a specialty of Capri—and make our way to the dock, passing weekenders arriving with suitcases and others who clearly are commuting from Naples. The 1720 hydrofoil is run by another company and is even fancier than the one that brought us, with sexy Italian television playing; on both it's possible to buy espresso and pastries.

We check the situation at the ship before Francesco drops us at the Ristoranto Europeo, near his office in what he says is a very dangerous area. We want to go early, but he warns that the pizza oven will not be hot enough yet. Few diners are inside when we arrive at 1930—it's Saturday, so fashionable dinner hour is even later than usual. Two young Japanese women whose language is even more of a barrier than ours mimic what we order. All of the appetizers are displayed, as are desserts, aiding choices. We have mozzarella again— jelly roll fashion with basil between the layers—with cherry tomatoes halved and doused with olive oil and big capers. Then linguine marinara with mussels, and great bread, then we share broiled white fish and grilled squid with salad, sweet chocolate cake and, of course, effervescent bottled water and dry, white house wine from a squat Italian pottery pitcher.

At 2100 Francesco returns, so we forgo espresso for the drive to the *Charlotte*. While we've played, the ship's been loaded. Again in the dark of night, thirty minutes after midnight, the tug *Vesuvio* pulls us forward. Out of the breakwater, we head for Livorno. It's very foggy, and except for the string of lights along the waterfront boulevard, the city has faded up the hills.

The scenery for tonight's viewing pleasure is Ischia, larger than Capri and closer to Naples. Next trip.

9. If the Pilot Refuses, Dock the Ship Yourself

9/17/90

Dear Mom and Dad and all,

Greetings from a place I never thought I'd be—"Arabian Gulf" as Saudis call it!

We are due into our port of discharge, Ad Dammam, Saudi Arabia, @1200 LT today—that's 0500 your time! It is very hot and humid—sea temp is at least 95°—engineers have a tough time lasting in the engine room for any length of time. Even the pool is too warm! As long as we're not rolling, we've had the pool full most of the time—nice especially @0630 every morning when things are still quiet.

*T*he view of Ad Dammam from the bridge, seventy-six feet above the water, was like that of any other harbor—full of fishing boats, gantry cranes, several ships, decent tugs—as we headed toward land. Slowly we maneuvered our way through the Persian Gulf—west past Shutaya Light and buoy two, then south to buoy five, then west again between buoys seven and eight, running between the reefs to the six-mile buoyed approach channel to the pilot boarding area. The *Lyra* picked up the harbor pilot about a half mile off the breakwater, passed the anchored *Green Island,* a Central Gulf Lines lash vessel, as she lowered her loaded barges to the sea, and glided up to the dock that hot, still September afternoon.

I had been feeling anxious about the unknown since we passed through the Strait of Hormuz into the Persian Gulf. My heart always beat a little faster when making my initial approach to a new port. Arrivals and departures are times when the master has the conn in directing the maneuvering to the pilot boarding area—giving the rudder and engine orders. As captain, it's your time to shine. This trip it also was time for additional concern because I was unsure of the reception I'd receive as a female master in a Muslim nation.

A new man-made commercial port, Ad Dammam was one of the funnels (the other was Al Jabayl) through which the U.S. military brought vast amounts of war machinery in anticipation of its face-off with Iraq's Saddam Hussein, and through which it all had to be hauled back stateside. It also has the most beautiful docks I've ever seen, with lots of fenders and bollards, and plenty of room for turning around.

The harbor was decidedly empty. One area had been segregated for commercial carriers, but the U.S. military had taken over two docks with room for about ten ships. We finished turning around and tying up starboard side to the dock about 1530. We were behind the *Cape Douglas,* like us a RO/RO ship, but owned by the military and operated by the Military Sealift Command (MSC). We lowered the gangway, an aluminum ladder—no one walks the plank any more—about twenty feet to the dock, and lowered the stern ramp in preparation for off-loading our cargo.

The Saudi agent, dressed in his caftan, had come and gone with the papers to clear the ship, and I was hanging around my office waiting for the MSC representative for a briefing on our expected port stay. Finally I went below, only to discover that we were being inundated by GIs. I tried to keep them on the cargo deck, but they all wanted hot coffee and I let them go. Suppertime is always at 1700 and, when I arrived at the officers' mess, I discovered that the MSC rep was already eating at my table, where the naval liaison had seated him. He, like the other military, was so hungry for a hot meal—logistics had prevented the field kitchen from arriving with the first units—that he had headed for the food before coming to see me.

And for 250 soldiers from the 101st Airborne Division, the *Lyra*'s visit meant much more than just receiving equipment. It meant their first real meal in a month. They were surviving on MREs—meals ready to eat. I saw those rations, featuring things like cold corned beef hash under the khaki-colored cover, and they looked terrible. They reminded me of our lifeboat rations.

Where there usually was everything from railroad cars to mahogany planking for bowling alleys, we were carrying Chinook, Cobra, and

Blackhawk helicopters for the 101st Airborne. Perfect cargo for a RO/RO ship, with its road-size ramp at the stern for loading and unloading. At that time, the *Lyra* was one of twenty-eight in the Lykes Lines fleet, and the first commercial vessel involved with Operation Desert Shield.

While under military charter, we're carrying billy clubs, Mace, leg irons, and six pairs of handcuffs for shipboard security purposes. We never used any of them. As on commercial runs, the unused .38 Smith & Wesson with a hundred rounds of ammunition was in my safe.

It wasn't the *Lyra*'s first time under military charter. She'd spent five years, 1981 to 1986, stationed in Diego Garcia. Mine either. As chief mate on the *Louise Lykes* in 1986, I'd been involved with a military charter to Midway Island, Guam, Korea, and Japan. For the chief mate, whose main responsibility is the cargo, sailing commercial or under military charter is virtually the same. But for the master, the communications under military charter are ungodly.

Although I'd made four or five voyages a year since sailing on my master's license in 1989, this was my first time into the Persian Gulf. I knew there was a potential problem with a Saudi harbor pilot refusing to work with a woman. In fact, when my boss, Capt. Rick Manchester, had indicated a concern before we left the States, I had offered to get off then and there. Captain Manchester declined, but he was curious about what would happen. He also said that if the Saudi pilot refused to handle the ship because the master was a woman, I was to turn over command to my chief mate. I told him I was not so sure I could do that, but I assured him that I would handle the situation as it presented itself—without international incident.

My husband, Jack, kidded me: "If the pilot refuses, dock the ship yourself."

As it turned out, a British pilot docked us and a Pakistani pilot sailed us the next day. The only local Saudi I saw was the Lykes Lines agent from the Gulf Agency Company (GAC). He was surprised to see a woman (I was dressed in my usual khaki shirt and pants), but he was most cordial. On a commercial run, a crew list precedes you to your destination, but on the Saudi run they had no way of knowing who we were in advance. But he and I did all of the paperwork together with no problem.

From the twenty-two-member crew's standpoint, we weren't doing anything different from a regular commercial run—just delivering cargo. But things going on around us certainly were different.

• • •

We had been in a war risk area for a day and a half since crossing twenty-four degrees north latitude in the Gulf of Oman—191 miles south of the Strait of Hormuz, the entrance to the Persian Gulf and the "point of no return." There was very little traffic. Because insurance rates were so high, commercial companies were staying out of the Persian Gulf. Uncle Sam could afford it! Each voyage when we crossed into the war risk area we had to send Lykes a message with the date and time we crossed twenty-four degrees north, because at that point the government took over the ship's insurance.

We'd been running past a bunch of small outboard boats. The naval liaison officer we had picked up the previous night off Muscat, Oman, explained that they were smugglers. From Oman to Iran they carry rugs, sheep, alcohol, cigarettes, anything. They run near to the ship to lose themselves in our larger return at the radar surveillance station. Then they figure they're safe.

We were carrying eleven supercargoes—military personnel who were responsible for maintaining the helicopters and support vehicles during the crossing, keeping the batteries charged, fuel leaks cleaned up, lashings checked and tightened. Two looked like they were about twelve years old and not very happy. But they all ate well, used the salt-water swimming pool every day, and watched all the video movies aboard. Because Sunday and Thursday are steak nights on Lykes's weekly menu, twice a week the officers have a barbecue, grilling steaks on deck. The final Thursday the passengers were invited to join us. The chief mate, Eric Wilcox, and I supplied the Budweiser, their last for a long time; alcohol is not allowed in a Muslim country.

The remaining beer and the girlie magazines, which Muslim countries—and some non-Muslim countries, like the United Kingdom—consider pornographic, had been locked up in the bonded stores locker in preparation for landing in the Saudi Arabian port.

While preparing the *Lyra* for military charter, we spent a week in Galveston, Texas, undergoing repairs to the stern ramp, overhauling several engine pistons—routinely done every ten thousand hours of operation—and the communications system.

The housing and a bearing for the Marisat (satellite communications system) antenna had to be renovated, because with the large quantity of messages the military sends, satellite communications are a must. It's a three-day job at least, and one we had been putting off for two years while we were on commercial run. First a mast and boom had to be welded in place to the port side of the wheelhouse and high enough above the satellite antenna to lift the dome clear of the antenna assembly. The antenna and dome are mounted on a separate ten-foot mast on the flying bridge, a deck above the wheelhouse level. The dome, which covers the satellite dish antenna, is four feet high and about four feet in diameter.

The vibration on the *Lyra* (which is common to most diesel ships, especially those with the house on the stern, over the engines) had so damaged one of the antenna's bearings and the housing that the antenna could no longer lock onto a satellite properly. The damage had required my climbing into the dome and tying off the antenna in the proper position for maximum signal strength so that the radio operator could send the telexes.

International Telephone and Telegraph (ITT) Mackay out of the Houston office was hired to do the repairs, and I asked their technician to show me what he had done before he left the vessel. Well, three days later the technician had the radio operator sign his completed work order—without looking at the actual repairs—as I was tied up elsewhere. The system, of course, was "completely operational" and checked out alongside the dock. The radio operator quit five days later in Jacksonville. Only later did we find out why the ITT technician had been so reluctant to have me check out his work.

We had no problem with the antenna until we were east of the Azores, when the ship did a bit of rolling. Again, the antenna would not lock onto the satellite and the signal strength was too weak to transmit. I climbed into the dome to investigate and I couldn't believe what I saw: Instead of hooking up the pitch and roll synchro motors that compensate for the vessel's motion at sea, the tech had blocked the housing with two pieces of Styrofoam. Again, tying off the antenna and frequent adjustments by our chief engineer, Brian Norton, were required to keep the Marisat in operation.

I believe that bill was $22,000. I can see why the company, despite the 50 percent duty, prefers repairs done overseas—especially in Germany, where the ship was built. The work is dependable.

The officers named the dome "Dempsey Dome" and threatened to paint it pink.

The U.S. Army had contracted with the Jacksonville Port Authority to use its deep-water docks on Blount Island to load. The week before we sailed, our cargo had arrived at the Florida port from the 101st Airborne's home base in Kentucky: Artillery. Fuel trucks. Forklifts. After we sailed, I sent MSC a list of military equipment we had loaded aboard ship, including five Chinooks MSC may not have known were aboard, because they weren't on the load list and they were the last we loaded. Apparently MSC took no notice, because we received no return message.

Actually, the last thing the army wanted to load before closing the stern door were fuel pods for the helicopters. Without them, the helicopters are basically worthless. Of course, the U.S. Coast Guard was opposed to having loaded fuel pods carried under deck, because it's a violation of federal regulations. The chief mate, Eric Wilcox, called me on the handheld UHF walkie-talkie about the problem. MSC told the Coast Guard that if they were unable to load the fuel pods, they would off-load all the helicopters they had just loaded!

I told the mate that MSC must have a waiver somewhere.

"Oh, yes, we do."

"Well, let's have a copy."

In about thirty minutes a reservist showed up with one.

"That's great," I said. "The only problem is this one expired in 1987."

Back to the dock office and, in good time, a current waiver was produced and we carried the loaded fuel pods under deck.

In times of national emergency, many regulations are waived.

Military regulations are confounding anyway, and infuriating at times.

When we finally got our orders to head east for the Suez Canal, for instance, we didn't know our destination port. The sergeant who headed the eleven men on board apparently knew, but he wasn't at liberty to tell me.

We were given orders to send messages while crossing the Atlantic to the MSC communications center in Washington, D.C., four times daily. They consisted of position, course, and speed at 0600 and 2000 LT (Local Time) and 2400 Z (Zulu or Greenwich Mean Time), adding weather to the fourth at 0800 LT. From Gibraltar to Port Said, messages increased to seven times a day. Unbelievable, and unnecessary at 16.3 knots!

Before leaving Jacksonville, I quizzed them about sending messages at 0600 and again at 0800. Because the charter speed was 16.3 knots or 32.6 nautical miles in two hours, it seemed superfluous. And, because I was new at this, I wanted to be sure I understood, so I contacted the MSC representative in Jacksonville. He called MSC headquarters in Washington, D.C., and the captain in charge there finally tired of my questions.

His solution: "Tell her to follow the orders verbatim. No other master has had problems with them."

Actually, the message requirements changed each trip, adding to the confusion. By my last trip under military charter, we were down to one advisory a day. I couldn't believe or understand the inconsistency and what seemed to me unnecessary expense—satellite communication is the most expensive form of sending messages.

Before we left Jacksonville, we received a two-page inventory that accompanied the chemical/biological warfare suits we carried for each crew member. But all we received from the inventory were three trash cans, brown kraft paper, and forty-two bath towels. Oh, and videos and thirty-year-old manuals on how to use the suits!

Two navy reservists who came aboard said we might get the rest of the inventory in the Straits of Gibraltar or the Suez Canal. Gibraltar seemed unlikely to me, as it would have to be brought out by launch, but we would be at a mooring buoy in Suez, so that seemed like a logical place. Nothing materialized prior to arrival in Ad Dammam, however.

En route to the Persian Gulf, we ran across the *Cape Inscription,* a government-owned vessel Lykes had owned previously and then was managing and crewing, on its way home from there. By this time we knew where we were headed, although the MSC had only told us the coordinates, not named the port—we had to figure that out for ourselves. I quizzed the captain, Jim Cullen, about the routine there and, in turn, he asked if we'd gotten our gas masks. A negative reply prompted a story. Captain Cullen said after seeing every GI on the dock in Ad Dammam with a gas mask on his hip, he had messaged MSC that his men were using "plastic bags and duct tape."

MSC's reply: "Don't worry about it."

Just before we sailed *from* Ad Dammam, we did get gas masks and other bits and pieces, but we never did get everything from the inventory that trip.

Every message we received from MSC reached us three days after being promulgated. We never got an answer to any query we sent them, particularly where it pertained to weather, which proved to be a real problem. Their weather reports would reach us three days after we left the covered area.

Because we were under military charter, we had access to the Norfolk-based Optimum Track Sailing Route (OTSR) that the navy uses for its vessels. We were told to use it for weather routing rather than Weatherways out of New York, Lykes's usual source as a commercial carrier.

As soon as we got sailing orders, I requested sailing recommendations from OTSR. No reply. Finally, two days out I subscribed to Weatherways for the Atlantic crossing. I think OTSR just couldn't handle it. They suggested I go to Washington, D.C., and see their nineteenth-century communications. In truth, so many ships were coming under charter that their system was overloaded with messages. Each message we sent or received through their system went to three feet of addressees, whether they needed it or not, and the list was repeated with each message. The resulting backlog of messages virtually shut down the system's usefulness.

Returning home from our first trip, we had the same problem. I needed routing once we cleared the Straits of Gibraltar headed, we were told, for Norfolk. The day after we transited the Suez Canal, 28 September, I sent a message to OTSR requesting routing. They had plenty of time to get it back to us, as we were facing a five-day trip in the Mediterranean to Gibraltar. Nothing. But on 1 October our orders were changed to Jacksonville, and I immediately sent our revised destination to OTSR, again requesting routing. Nothing. We cleared Gibraltar 3 October. Nothing. So I made our own route—a rhumb line from Gibraltar to Santa Maria, the southernmost island of the Azores, then a great circle to Jacksonville.

Then a day west of Gibraltar we began hearing weather reports that hurricane Josephine was approaching the Azores. Right then I contacted Weatherways. Within forty-five minutes they gave me Josephine's track, with a recommended route to Jacksonville. The problem was that Josephine forced a cut-off low pressure system to go south, which in turn became tropical storm Lillie and then hurricane Lillie.

Initially we did fine, sailing around Santa Maria Island and southwest of Josephine. That night at 0200 I got a telephone call from OTSR in Norfolk. "What are you doing about Josephine?"

I told them what I'd done, and that we had it in hand. In return, I asked if he had gotten our messages through the District of Columbia. He hadn't. I asked if we could communicate directly instead of through Washington. We couldn't. He asked if we'd been getting their hurricane reports every six hours. We hadn't. He said he'd put us on the list for them immediately. We never did get them!

Moving north of Lillie—our only choice, because trying to go south would have taken us too far out of our way—gave us terrible weather going into Jacksonville. The only advice Weatherways could give us was "best speed" to outrun it, and on a diesel ship that's impossible because you're already doing "best speed." We were doing thirty-five-degree rolls as we passed north of its center the day after it became tropical storm Lillie.

With a "tender" ship, you experience five-degree rolls in flat calm; ten- or fifteen-degree rolls aren't much bother. We had taken on so much fuel—I hadn't wanted to, but the military insisted—before heading toward Jacksonville that the ship was "stiff." As a result, those thirty-five-degree rolls were snap or quick rolls. They took their toll.

My chief engineer, Brian, is a Coca-Cola freak. He was down to twenty-five cases of Coke, stacked in a corner of his quarters. A metal wastepaper basket took off and repeatedly hit the Coke, which exploded all over his overhead. And because the microwave oven had hit the deck several times, the damaged door later fell off in his hand while he was nuking popcorn.

The steward lost a bunch of plates in the galley.

The door to my office jammed closed, and I couldn't get out for a while.

After that we took evasive action, sailing northwest until after supper before rejoining our great circle to Jacksonville.

The only other time I've been in weather like that on the Persian Gulf run was during the June–July 1991 crossing from Houston to Dammam. I still have a queasy stomach, courtesy of the seasonal southwest monsoon we encountered that trip. It took thirty-two hours to change a piston, with winds buffeting the ship with 35-knot force while we were making bare steerageway, about 5 knots, well below our charter speed of 16.3 knots.

Brian had already run into problems with high crankcase pressure in the starboard engine in the Gulf of Suez. He shut it down and pulled the number six piston, thinking that would fix it. Nothing had been wrong with the piston, as it turned out, but he did find a burnt exhaust valve on it. That job took the engineering department thirty-two hours, too.

We'd already been having trouble with the port engine because the turbocharger wasn't working to capacity. That was bad enough. With the starboard engine shut down to change that number six piston, we were down to seven knots on the port engine. And when the starboard engine was restarted, the crankcase pressure was still high.

Then we cleared the Red Sea, and the monsoon confronted us. The seas are pretty rough with a thirty-five-knot wind. Going around the coast of Oman in the Arabian Sea they were on our starboard quarter, the worst possible condition for ship's motion, and there was no place to run from the monsoon. We were committed. Once again we were empty, with just a bottom full of fuel oil and ballast, so the ship's stiff condition was causing repeated thirty-five-degree snap rolls. That's when we had the number two piston seize in the starboard engine—it had been causing the high crankcase pressure all along.

If one of the nine pistons doesn't move, the only thing to do is shut down the engine. Then the piston, a couple of feet in diameter, has to be lifted out by a chain fall (a hook attached to a chain) and, in turn, the piston liner, a piece of steel weighing at least a couple of hundred pounds itself, has to be replaced. Next, a new piston has to be moved about forty feet and lowered by forklift from the number two deck through a hatch to the engine room, and the whole process reversed.

Despite the weather, the chief engineer decided to try to change the piston, a second thirty-two-hour job. I was quite concerned that someone would get hurt by the piston liner swinging off the chain fall. I advised him if his crew had anything swinging to allow me time to maneuver the ship so she had the least motion. He never alerted me. Afterward the crew told me the swinging liner did take out a steel catwalk guardrail in the engine room. Luckily no one was injured, but those weather conditions just wore everybody out.

None too soon we sailed from Dammam for Bremerhaven and a long-overdue dry dock where, among other things, both engines were overhauled and the bottom cleaned. Normally Coast Guard requires it every two years. This time it was thirty-five months.

That first trip we reached Ad Dammam after nearly a month at sea, spent nineteen hours unloading the cargo and another four picking up dunnage and lashing gear on the cargo decks, and turned around. And all we saw were the dock and the warehouse, which was both office and barracks. The rest was off limits. There was absolutely no shore leave. And it was like that each trip, although the stays in Dammam got longer and longer. You can imagine that by the time we were in dry dock for those eleven days in August 1991, after more than two months without substantial shore leave, the ship's crew was in high anticipation. While we were there, I gave out $17,000 in draws for "port entertainment." I was told girls there ran $100 for thirty minutes.

First trip we had left Jacksonville at 2400 on Friday, 24 August 1990, less than a month after Iraqi President Saddam Hussein invaded Kuwait. The two-week, 5,840-mile passage to Port Said, Egypt, was uneventful. Our route took us five miles north of the Azores, close enough to sightsee—Corvo, which is fertile, green and steep, and Flores. As we often do in that area, we spotted whales nearby. We passed through the Straits of Gibraltar on 3 September. It felt good to transit them again. The previous time was with Jack on the *Howell Lykes* in December 1987. From Gibraltar to Port Said we followed the "J. C. Dempsey coastal route"—five miles off the North African coast to Cape Bon, the northeast tip of Tunisia; then Cape Passero, the southeast point of Sicily, then Egypt. That way you get about one knot favorable current all the way. And we did. Orders were for a 16.3 knot passage. Ours was 16.96, and we had to slow down the last three days to do that!

We arrived in Port Said on the Mediterranean Sea side at 0742 on 8 September. We tried to stay out at anchor until our canal transit that night, but at 1100 gave in to authorities and came inside the breakwater and tied up to mooring buoys. Then it was nonstop Egyptians, begging and stealing, until SBE (Stand By Engines) at 2354. I put a sign on my door, "Gone to Cairo. See the Mate on Watch," trying to get an hour nap, but that didn't work either. I went through a case and a half (thirty-eight cartons) of Marlboros— that's pennies, really. If you give them Salems, they throw them back! Egyptians don't smoke the Marlboros, but sell them for $15 a carton. They smoke Egyptian cigarettes that cost $10 a carton.

Who gets the cigarettes? The harbor pilots. The pilot launch. The tugboats. The mooring boats. The electrician sent to man the canal search light. The boatmen ordered aboard in case we have to tie up along the canal. Beggars. Hawkers. The Egyptian agent. Even Ali Lami from China Mitchell's garbage scow, as that was one of three places on the voyage—the only others were Suez and Ad Dammam—where we could dispose of plastic.

The hassle was the reason I had resisted coming into the harbor. The port authorities began questioning me whether the cargo was dangerous, and at that point it seemed a better idea not to resist. Only afterward did I find out the local Lykes Lines agent had overheard the radio transmission and had known I wasn't required to come inside the breakwater, but didn't come to my rescue.

The sixteen-hour Suez Canal transit was no problem. We were number three ship in our convoy. Because the channel is too narrow for two-way traffic, we had to anchor in Bitter Lake in the canal from 0630 to 1130 on 9 September to allow northbound traffic to pass. Then, because of our military cargo, we became number one ship (instead of number nine behind the bigger, faster containerships and car carriers). They were all mad, too. We dropped our last pilot at 1540 that day. After Port Suez it's another ten hours of fairways down the Gulf of Suez. The faster ships all soon blew by us.

Because I was required to be on the bridge during both the Suez Canal transit and on down the fairways, the vessel's speed is a major consideration—that's a long twenty-six hours.

At the mouth of the Gulf of Suez and the Gulf of Aqaba were U.S., Spanish, and French navies. Every ship was challenged frequently, asked to give last port, next port, cargo, and call letters—in our case, WSDG. I heard the U.S. Navy tell one ship to slow down for boarding. As we continued south through the Red Sea, we were told to stay twelve miles off the coasts of both Yemen and Ethiopia because the United States wasn't sure where their sympathies lay. During a forty-minute period passing through the Bab al Mandab Straits at the southern end of the Red Sea, the channel forces you within nine miles of the coast. After that we stayed thirty miles off, not out of fear but for a practical reason. It's called trash.

Outside the twenty-five-mile limit, we could drop wet garbage and biodegradable trash, such as cotton and paper, at sea. If not, legally we had to hold it and, believe me, it's a problem. We're already stuck with plastic, which was not dumpable anywhere. Because we couldn't dispose of plastic at any U.S. port except Jacksonville, the only one with receptacles that meet U.S. Department of Agriculture regulations, we're forced to dump it on Third World countries as we traveled. And what do you think Egypt did with it when we dumped it there? Bury it in the desert? The last trip, I brought the ship back into Newport News with sixteen fifty-five-gallon bags of plastic piled up on the stern, and my relief had to take those bags back out, plus whatever had already accumulated on his crossing, and dump them at Port Said with our contractor, Mitchell Brother Co. And that cost the company $185 per ship per trip.

After departing the Suez Canal we learned that we'd be picking up a naval liaison officer. He started communicating with us directly from Bahrain, and vice versa. Three days before our rendezvous he called us on the Marisat phone.

I heard, "Hello, Captain, this is Doug Lloyd."

"Is this the Cdr. Doug Lloyd I know?"

"Yes, it is."

What a relief—a familiar voice in an unfamiliar place.

Doug Lloyd was a 1975 graduate of Kings Point and worked ashore for Lykes Lines in New Orleans as a port captain. When the company cut back on the shoreside staff in 1982, Doug lost his job. From there he worked for the port of Milwaukee, Wisconsin, and I had seen him there when I ran into the Great Lakes. Then he was with MARAD, and was in the Persian Gulf as a navy reservist.

At 2249 on 15 September we slowed down at a predesignated rendezvous point off Muscat, Oman, to pick him up. His job was ensuring that we stayed clear of the minefield and at least twelve miles off Iranian-owned islands, among other things. But he also boarded with all of the answers to our questions—check-in points, recommended route, port routine. It was really nice to see him again.

Doug rode into Ad Dammam with us but not back out. On later trips the naval liaison officer just met with us for about an hour off Muscat to brief us.

Our Persian Gulf transit involved three checkpoints—Alfa, Bravo, Charlie. Alfa is fifty-five miles south of the Strait of Hormuz, the entrance to the Persian Gulf. We were required to check in via telex at each point, with our ETA at each remaining checkpoint and our port of discharge. If you do not check in at the next checkpoint within thirty minutes of your ETA, they come looking for you. We were unescorted—just being monitored. Cuts down on collisions!

The route into Ad Dammam is north of Bahrain to Buoy RTE2, around the reefs, through the East Channel rather than the longer route via Ras Tanurah Channel. The East Channel is limited to thirty-five-foot draft. From RTE2 to D12, the entrance channel to Dammam, is eleven miles or about forty minutes. From D12 it's another six miles and forty minutes (due to an eight-knot speed limit) to the pilot boarding area at Buoy D13, a half mile off the breakwater. The only extra pay a captain gets is for taking the ship through a buoyed channel like that without a pilot aboard, two hours minimum going in and the same coming out. Believe me, I earned that!

We took arrival at 1300 on 17 September, FWE (finished with engines) at 1530. We had a British pilot with two Pakistani apprentices. As I'd mentioned, the Saudi agent was a little surprised to find a woman captain, but no other locals came aboard. Where we docked was totally controlled by the U.S. Army.

I was able to call Jack that night—Uncle Sam paid for one call from each person—and with the ship almost finished discharging its cargo, I posted the sailing board for 1400 the next day for the Suez Canal, with a stop first at Al Fujayrah, United Arab Emirates, for "bunkers"—fuel oil—and then home.

Taking on bunkers was an experience.

We were advised by our supervisory office, Lykes Lines in London, that we would receive capacity bunkers after leaving Ad Dammam. Because we had enough on board already, we did not need the fuel to get back to the States. Besides, the chief engineer was concerned about receiving fuel oil of unknown specifications—it's hard to know what temperature is required to burn it out. And because we were returning without cargo, we would be extremely stiff, which is dangerous in heavy seas and caused the unpleasant experience during hurricane Lillie. I later learned that 80 percent capacity was required.

I sent about four messages, trying to avoid capacity bunkers. No dice. We were ordered to stop in Al Fujayrah, outside the Persian Gulf just south of the Strait of Hormuz, at a certain point (they gave us the coordinates) and meet a fuel barge at anchor.

We passed through the strait about 1500 on 19 September. The ETA for the bunkering anchorage was 2100. We were off the anchorage at 2100, but it took us another hour to weave our way through the anchored ships.

I quit counting at seventy targets on the radar scope.

We traveled about six miles in and around the ships at various maneuvering speeds. It got to be fun after awhile, but I think the third mate is still shaking his head.

The anchorage was in very deep water, about two hundred feet. Before we let go the anchor, I had the mate walk out two shots of anchor chain (180 feet), instead of letting go just outside the hawsepipe as you do when anchoring in shallower water. Otherwise you may not be able to stop the chain from flying out.

We finished bunkering about 0900 on the 20th. And, yes, the chief had trouble burning it. Fuel pump seizures became a common occurrence. About once a day we lost an engine until the pump was freed up. Each time that happened, it took about twenty minutes. It was no problem in open water, but it was in the Straits of Gibraltar.

And we paid for that bottom full of bunkers in the Atlantic with Lillie.

On my last trip back to Newport News from Dammam we had a full complement of supercargoes—twelve military men (and women— some male captains wouldn't take female soldiers, but I was a soft touch) who were responsible for maintaining their cargo aboard. That number resulted from a mixup. The female captain running the unit asked how many I could take and, when I said twelve, she thought that's how many I wanted. The U.S. Coast Guard Certificate of Inspection (COI), our most important certificate, limited us to twelve. If you violate the COI, then you jeopardize the vessel's insurance. I didn't mind having the passengers, although it meant feeding that many extra people for three weeks, that many more sharing the videos and the pool. Our biggest concern was using up our precious fresh-water supply, which we made ourselves, for showers and laundry.

It turned out okay, although I did have one scare. Military passengers were not required to stay in uniform aboard ship, and almost immediately after embarking one fellow changed into his flowing robe of Islam (I understand many servicemen converted while in Saudi Arabia) and wandered up to the bridge as we were getting underway. I thought, *Whoa—did someone sneak on while I wasn't looking?* I put a stop to his wearing the caftan on the *Lyra*—it was a danger to him as he made his way up and down ladders, or stairways, especially in any kind of seaway with rolling or pitching motion—but he proceeded to try to convert crewmen on the ship. One day I caught him proselytizing with the saloon messman while he was setting up for a meal, and I let it be known that whatever that soldier did, he was not to interfere with my crew during working hours. After that I think he slept from 0700 until I went to bed and did God's work the rest of the time. I never saw him again!

Stowaways are a serious problem, and we did a stowaway check whenever we left one country for another. To try to avoid the problem, ships have had to weld shut each extra door to a space and every crawl space that isn't being used. Each stowaway costs the company at least $30,000. Some never are able to leave the ship. Once you get them to the States, they have to remain under guard until you can send them back. Some have to be flown back to their country with an escort, and sometimes it takes months to know their country of origin. In one case in New York City, a "do-gooder" was able to obtain a court order preventing the stowaway's "deportation" because his rights were being violated. So the company on whose ship he stowed away was paying for him to be housed for the foreseeable future at $100 per day. We had one stowaway on the *Lyra* before I started sailing as captain aboard her. He had sneaked aboard in Berbera, Somalia, in 1988.

Passengers have been known to cause problems unintentionally and, because they were not our primary reason for existing, Lykes went out of that business in the spring of 1995. That's the trend. Several years before that, American President Lines discontinued passenger service after a chief mate raped a female passenger and she sued the company.

Although a ship could carry twelve passengers, toward the end it was usually more like seven, and they weren't always prepared by Lykes for the pace of travel when they made their reservations. For instance, on containerships the time in port is so short, only hours, that passengers become frustrated. Port time could be 2000 to 0600. Another problem: The company listed a number of *possible* ports of call, but many were remote possibilities or were no longer used. For instance, we no longer stopped at Valencia, Spain, or Piraeus, Greece. Passengers complained to the captain, and the passenger service didn't want to hear the captain complain.

Zaghoul. That's the name of the only bad harbor pilot I saw over there. I warned other ships about him, too.

My second trip into Ad Dammam we had a tugboat made fast on our port quarter helping us dock. We had to spin the ship around, with the bow toward the dock. There's plenty of room to turn in the shipway, the space between the two docks. With two bow thrusters and a tug on the port quarter, you can spin the *Lyra* around pretty quickly. The tug kept pulling her forward toward the dock, and I could see we were closing too fast. So I stopped the turn, but the tugboat was still pulling us toward the dock, even though we had the engines going astern, working in the opposite direction. I kept trying to get the pilot to stop the tug, but I could see he was still pulling us forward. We had to go full astern to miss the dock. The second mate was advising me of the clearance on the bow, as it's impossible to judge the distance between the bow and the dock from the bridge, 486 feet away. Finally, we drew within six feet of the dock and I could see we weren't closing on it, so we were okay. Otherwise, my next move would have been to have the chief mate cut the tug hawser and the second mate drop the anchors.

In that case, a miss was as good as a mile.

The military efficiency at Dammam seemed to deteriorate after my first trip there in September 1990 during the newness of the engagement. Home for six months after my first trip, I went back to work in April 1991. I left Savannah for Dammam, returned to Houston in mid-June, turned around to Dammam, then Rotterdam/Bremerhaven, Germany, with eleven days in the Lloyd Werft yard in August before the final pickup in Dammam and home to Newport News in October 1991.

My first trip into Dammam was the shortest stay—nineteen hours. By the last trip port time stretched to eight days, and I had heard that, despite Saudi rules, it was possible to sneak into town wearing camouflage fatigues. So halfway through our stay I made a trade. Lieutenant Robinson from a Ft. Eustis stevedoring unit asked me to get a letter of recommendation for the twelve-hour night-shift crew (and a case of beer for her birthday party), and I agreed. I asked her to get some uniforms and a couple of us off the ship and into town, an hour's ride away.

The chief engineer, Charlie Kyle, and I put on military fatigues (although, without the dark T-shirts and boots, we still felt conspicuous), plus the big floppy camouflage hats shielding our faces, and borrowed plastic clip-on badges, like a driver's license without a picture, identifying us as army. My uniform was much too large, so I really looked like I was out of uniform! Charlie was willing to shave off his beard just to get off the ship, but it was unnecessary because some civilians there had beards.

Lieutenant Robinson drove her army-drab four-wheel drive Chevy Blazer onto the stern ramp of the *Lyra* and picked us up so we didn't even have to walk onto the dock where there were always Saudi guards with machine guns, one at the stern ramp and one at the gangway amidships. I climbed in back, Charlie sat in the front passenger seat, and about 1900 Lieutenant Robinson drove us through the Saudi checkpoints. The port is huge. We went through a couple of gates before we came to the main gate. Customs was there. Sometimes they asked for IDs, but not this night. We worried more about being able to get back onto the dock, but that didn't prove to be a problem either. We did take our Z cards, our U.S. merchant mariner's documents, with us for identification. And I also had my U.S. passport with me just in case I had to prove who I was. The chief mate knew where we were, too.

We drove down a long causeway into town. It was dry and dusty, and so hot you didn't want to be outside. We stopped in a couple of Saudi stores, including a grocery store to buy Gatorade, American newspapers and magazines (cover photos of Madonna on *Newsweek* and *Time* had her body blacked out with marker pen), then headed for a huge, modern Saudi shopping mall. Charlie bought some gold jewelry for his wife—gold shops were everywhere, and loaded. I was intimidated because I know nothing about gold, and I settled for a couple of souvenir T-shirts.

Military were abundant in the stores. And the Saudis were milking the GIs. They were allowed. I was self-conscious because my borrowed uniform didn't fit. While we were in one of the stores, I saw a soldier who had been checking the cargo being loaded aboard the *Lyra,* and he recognized me. That was okay. But it would have been a problem if we'd gotten caught by the Saudis, because our jaunt into town was against their rules. We were the only ones not allowed in town. Ship personnel were even allowed shore leave in Al Jabayl, the next port up. There was access to phones there, too, and people could walk throughout the port. I guess the Saudis at Dammam didn't want a bunch of drunken sailors wandering around!

We also sneaked off one time to use the telephone. It was at a whole building full of telephones just outside the gate, adjacent to a seven-story barge some army stevedores were living on. After the

John Lykes had been in Dammam loading ammunition for about three weeks, the army chaplain did take that crew in groups of six to use the phones because they had been in port so long and still had another two weeks to go. Otherwise, shore leave there was limited to a walk on the dock the length of the ship.

And the first day I was there, Edward Ellis, a navy yeoman second class reservist from Lake Charles, Louisiana, drove me about a quarter of a mile down the dock so I could visit Capt. Greg George on the *John*. I put on a hard hat and a color-coded badge that I borrowed from another MSC runner. Since Captain George is rather plump and short—and conspicuous—it was easier for me to blend in with the American soldiers. Besides, he'd already been caught once trying to sneak off his ship to visit his brother, who was chief mate on the *Ashley Lykes,* and had been told to go back!

It was even difficult to get off the ship for legitimate reasons. One trip I had two crew members who needed medical attention. Chief Engineer Brian Norton needed to see a dentist, the other a doctor for his back. I had to get the ship's agent to come get their passports and Z cards, drive all the way into town to immigration to get visas for each one, and come back for them. A Saudi driver took them and brought them back at $96 a man. That $96 didn't even include the doctor bill. I don't know how much that was—that bill was sent to Lykes's headquarters in New Orleans. The escort was under orders not to stop anywhere, but he was nice enough to let them shop at an outdoor fruit stand. Brian, a junk-food addict, brought back baked goods for himself; knowing how much I like fresh fruit, he brought back all kinds of it for me. The driver paid for it, and the chief paid him back in U.S. dollars. I think the Saudis prohibited that practice later on. Initially you could get five or six people off the ship, at $100 a head, to go to town with the agent. Later that was prohibited, too.

I never even got to the MSC office, a ten-minute ride from the ship. But I had a VHF radio to summon a rep when I needed one, which I did.

The MSC did little to make our lives pleasant in Dammam, despite our confinement. The only one who did was YN2 Ed Ellis. He was a real sweetheart of a guy. He did more for the ships than anybody else. He'd make pizza runs, even when he was off duty. He made grocery store runs for us, brought us fresh fruit and things, traded movies between the *John Lykes* and the *Lyra.* I did write a letter of commendation to his boss after we left.

Mostly the MSC seemed indifferent to us, and mighty disorganized. My last trip to Dammam was the worst.

Along with the regular twice-daily radio messages to the appropriate MSC office, I always let the MSC office in Dammam know our position and our ETA into Dammam. And several days before we'd arrive, I'd ask, as usual, for berthing instructions (where we dock), and whether it's port or starboard side to, or straight back as we had before. It's nice to know. Particularly with the ramp, it was a lot easier if we could dock so the ramp came straight back rather than slewed to the side at a thirty-three-degree angle. I asked when loading gangs would start. And I always asked ETD—estimated time of departure. In this case, it should have been EDD—estimated date of departure! And I never heard back. We always got a message from them even before we reached the Suez Canal, saying, "Welcome back to the Port of Dammam. If your ETA changes even one hour, please advise us." And we're nine days away!

This particular trip they told us before arrival that we'd be berthed immediately. Instead we had to anchor overnight because the *Elizabeth Lykes* was at the berth that had been designated for us, and she hadn't finished taking on cargo. That's not terrible, as it meant we had a free night at anchor. But it caused a lot of extra work, shutting down the engines, anchoring, restarting the engines, and shifting to the dock, which we finally did the next morning. FWE was just before noon. And they indicated ETD three to four days.

I also expected them to be ready to load us when we arrived, but I could see there was no activity around the dock. YN2 Ellis came aboard; the agent finally showed up. But nobody was set up to start loading us, and no cargo was waiting. Everything was dead. And the MSC was paying Lykes Lines $35,000 a day to charter the *Lyra,* whether the ship was working or not. We finally got word that the pre-stow meeting would be at 1130 the next day.

The Persian Gulf run was not without its humorous side.

Ridiculous requests came to the ship, such as, "*Lyra,* please advise when you've picked up your anchors." We weren't anchored—we don't usually drop an anchor when we're tied at the dock. Usually the time of "last line" at the dock is what's needed for port documents.

One memorable moment occurred when we were loading tanks and a poor female ensign asked, "What are we going to do with all the tank tops when there are no more tanks to load?" Evidently she'd heard a reference to our tank top—the very lowest deck, on top of the double bottoms where we carried our fuel and ballast.

Usually loading took thirty-six hours top to bottom. This trip it stretched to eight days. And it was one fiasco after another. At the pre-stow meeting we asked that the twenty-one RHTCs (pronounced "retches"), each a forty-eight-ton forklift with its own spreader bar for lifting containers, be the first equipment loaded on the open deck, as far forward as possible, because of their weight. The engine room, and the "house" or living and working quarters of the ship, and the stern ramp were all aft, so that would get rid of all the extra drag. No problem.

The hitch was that they expected to have to load them with a floating crane, which only worked five days a week. And we were going into the Muslim Sabbath and the day following, both non-work days. But when they started loading those RHTCs, sure as shootin' they were driving them up the main deck ramp. They were so wide that their tires hit on either side, and it was tearing them up a little bit. But they grew to be very careful with them. Overhead clearance was less than an inch when they went up the movable ramp. And they couldn't let any air out of the tires to decrease their height, because that increased the tire width, already at the absolute maximum to make it up the ramp.

The lashers, who work twelve hours at a time, five or six days a week, had the hardest job. They secured each RHTC to D-rings on the deck as they were loaded. Additional cargo was loaded that blocked them in. About the sixth day, the army decided to take six back off the ship. They were needed to equip a full unit to be left behind in case hostilities ignited again, and nobody had counted before they were loaded. And the army didn't want just any RHTCs, but certain ones. We did talk them out of retrieving the accompanying spreader bars, which were loaded on another deck. Unbelievable!

It was a Sunday afternoon, and I finally put out the word, "I want to see someone from MSC who knows what's going on." Only YN2 Ellis had been visiting, and he didn't know what the army was doing. I finally got the major to come down about 1400. I wanted to know when we were sailing. He said we would be delayed because we were waiting for a broken-down RHTC to be brought in from the desert and washed according to Ag Department regulations before loading. I'd heard we were going to finish loading Monday. He indicated Tuesday. The last three RHTCs were to be the last cargo loaded, and there went our plan. Optimum sailing is with a three- to four-foot drag; those three RHTCs meant we sailed with a seven-foot drag.

I managed to keep my cool until the last day. Then I finally lost my sense of humor and had to leave the deck and let my chief mate, Bill Mago, and YN2 Ellis finish. The last straw was actually scrap wood. Dunnage.

But let me back up. When the ship's working commercially, the paperwork usually accompanies the last load. But the army needed time to run the paperwork—the cargo manifest and the dangerous cargo manifest—after all of the cargo was loaded. Written in triplicate, it sometimes ran 120 pages. Typically, no one on the discharge side asked for it. Later we'd just toss it overboard.

The first time we took materiel home from the Gulf we were told by MSC to post our sailing board four to six hours after last load; it was eight hours until we received the manifest. Next trip we were told six to eight hours and it was ten. Each trip that elapsed time lengthened. This last time, at the pre-stow meeting I was told we could expect the paperwork within three hours of last load. I couldn't believe the three, so I made them repeat the guarantee!

Finally it was the 17th, the eighth day since we had arrived. The last RHTC showed up at 1800 and all that was left on the dock were seven steel spreader bars sitting right behind the stern ramp—where they had been all day. To expedite the paperwork, the checkers had already scanned everything on the dock to be loaded, just like the checkers at the grocery store, for the manifest.

Because 1800 was also shift change, we were delayed again. But I was assured by Ellis the paperwork was being processed and should be ready at 2200.

At 1900, as they started to load again, the chief mate said, "I hate to tell you this, but they won't start the paperwork until the last load is finished." So I went to see the damn checker, who was sitting on the stern ramp. I said, "You are kidding, right?"

"Until those spreader bars are on the ship, we will not start the paperwork," he repeated.

I asked, "Why is that?"

"What if they don't make it?"

Another holdup. The loading gang foreman had sent a forklift to get dunnage to put between the spreader bars to keep them from sliding, steel on steel. "What's the matter with that pile of dunnage, which came off the *Lyra,* over there on the dock?" I asked in disbelief. "I didn't see it," he answered. An hour and a half later, there was the forklift with the dunnage.

You talk about waste. We had brought three tons of grade A lumber from Houston with us, some of it the nicest birch and cherry you ever saw, more expensive than you would use in building a house. But it wasn't to build anything. It was intended to sheath the hatches of ammo ships as required by the U.S. Coast Guard so the ammo wouldn't touch any steel. When pieces of this wood got dirty or broken, as it did in using it through the two previous trips, we just threw it over the side. And we carried it for nothing. Dumpsters on the dock were full of it. They had more dunnage than they knew what to do with.

At 2217 we logged last load. And despite promises of paperwork in one and a half to three hours, we finally got it four hours later.

It's a lengthy procedure to sail. It involved posting the sailing board eight hours ahead to satisfy the crew's union contracts, alerting the engine room, calling Port Control for the harbor pilot to take us out, the mate doing a stowaway search. And we were all very tired. I was just resting on the settee in my office. Finally, about 0330 we got a pilot. We blew that one long blast as we eased forward, at 0400 we dumped the pilot, and at 0500 we took departure out of the channel. As we passed the *John Lykes,* with supercargoes waving from one ship to the other, I let loose three unanswered blasts as a farewell. In the quiet early morning they echoed throughout the port.

I prefer to remember the happy ending from the first trip, for which I received the U.S. Navy's Meritorious Public Service Award. Any captain could have received it, but they singled out nine of us. As usual, I was the only woman.

That trip we left behind 250 very grateful GIs. In a thank-you letter to my boss, Captain Manchester, Col. James H. Pillsbury of the 101st noted that the combat power the *Lyra* brought arrived in "excellent condition" and the injury-free, nineteen-hour off-load went "quickly and efficiently."

But the letter from the port crew to the *Lyra* crew really tells the story:

The hot chow you provided was a bright and happy moment for us all. It was nice to know that no matter how far from home you are you have friends and support.

The story unfolded this way: Colonel Pillsbury and his number two man came to my office the day we arrived, about 2100. He introduced himself, and asked if we could do him a favor.

"Yes," I answered; anything I could do, I would.

"Could you put together 450 sandwiches for us?"

I replied that I didn't think we had enough bread, but perhaps we could do something else.

He explained that his troops had not had a real meal in thirty days, but had been surviving on MREs, sort of military TV dinners, unheated, because the men had preceded the kitchen facilities. He hoped to get the *Cape Douglas* to feed some of them, too. I promised I'd get together with my steward, James Narcisse, and do what we could.

Narcisse is a good man, a real morale booster. A New Orleans resident in his fifties, Narcisse is the kind who surprised us at coffee with homemade date-nut bread or cookies. Sometimes he'd make homemade pizza. When he found out lemon meringue pie was my favorite, he baked five—two for me and three for the rest of the crew!

Anyway, thirty minutes later I found Narcisse, and he suggested we cook fifty pounds of beef and give the soldiers a roast beef dinner. Before we left the States, the ship had loaded stores to last 120 days—we didn't know how long we'd be out—and we expected to be back in 52 days, so we had plenty of food to share. In fact, when I put in a call to Lykes Lines' office in New Orleans before we arrived stateside, I had a question posed to me through my number two boss from Commissary Supt. Larry Wadkins: "Where'd you get the beef?"

I took Narcisse with me to Colonel Pillsbury's office and made the proposal to serve it the next day.

"Sounds good," Colonel Pillsbury said.

Next morning Narcisse got up at 0400 and started cooking. At 0700 I was on the cargo deck and I grabbed three GIs for KP duty. They helped him until 1100, when we served the dinner under the warehouse roof on the dock. Besides the roast beef, we offered mashed potatoes, gravy, cooked turnips, broccoli, coleslaw, rolls, and French bread. The soldiers brought their own soda—they had cases and cases of that!

Colonel Pillsbury had said they didn't even have plates, so we found some heavy-duty paper party plates to serve on. That's how we knew we served 250 GIs. We ran out of food with eight still in line, and we fed them aboard. We finally finished serving at 1230, and Colonel Pillsbury and his second in command came aboard fifteen minutes later to thank us. When I found out they hadn't eaten, the chief cook helped me put together two submarine sandwiches for them with pork he was cooking for dinner, and we opened a can of pears to go with them.

There went our feeding costs, but we were glad to do it! It was James Narcisse who deserves the credit, but being the female I got it.

Landlubber's Log
27–28 February 1994

Sunday, 27 February

Today starts out rather cloudy, but we're doing great speed, better than nineteen knots, and expect to arrive Livorno 1530, earlier than planned. No gangs today, but they'll start bright and early Monday: two gangs, two cranes, and unfortunately that means we may leave at 1500. Maybe there'll still be time for a quick trip to Florence.

After staying up until 0240 with Debbie while we ran the islands, I wake at 0645, decide to rest for just a few minutes more, and suddenly it's past 0830! Never mind: she has had the galley put away breakfast for me. You think no one notices? The chief mate comes out with a snappy, "Hello, sleepyhead." Afterward it's time for a little work, and just before 1100 an island goes by to port.

At 1330 my presence is requested on the bridge. A reprise of the Piombino Straits; it looks easy today as there's no traffic. We pass only a mile off the island to our right. Under heavy clouds, the sea has a decided turquoise cast. Time passes, and the heavily industrialized city of Piombino is to starboard, with many smokestacks rising. Elba is on our port; the harbor, set way back, is gorgeous, low white buildings with red roofs everywhere.

"Put that on our list of places to return when we get our yacht, okay?" the captain says.

Now we're four miles off the islands to starboard. It's nearly 1500. The temperature is dropping. The visibility is dropping. The radar shows several ships ahead, but we can't see them. As Livorno ship's information and pilots have told us to do, we let them know when we take arrival at three miles from the breakwater. The GPS beeps arrival. "Time to go," the captain says, and the usual routine begins. With the bearded pilot aboard, it's very quiet as we head for the container berth, dead slow ahead, on by now familiar territory at second call this voyage. Last stop's ships have been replaced; the *Rose Bay* and *Orinoco* are the names on the hulls this trip. A passenger ship from Moby lines, with a big blue whale on her hull and a blue stack, is docked. The rolls of kraft paper and bundles of shredded newsprint are still on the same dock. The *Blue Light* is there. So is the *White Stone*—just can't get away from home. We dock the same place, too, with the burned-out hull of the ferry across the channel from us.

The usual whirlwind of immigration, agent, and so on, and just before 1730 Sabrina is there to drive us off to dinner. It being Sunday night, few places are open, but we try a new little restaurant near the harbor. After a wonderful Italian dinner, our last of the trip, we crave sleep before our last day on land, and more sightseeing.

Monday, 28 February

The game must be "can you top this?" Debbie has work to do, and reluctantly remains on the ship. After a quick breakfast, the agency's driver, Ilio, is there and at 0800 he and I set off for Florence.

The drive there, about an hour and a half, is picturesque. There is a toll road, but we take another way through the countryside. Lots of very old, deteriorating, Italian-yellow buildings—Ilio explains that they can only be restored if they are used for their original purpose, not always feasible. Lush farmland—vineyard after vineyard up and down the hillsides. It's particularly good for grapes because they get sunshine and rain, but they don't drown because the land drains. Memorable chianti comes from here.

The outskirts of Florence are modern-looking; apartments, shops along a busy boulevard, but turn a corner and we're in the old city and back centuries. In the shopping district everything is closed until about 1430 because it's Monday, but we spot the owner in a leather shop. He's kind enough to let us in for a quick purchase.

We walk by the Medici Chapel, but it too is closed, so we head for the Duomo and Giotto's Campanile adjacent. It's a climb—414 steps, the last very narrow and spiraled, just wide enough for two thin people to pass side to side. Again, the endless climbing on the ship is put to good use.

Begun in 1334, the many-storied bell tower offers a magnificent view of Florence from the top. All around the cathedral are points of interest. On a far hill are houses for the rich. Lower, the Pitti Palace, Boboli Gardens, the Uffizzi (the crane marking the parts being repaired from the past year's bombing), the Ponte Vecchio, and the

Mayor's House. Ilio points out top-floor residences with roof gardens, his great desire.

Once again at ground level, we head for the Palazzo Vecchio in the Piazza della Signoria with its magnificent state rooms, lavish in size and splendor. Next, we walk across the Ponte Vecchio, the oldest bridge over the Arno River in Florence. Its gold shops are closed. It's Monday, after all. There's another apartment up top Ilio longs for. Back near the shopping district, we detour through the Loggia of the Mercato Nuovo. Sometimes it's a souvenir market, but today only the pig—a famous bronze statue—is there. Legend has it if you rub his nose, you will return to Florence. I do and I will.

We need to check on the ship's loading progress. To phone Livorno, we stop in the post office—it's a work of art in itself. We pick up mozzarella in a cheese shop for the cruise back to the States and lunch for us at a sandwich shop Ilio has been patronizing for twenty-one years, then head for the car and Livorno. One last stop—near Ilio's house, which he points out—at his favorite gelateria. We buy lots of gelato to last the trip home.

While we've been gone, the chief mate has found the elephant feet, in the nick of time—in another couple of hours the captain would have sent a message to the States requesting another set and explaining that the *Charlotte*'s set was somewhere in Izmir.

Good-byes again, and at 1600 the pilot is aboard with his apprentice and we're homeward bound.

After we leave Livorno, the captain asks the AB on the bridge to wash the windows, and ends up standing on the rail, her head in a compartment, trying to figure out why the water won't stop coming. If it isn't one thing that needs fixing, it's another. A comment to the engineers at supper brings immediate response.

After dinner, the captain wins the cribbage marathon, four games to three, with the second mate kibitzing. Then it's retard clocks, or as Amy says not too kindly to one AB, "Retard, clocks." First full night's sleep in a while is very welcome.

10. "How Long Have You Been in the Captin Buessness?"

Captain's standing brings admirers, including classes of elementary schoolchildren who became pen pals after adopting my ship.

I found them—or, rather, they found me—through the Adopt-a-Ship Program sponsored by the Propeller Club. Similar programs are also conducted in other countries, such as England and Norway. The Propeller Club, comprised of shore-based personnel related to the marine industry, is the largest nationwide marine organization.

Adopt-a-Ship dates from the same period as the Merchant Marine Act of 1936, and is designed to teach the "citizens of tomorrow" the need for an adequate American merchant marine for both domestic and foreign shipping. For many years it was administered by the Women's Propeller Club and, since 1958, again by the Propeller Club.

Through this program, all Lykes ships are adopted each school year—usually by landlocked Midwestern schools. It is the captain's responsibility personally to answer the students' letters and, in most cases, it is hard to get anyone else (but cadets) on the ship to take part. Many captains see it as just one more chore.

The kids wrote. I wrote. The teachers wrote. I got lots of attention, and hopefully the students learned a little something about the sea, ships, geography, history, transportation, foreign and domestic trade, and English.

Kids ask all the questions you'd want to, but were too polite to ask.

The Evans School in Fond du Lac, Wisconsin, was the most active school Lykes had adopted, and it was already in touch with the *Shirley Lykes* when I joined her just before Christmas 1986 as chief mate.

She had the unique position of having a local man, James J. Robinson, as captain, and he made periodic visits to the school—including one in his honor when he logged his millionth mile at sea—which piqued their interest. Nell Bourgeois, secretary to the vice president of Lykes's marine division, sent the *Shirley*'s schedule for each voyage to the fourth-grade teacher so her students could follow along on the map.

When I joined the vessel, Adopt-a-Ship was one responsibility I took willingly from her captain. In my first set of letters from the students in February 1987, each began with the teacher's prescribed introduction:

> Welcome aboard our *Shirley Lykes!* We are proud to have you as our adopted shipmate and Chief mate. We hope that you have had a safe and enjoyable voyage so far. When your busy schedule permits would you please be so kind and write and tell us about voyage 105?

From there each was on his own, asking what cargo we carried, which was my favorite signal flag, and comparing weather notes. They asked my age, hair color, favorite subject and sport, in return sharing family and friends, school and Scouts.

Their packets were sent to many ports, offering St. Patrick's Day greetings, Easter greetings, and Christmas letters to individual crew members. One Christmas the ship received a ten-foot-long computer-generated banner. In return, I kept those cards and letters coming back to the school.

When I became master of the *Lyra* in 1989, there was so much publicity that fifth graders at Stansbury Park Elementary School in Stansbury Park, Utah, started writing in addition to the fourth graders at Goliad Elementary School in San Angelo, Texas, who had officially adopted the *Lyra.* That doubled the fun. When I became captain of the *Charlotte Lykes,* I inherited the fifth-grade class at Edith Tether Elementary School in Fairplay, Colorado.

Here's a typical letter from a student in Utah:

Dear Captin Dempsy,

. . . Ive never seen a lady that drives a ship. I think that it would be sort of fun. What kind of ship do you ride on? Is it Big? Is it fun, or do you get sick? How long have you been in the Captin Buessness? . . .

Your friend,
Mattie

In addition to nearly unanimous praise for their teacher, Mrs. Pat Atkins, letters from the students at Goliad Elementary School provided many variations on a theme. My favorite, just because it was so personal:

Dear Master:

Thank you for sending those letters. I have some questions to ask. Do the men like you as captin? Why don't you send stuff for just the person that writes for you? Do you like in New Arealns? Sorry if I spelt that wrong! Are you very pretty? If you'r hair brown, blond, black or red. Could you send us a picture.

Sincerely,
Amber

P.S. Are you married? Do you have children? I bet you'r butiful.

The students shared some Texas products, including green jalapeño pepper lollipops, bean dip, and chili mix. They also shared school pictures of themselves with their introductory letters and, throughout the year, personal tidbits. Always they let me know they would be waiting for my answer.

In return, the ship sent everything from postcards and foreign currency, coins, and stamps, to dolls and Egyptian paintings on papyrus. From the ship I sent menus, pilot charts with our track, and a few samples of MREs—the military "meals ready to eat," packaged in heavy-duty army-drab green foil. And I wrote letters such as the following:

3/3/90

Dear Mrs. Atkins and the fourth grade class,

Greetings from your ship and your other captain. Since I joined the vessel in Wilmington, N.C., on Jan. 20th, we have been nonstop. But now I would like to catch you all up on what your ship has been doing.

Jan. 20th in Wilmington, N.C., we loaded some military vehicles to take to San Lorenzo, Honduras, via the Panama Canal. I've included some literature on the Panama Canal. We sailed from Wilmington morning of the 21st after a seven-hour delay due to fog. We arrived at Cristobal, Panama, the northern entrance, Atlantic side (yes, the Panama Canal runs in a north-south direction from the Atlantic Ocean to the Pacific Ocean) morning of the 25th. Canal transit was delayed until very early on the 26th. We spent the whole day transiting the canal and sailed from Balboa, Pacific side, evening of the 26th.

To transit the canal, we must travel through locks with the assistance of "mules." These travel like railway cars along either side of the locks to hold the ship in the middle of the lock. They tie the mules to the ship with heavy mooring wires. We always use four mules on the bow and two on the stern.

In order to get the ship up the river to San Lorenzo, we had to have daylight to see all the navigational buoys and the right tide. We needed high water since our draft was 25 feet. That is how far down into the water the bottom of the ship is.

San Lorenzo is on the west coast of Honduras. You must enter the Gulf of Fonseca between the countries of El Salvador and Nicaragua. It is a very small port with only one dock. The countryside is mountainous, with several volcanoes, and the people are very poor.

We arrived the afternoon of the 29th of Jan. We discharged our cargo that night and left the next morning at 0600 on Jan. 30th.

On the way back to New Orleans, we stopped in Balboa to pick up some POVs (private owner vehicles), cars owned by people in the military like vans, small trucks, station wagons, sports cars, etc., to bring back to the United States. Then we transited the canal the night of Feb. 1st. We arrived in New Orleans on Feb. 6th.

The two-week trip to Central America was short and fast, but also a good break for all the crew from all the terrible weather of the winter North Atlantic and North Sea. We even used our swimming pool on the ship for several days.

Then we loaded in New Orleans, Charleston, and Norfolk to return to northern Europe. We have discharged the cargo in Rotterdam, Felixstowe, and Bremerhaven.

Since Feb. 24th, we have been undergoing repairs, which will be completed on March 5th. These repairs are for a normal overhaul of our diesel engines. We have two, and after 10,000 hours (how many days is that?) of operation, the cylinders and pistons must be cleaned. Also during this time we are fixing many other things.

Perhaps you have heard about all the bad weather that England, Belgium, France, Germany, and Holland have been experiencing. Well, that was our week in Bremerhaven! We had winds of force 12; that is hurricane force. The highest was 90 MPH. We had 17 mooring lines out and two tugboats pushing alongside the ship to keep us *at the dock. It was the first time I ever saw a snow shower with thunder and lightning!*

Unfortunately, we were not able to do much maintenance on deck because of the weather, and no one could do much sightseeing.

I have included copies of our barographs, record of the barometric pressure, for the period we were here. As you can tell, first an extreme high pressure system and to the other end with a bad low pressure system. Also, some of our weather maps for our Atlantic Ocean crossing and also here in the North Sea.

I have asked some of our officers and cadets to write you and tell you what they do on the ship. Hope you enjoy hearing from them also.

We have all enjoyed your letters. The only question you all seem to ask is what was on the postcard from Holland that Captain McNamara sent you. I am sure it was cheese.

We wish you all an early spring and good luck in school!

Best wishes,
D. D. Dempsey
Your Captain and Crew, MV Lyra

As school began the following fall, I sent this typical introductory letter:

9/22/90

Dear Mrs. Atkins and 4th Grade Class,

Greetings from your adopted ship, the Lyra, once again, and your Captain, Debbie Dempsey, once again!

Due to the crisis in the Middle East, your ship has been chartered by MSC (Military Sealift Command) for one year to transport military cargo and soldiers from the United States to Saudi Arabia. We loaded a full load of military vehicles consisting of helicopters, trucks, jeeps, trailers, refuelers, etc., in Jacksonville, Florida, and delivered them and 11 Army sergeants to Ad Dammam, Saudi Arabia. Our route took us across the Atlantic Ocean, just north of the Azores, then through the Straits of Gibraltar into the Mediterranean to the Suez Canal. We transited the Canal into Suez Bay, south through the Red Sea, into the Gulf of Aden, the Arabian Sea, the Gulf of Oman into the Persian Gulf through the Strait of Hormuz to Ad Dammam. We left Jacksonville on August 24th, transited the Suez Canal on Sept. 9th, and arrived in Ad Dammam on Sept. 17th. We sailed from Ad

Dammam on Sept. 18th, stopped in Fujayrah, United Arab Emirates, for fuel oil on Sept. 19th, and are on our way back to the Suez Canal. We are not sure if we are returning to the United States for another load or if we will be stopping somewhere in the Mediterranean or northern Europe for more military cargo. When we get to the Canal then we receive our orders for the next port. We expect to transit the Canal northbound on Sept. 28th.

Your ship is what we call a RO/RO. That's short for roll on/roll off. We have a big stern (back of the ship) ramp that we lower onto the dock. Then they can drive the cargo on and off the ship. The stern ramp leads into the ship, which is like a big parking garage inside with four different levels. The first, second, and third levels are all accessible via ramps. The fourth or bottom level is accessible only by two big cargo elevators. These elevators are 40 feet long and $10^{1}/_{2}$ feet wide and can hold 80 tons. We always work in long tons, which is 2240 lbs. equals one ton. So, how many pounds can the cargo elevators raise and lower from 3 to 4 decks? The stern ramp can support up to 160 tons! That is a lot. For instance, an army tank weighs approximately 54 tons. A big helicopter weighs about 6 tons. Your car weighs about 1 to $1^{1}/_{2}$ tons. This ship weighs 9,687 tons. When it is fully loaded with cargo, fuel oil, water, and stores, the Lyra weighs 24,555 tons.

The Lyra is 634 feet long and 89 feet wide. It is 162 feet high and, when fully loaded, draws a little over 28 feet of water. That means if we tried to enter a harbor that had only 27 feet of water alongside the dock, we would go aground. Consequently, we always keep her in deep water!

The Lyra was built in Germany in 1977. The MV designates us as a "motor ship," which means our propulsion comes from two diesel engines connected to one propeller. Maximum horsepower is 18,972 hp and for normal use is a little over 16,000 hp. Our fuel consumption is about 310 barrels a day and we travel at an average of 16.5 knots (one knot equals 1.15 miles per hour—so 16.5 knots is the same as 19 miles per hour). In one day, we travel about 400 miles. That is about 0.75 barrel fuel oil per mile and, since there are 42 gallons in one barrel, our mileage is not very good when compared to your car. But, don't forget: we are moving a lot of weight. That's a little over 30 gallons of fuel oil per mile! And since one barrel of fuel oil costs about $22, the cost of fuel oil is the most expensive part about running a ship. We carry a little over 18,000 barrels and travel 22,000 miles.

The normal size crew on the Lyra is 22 people, divided into three departments: deck, engine, and steward's. The deck department is run by the chief mate. Under him is a second mate, third mate, and six deck hands. Deck department is in charge of all cargo loading, discharging and securing, painting and cleaning of the outside of the ship, and also tying up and letting go in port. The deck officers stand watches of four hours on and eight hours off day and night. Each watch has two deck hands to help. At sea we make sure the ship goes from A to B, called navigating. In port, we make sure the cargo is taken care of properly. The chief mate is also the ship's doctor. There is also one radio operator who sends and receives messages from our company, agents in all the ports and, in this case, the military.

The engine department is in charge of keeping the ship's engines running all the time. If anything breaks down, they have to fix it. We carry lots of spare parts and tools to do that. There is a chief engineer, who is in charge of the engine department, a first assistant engineer, a second assistant, a third assistant (who is also a woman), an electrician (another woman), an oiler, and a wiper. They all get very dirty, but they also keep everything going including the air conditioning! And in this area of the world where air temperature is 100° and sea temperature is 95°, that is very important! Just like in Texas.

The steward's department is in charge of feeding everyone three times a day, keeping the inside of the ship clean, and giving everyone clean sheets and towels once a week. There is a chief steward in charge, a chief cook, and two messmen. Everyone eats the same food.

There is just one captain. I'm in charge of everything. I tell everyone what to do! But right now that is an easy job because the crew is good and they pretty much already know what to do.

There is also a small swimming pool on board. Right now we have it full. We all use it, and on these hot days it feels good and relaxing.

We are due at Port Suez, Egypt, on the 27th of Sept. We will transit the Canal northbound on the 28th. The Canal is about one hundred miles long. It goes from Port Said on the Mediterranean to Port Suez on the Red Sea. There are no locks like in the Panama Canal. Northbound transit should take a little over ten hours. Then we will continue west through the Mediterranean, the Gibraltar Straits on to the East Coast of the United States. What port exactly, I do not know. The military will tell us eventually.

I have asked other officers to write you about what they do. Also, I *have enclosed some menus, a pilot chart showing our route, and some postcards from Egypt.*

Please write with all your questions and we will try to answer them. Everyone on the Lyra wishes you all a good school year and hope you all study hard.

Very truly yours,
Debbie Dempsey, Master
MV Lyra
Voyage 50

With the end of school came the traditional last letter:

5/11/91

Dear Mrs. Atkins and 4th Grade Class,

Greetings once again from your other captain. Captain McNamara and almost all the crew got off the ship in Savannah, Georgia, on April 20th. Your ship was gone from the U.S.A. a long time—a little over six months. We all thank you for all the letters and support you gave the Lyra and her crew throughout the Persian Gulf crisis.

I guess this will be the last letter you'll receive from your ship this year since school must be approaching summer vacation.

Well, we are presently on our way back to Ad Dammam, Saudi Arabia, to pick up another load of military equipment and either bring it back to the U.S.A. or to Europe.

We sailed from Savannah on April 21st. The ocean crossing was uneventful. We passed just north of Bermuda and well south of the Azores. We passed through the Straits of Gibraltar on May 1st. From Gibraltar we followed the North African coast by Morocco, Algeria, and Tunisia, just south of Sicily, well south of Crete, and arrived in Port Said, Egypt, on May 6th. We made good time since for most of the Mediterranean we had a force 7 (that's from the Beaufort scale indicating wind and sea conditions—0 is calm and the highest, 12, is hurricane) tailwind—about 35 knots helping us.

In Port Said we bunkered—received fuel oil. We started our south-bound Suez Canal transit at 0018 on the 7th of May. We were the first ship in the convoy out of 23 total. We anchored in Bitter Lake at 0724 until 1230 while the northbound convoy passed. The second half of the canal transit we became number 8 ship. We finished the transit at 1642.

Since being in the Red Sea and now the Gulf of Aden, sea water temperature is 94° F and air temperature 98°. It is hot and humid! Just as hot as it was last September when I wrote you. We are not making very good speed since the high sea and air temperatures reduce the efficiency of our engines. We are due in to Ad Dammam early on the 16th.

The seas have been calm so we filled the swimming pool a few days ago and are all enjoying it.

We have noticed that there is a lot more shipping traffic since the cease-fire than there was my last trip through. Also the Suez Canal pilots commented that commercial traffic is picking up, which is a good sign that things are getting back to normal.

Yesterday I talked with another Lykes ship also on this run, which had just left Dammam. He said the visibility was worse than being in fog due to the smoke, haze, and pollution from all the Kuwaiti oil fires. That is terrible, and we are not looking forward to that problem.

By the way, it was 5,688 miles from Savannah to Port Said and is 3,153 miles from Said to Dammam. At 16.3 knots, how many days is the passage?

But I will let you know how we make out and write more after we get into Dammam.

Well, we made it into Ad Dammam morning of the 16th. We arrived at the entrance to the approach channel at 0306 and finished docking at 0542. The army started loading by 0900 and they are doing such a fast and good job that we may sail tomorrow evening. We are loading just about the same equipment—helicopters, tanker trucks, M-1 tanks, Bradley tanks, and various utility trucks. We also will be carrying 12 military personnel as supercargoes—that means they take care of the equipment on the way home and make sure they are in running order for discharge.

The port of discharge will be Houston, Texas—your home state! This equipment and military units belong to Fort Hood. From Dammam to the Suez Canal it is again 3,153 miles (about eight days), one day for canal transit, and then it is 6,739 miles from Port Said, through the Mediterranean, past Gibraltar, across the Atlantic Ocean, through Hole in the Wall (the Abaco chain of the Bahama Islands) and Northwest Providence Channel, around the Florida Keys and on across the Gulf of Mexico into Galveston and on up to Houston. Sound like a long way? It certainly is—about 17 days.

After Houston, we will go into the shipyard for about two weeks. The bottom will be sandblasted and painted—you can see the grass growing on the bottom of the hull now. It has been three years since the Lyra was last dry-docked. We put the ship into a slip with doors like a lock in a canal. Once the ship is inside the slip, the doors are closed and the water pumped out, leaving the ship high and dry so all kinds of maintenance and repairs can be done. These periodic dry-dockings are required regularly by the U.S. Coast Guard to make sure all U.S. flag vessels are kept in good condition.

Then after the yard we will come back over here to continue bringing equipment home to the U.S.A.

We are sending you a house flag—the flag of our company, Lykes. The "L" stands for Lykes. We flew it here in Ad Dammam, Saudi Arabia, during Operation Desert Shield and Operation Desert Storm. Please display it in your classroom. Also, the picture of your ship, the Lyra, was taken as we entered Port Said on the 6th of May. As you can see, there is no cargo on board.

Again, we thank you all for your support and letters during these long voyages. We have enjoyed being your adopted ship. We wish you all much success in your years ahead and a great summer vacation! So long for all on the Lyra,

Very truly yours,
D. D. Dempsey, Master
MV Lyra,
Voyage 53

P.S. Also thought you might like to see what "MREs" are like!

A number of students asked the same questions. And questions require answers, so I had a stock:

- It took me eight years to get my master's license, and thirteen years to get the master's job. But before that were four years of college, another two and one-half of intense study at Maine Maritime, and working my way up through the ranks. My eyes are blue and I have short brown hair—now. I didn't have to cut it to be captain, but I did because it's easier. At school I had it long, but it would have been easier to have it short.
- I like being captain, but being the first *girl* captain is a pain in the ———.

The advantage of being captain is that you get your way. Your way is it! The disadvantage of being a female captain is the fact that you are so visible and, like every captain, that you are lonely. You can't ask anybody. You're it, and if you make the wrong decision, you have to live with it. You can't be liked by everybody; you can't be one of the boys any more.

It's an easy job—sometimes—with good help. Remembering things like latitude and longitude is easy—just part of the daily routine. And I do steer the ship, but not very often. Only when I have to. Usually ABs (able seamen) steer when necessary; at sea the ship's usually on automatic pilot. For so large a ship, the *Lyra* has a small, wooden steering wheel—slightly less than a foot in diameter.

- I've never gotten seasick on the *Lyra,* but I have on sailboats—twice. The first time was in 1973 on a yacht delivery to the Virgin Islands. The boat was all closed up, with me down below cooking hamburgers on a kerosene stove. The second was as part of the all-female crew aboard the forty-six-foot yacht *Dancer* during the 1992 Newport to Bermuda race, during *very* rough weather. We still finished the 635-mile race in three days, fifteen hours, forty-three minutes, and forty-six seconds, a remarkable twelfth of 118 boats.

- The merchant marine is the commercial end of shipping and is civilian, not military. The confusion comes when ships, such as the *Lyra,* are chartered by the military as we were during the Persian Gulf War.

- The food's good—if you like red beans and rice and grits and overcooked vegetables! It's adequate, not good. It's a twenty-five-year-old Louisiana menu, and you know what day of the week it is by what you're eating. Every Lykes ship around the world has the same food; how good it is depends on the individual ship's chief steward and cook.

Union regulations have prompted the choice of more than one entrée at each meal. And I understand the radio operators in a recent contract negotiated for better salads, and so forth. Shift changes dictate meal times to accommodate everyone. Breakfast is from 0730 to 0830, taking into account the four-to-eight and eight-to-twelve watches. Likewise, lunch is 1130–1230 and dinner, 1700–1800.

I usually lose weight when I go to work, and I always bring Granny Smith apples and yogurt with me.

- We do make our own potable water. We distill sea water into drinking water to be used in the galley, for showers, for the sanitation system, and so on. Each day we can make about twenty tons of water, and we consume about fifteen tons.
- The *Lyra,* like her sister ship, the *Cygnus,* is named for a constellation, which in turn is named after the small harp-like instrument carried in the arms of angels, the lyre. She was built in Bremerhaven, Germany, and construction took two years from keel-laying until she was finished in 1977. Built as a commercial ship for Hansa Lines of Germany, she was the *Reichenfels* until she was bought by Lykes Lines in 1981 and renamed. Lots of labels on equipment around the ship, from the elevator to the ballast tanks, are in German, a reminder of her beginnings.

   She has a black hull and white house. The *Lyra* is a RO/RO ship, designed to carry big equipment that can be driven on and off, and it's longer than two football fields. She carries airplanes, helicopters, tanks, trucks, cars, mining equipment, reels of cable, and other cargo loaded in twenty- or forty-foot containers. It's all big, bulky, and heavy.

   The *Lyra* has eleven levels altogether. From the top down, first are the flying bridge with all of the electronic equipment and antennas, and then the bridge—where the wheelhouse is, and from where the ship is driven and navigated. Next down is E or captain's deck with officers' (captain, chief mate, chief engineer, and radio operator) living quarters and offices, including the radio room. D deck houses more officers, the hospital, and swimming pool. C deck, down one, houses crew and the ship's office; B deck is noted for the officers' dining saloon, recreation room, and gym. On A deck is the crew mess, recreation facility, and quarters. Below that is the number one deck, the main deck or weather deck. It's strictly a cargo deck. Next lower is number two deck, the main RO/RO cargo deck. Then comes number three deck, with the engine room aft and cargo forward. Bottom-most is number four deck, strictly cargo.

   Each of the twenty-two crew members has his or her own room. Officers have private bathrooms, while some crew have to share.

   The reason the ship doesn't sink harks back to physics: Mass displaces its own weight. The 24,000-ton ship displaces that much in sea water. If the ship had a hole in her hull she would sink, but she doesn't

- From the ship, we see whales, flying fish, dolphins, turtles, and Portuguese men-of-war, and algae and seaweed. In addition, of course, we see other ships and sailboats and an occasional island. We see empty barrels and trash. I have seen a shark, but not from the *Lyra*. That I saw from a sailboat between the Virgin Islands and Bermuda.
- We have taken water on the main deck, but it runs off through scuppers or deck drain holes leading overboard. Water also drains off through freeing ports, which are cutouts or holes in the bulwark along the weather deck. We've never had water as high as the bridge deck. We've never had anyone drown on my ship or any serious injuries. But the worst times are definitely during rough weather—it's difficult to cook, even to eat, sleep, or move around.

All of these letters followed by at least ten years my first attempt at speaking to students in the classroom. In April 1978, when I was second mate on the *Aimee Lykes*, I spoke and showed slides to two classes in Essex, Connecticut, where my niece was a student. They were only first and second graders. One thank-you note reflects the whole passel:

Dear Debbie,

Thank you for the thing you showed us. will you come back neks year your pal
Warner

Unfortunately, the way the program is structured there is no follow-up next year with any class. I often wonder about those "shipmates."

Landlubber's Log
1–6 March 1994

Tuesday, 1 March

Another magnificent day! The strong winds of last evening are gone, the breeze is drying the earlier rain from the tops of the containers out the forward porthole. It's cool but sunny.

After breakfast it's time to organize the loot and haul it from the passenger and captain's decks to the hospital on the main deck for easy removal in Norfolk—just in case of bad weather. The steward's cookies (pecan), brought warm from the oven to the bridge, are ignored today at coffee. We have pastries from Giovanni Scaturchio in Naples: miniature cannoli, chocolate-filled cream puffs, and tiny round chocolate ones filled with a liqueur-soaked bit of cake—wonderful. Steve's still working on the radar. There's no traffic. Many flat places appear on the water from the breeze. It's barely possible to spot Minorca way off in the distance. The entertainment is pilot whales; they seem to be sleeping, only showing a rounded dorsal fin and swimming along the surface.

"Want to go anywhere?" the captain asks the chief mate, who shakes his head side to side. Instead he fills in the cargo charts for each U.S. port. It looks full on deck now, after watching empty holes appear as we swung north in the Med. Most intriguing are eight wooden crates marked "Simonazzi" and, on a box, "Gruppo SASIB." A blue container that had needed to have its doors tied shut, part of the view since we left the States, is gone. So is the farm equipment, and the odd long paper-wrapped poles. We loaded almost four feet (the ship is sailing four feet lower in the water) in Livorno—the cargo is 10,669 tons.

At lunch today—poor-boy sandwiches on real Italian bread—the conversation about the expensive "thrones" continues. It's hard to remember when it began; it seems like eons ago. The three heads on the passenger deck never have worked right; a short course in plumbing indicates they have the wrong kind of float for a moving vehicle. They supposedly were fixed in Texas one trip, at a cost of $800. Each engineer has had a crack at them this trip, particularly the one in the only passenger stateroom in use. It's not just an annoyance: the ship makes her own water, and the system has been losing tons a day. Lots of joshing about it being a contest to see who can fix this head, and who gets the patent for the best design. Is it fixed? It's had a new float, new wires and such, washers and a heavy nut to weight the float down. Stu Negoescu, a second assistant engineer, worked on it today; now it's only trickling a little. The captain says it was a constant problem when her parents were in that stateroom last summer.

Fire and boat drill today at 1530, followed by survival suit practice, then slop chest.

The afternoon's entertainment is Mallorca to the west, only two miles off. Anything for the passenger: On the bridge appears a two-bit plastic cup with a slot in the top, marked "Sightseeing Tips." Although there are no tips one through four, Amy put in number five: "When traveling to foreign ports, be sure to bring Pepto-Bismol." Somehow that's not what the captain expected in the way of tips!

The engineers have decided the weather is too good to pass up the chance for another barbecue on the second deck of the house. It's a warm and beautiful sunset, with just an instant of a green flash. And savory hamburgers.

From the start, tonight's cribbage game is doomed: The gyro repeater is on the fritz. Each time there is a course change, it goes haywire and needs to be reset. It's quite a disruption to navigation, and requires the captain's repeated attention. We start the game before dinner, are interrupted, try to continue after dinner, are interrupted, finally take a look at Ibiza and the fishing boats off the coast, the beautiful night sky, and decide to hit the sack before 2100.

Wednesday, 2 March

It's another magnificent sunny shirtsleeve day as we spend the day running the coast of Spain, about five miles off all the way south. It's hard to know where to look first—at the scenery along the coast or the schools of porpoises swimming with us. We pass Cape de Palos at 0200—asleep—but manage to throw in laundry and head for the bridge to see Cape de Gata just before breakfast at 0800. Good news: we expect decent weather going home, and have been routed on a rhumb line all the way.

With *Sailing Directions Western Med* in my lap, I have a perfect sightseeing guide. Spain looks very different from Italy. The buildings are white and without the red tile roofs, and they're clustered along the shore, not creeping up the hills. The Sierra Nevadas are reminiscent of the Rockies where I grew up in that the slopes are without towns, and the towns are situated as if in valleys. Lots of saltpans, too.

The Sierra Nevada mountains are the highest in Spain and, the guide says, are "covered with perpetual snow." Pico Mulahacen at 11,424 feet and Pico Velata at 11,129 are certainly white today under bright sunshine. Descending, there is terracing down to the flatland, and numerous inviting harbors. Cabo Sacratif is the high point of the morning; after lunch and a nap, at 1430 it's Malaga, large and lovely, then Torremolinos.

At coffee, the chief mate remarks, "Looks like you'll get the scenic tour for dinner again tonight." Sure enough, just before 1700 the captain drags the armchair up by the rail, with a bottle of wine for the passenger and cranberry juice for her, Turkish olives, and Florentine mozzarella. Oh, and the Rock of Gibraltar. It's a clear night, and the rock is sharp—even after only two weeks, I'd forgotten how green it is on the west side, and how much building is there.

Look the other way, and there's Tangier, a flat city between two rises. The captain remarks that Hannibal rode elephants across the mountains there, and could he now?

When we're four miles south of Europa Point, the captain calls Tarifa traffic with our particulars, including our speed—15.5 knots, slowed by current—and the fact that we are carrying 489 tons of hazardous material. We have company as we make for Tarifa light. A huge school of porpoises is playing around us. The sun, bright orange, begins to set dead ahead, right behind the foremast. A Nordana containership is to port, Sea-Land's *Sea Leader* to starboard. *Sea Leader* crosses our bow, then slows, decides to cross back, prompting the captain to call her. She's heading north to Rotterdam. As we turn east into the Atlantic, the *Charlotte Lykes* starts to pitch.

Livorno to Gibraltar Junction, at 35°58' N, 6°12' W, was 912 miles—it's another 3,225 to Ambrose Light. Now we're steering 274. Next course change is in 3,090 miles at the entrance to Hudson Canyon, 40°7' N, 73°16' W, and the approach to New York

Tonight's menu is the pits, or maybe we're just not willing to settle for the *Charlotte's* repetitive fare after the culinary treats of the Med circuit. We opt instead for dinner in the captain's office: sandwiches made with prosciutto and bread that Steve Ballor, the radio operator, brought the captain from Livorno, avocado and homemade mustard, plus garlic-laced eggplant an Italian friend has given the captain. Dessert is vanilla gelato from Livorno with fresh strawberries from Haifa. Although the patch isn't great, Steve does get through to Deb's neighbor, a ham radio operator, enough to learn there is water, water everywhere at home. Under the prearranged schedule, they'll try to talk each day. After tonight's comedy, our worst choice so far, near midnight we retard clocks and head for bed.

Thursday, 3 March

Soft cotton clouds this morning belie the seas. To last night's pitching we've added rolling. It'll sure keep the nail polish stirred, but so far it's no trouble. The captain doesn't like the motion of this ship: it's too unpredictable, she says. She eats her favorite breakfast today—cottage cheese mooshed with soft poached eggs on toast; I use pitchers of orange juice and water plus jars of jelly to erect a visual barrier between us!

The ship has enough trouble of her own—the second mate called the captain at 0545 to tell her they've finally resorted to steering by the magnetic compass, the only one they trust. And the U.S. Coast Guard may not let the ship dock in New York without first fixing the gyro.

Despite the swells and force six winds today, we're doing 16.7 knots, about 0.3 better than Debbie expected. When we get into the Gulf Stream, we'll have 0.7 knot against us, and closer to Nantucket it will increase to a knot.

As we walk this afternoon, the swells seem to be building to a good roller coaster ride. We check out the wire, lines, and winches on the bow, and each lap around the captain picks up trash. "The Mahoney gang (the longshoremen in Alexandria) used to say, 'She wants the ship as clean as her house,'" Debbie laughs, as she talks about the time when she cleaned out the hatches as chief mate on the *Marjorie Lykes.*

Finally, a few minutes on the computer before cocktails with mozzarella and olives, a losing game of cribbage, dinner and a movie, vanilla gelato with the last of the Haifa strawberries, and sleep.

Friday, 4 March

It's gray this morning, but warm and no rain. Virginia, on the other hand, is still under a state of emergency, according to this morning's news. Too much rain again, and power outages. Snow is expected on the back side of the rainstorm. Here swells are smaller and no wind to speak of; the ship is doing eighteen knots. And the weather forecast is for no westerlies all the way back. ETA New York: 1800 on March 10. Unbelievable.

The only way to tell it's Friday here is the menu. Fish, fish, and more fish! I have kippers for breakfast—the steward tells the captain I can have all I want—no other takers. It's Debbie's turn to put up the barricade today. At coffee on the bridge (peanut butter cookies and the last of the Naples pastries), today's lesson is on filling out the weather report that NOAA depends on. It is recorded every six hours—every three hours during severe or unusual weather—and sent whenever the radio operator is on duty, so it's not sent at night.

By lunchtime, the temperature is sixty-one degrees under a bright, sunny sky. Another good day for a barbecue—grilled chicken and baked potatoes tonight. After a quick nap, time to walk. Wind is picking up a bit, and it takes a lot of stamina to get around the bow four times against it. Today the ABs are noisily scaling the deck— then it will be repainted, good for a couple of years if done right. The boatswain is "lamping up"—outside lights are shining here and there on the main deck, so he can see which ones are burned out, and replace them.

We work a while, then knock off for cocktails and cribbage. I win. After dinner we start watching a video, play a cribbage marathon with Amy and Don and lose big, watch a bit more, then head for the bridge to see Santa Maria pass about five miles off our port side. We're sailing north of the island, but the light at Castelo on the south side is so strong and the configuration of the island such that we can see it for a long time before it's obscured. So much for the Azores. Finally, after midnight we watch the last of the movie, retard clocks and retire. Ha. The weather gods know, and that's when the rolling and pitching increase. Not much sleep tonight.

Saturday, 5 March

The gyro's working! We've pitched and rolled and the gyro repeaters are following along. Who knows why. The system was shut down yesterday, though, then restarted. In the meantime, we're sitting in nice sunshine.

Write a while, then it's time for coffee (pecan cookies) on the bridge, discussion about the fact that John Candy died, and a quick glimpse of pilot whales, hard to spot among the swells today. Bob saw porpoises earlier. It's sixty-one again—no complaints. Write some more, lunch, and sleep just a minute or two—I can see why Debbie returns from back-to-back voyages exhausted. Shortwave radio, then we walk, a mile and a quarter through the course—it's easier to climb steps when the ship is rising than when it's falling—about 1,400 steps to a mile. More work, then cribbage (I win one and lose one). Gin and beer and mozzarella and olives, prosciutto and Swiss cheese sandwiches, and lots of chocolate ice cream instead of red beans and rice in the saloon. Good choice. Then we watch, or doze through tonight's movie. Lack of sleep is definitely taking its toll.

Sunday, 6 March

The days are going much too fast! Wake up early today, to gray skies, and laze in bed with a book. Breakfast, "Car Talk" on National Public Radio, and writing. The sky is brightening and there's not much swell, but there are whitecaps, so the wind must be picking up.

Coffee (oatmeal cookies), lunch, work, walk. A highlight of the day: take pictures for the book. It's a good excuse to talk to everybody. We only miss taking pictures on the bow—too windy. But we manage to take them in the engine room next to the pistons, testing gear in the steering gear room, even down three ladders into the stabilizer room; even snap Bob at the last slop chest for Voyage 87. Very hot and humid today, going through the Gulf Stream, and we're warm and soaking wet before we're through.

T-bone steaks are on the menu, and after much discussion and negotiating, the steward has given Debbie one box, eleven steaks, to grill outside. We take them out there to cook at 1630, only to find the steaks are still frozen. Never mind. We sip wine and wait for them to thaw some on top of aluminum foil placed on the lid. It's no wonder the winch still isn't fixed—first things first. Make the basketball hoop, then the grill and a stand for it . . . As we stand by the barbecue, even the chief engineer talks to me, about the captain and the book, for the first time since Norfolk. Stu, an engineer shipping out since 1982, talks about his family—father and grandfather both went to sea, and he's the only one in his family to carry on the tradition. His brother's a computer type, into laser lighting in Austin, and at some point Stu may opt for that, but not yet. He and John, both married, like to cook, even when they're home. Steaks are wonderful. Then cribbage (I win two), movie, and biscotti and lemon gelato from Livorno.

Retard clocks, and after reading a bit of *Going After Cacciato,* about 2230, try to sleep. But it's like riding a roller coaster in the dark, very exciting but disorienting. Finally turn the light back on about 0030 and read. Things keep going bump in the night, and finally, just after 0600, I give up and get up.

11. The Best View of Alexandria, Egypt, Is Over the Stern

*W*hen I left Exxon and coastwise sailing in favor of breakbulk shipping and foreign ports, I began an odyssey through some of the best and some of the worst. The routine voyages seem to blend together, leaving general impressions of times and places. For one reason or another, some stand out. Some of my most memorable trips were on the *Marjorie Lykes.* Just after we were married, in 1979, Jack was permanently assigned to the *Marjorie* to clean her up. Except for one trip on the *Ruth* in 1985, he remained on the *Marjorie* until 1987; then he was permanently assigned to the *Howell Lykes* as captain until he laid her up the end of 1992. He laid up the *Mason Lykes* next, made his last voyage on the *Marjorie* in August 1993, and retired in 1994.

The adventures on the *Marjorie* began at the end of 1979 when I was second mate; Jack had just been reinstated as captain after our union troubles, and Mark Robinson was chief mate. It was the first of two trips back-to-back, and we were running from the Great Lakes to the Med, with cadets on board. We called in Morocco, Algeria, Tunisia, Egypt, and Italy and headed for home.

Mark knew about a tradition of having a goat barbecue on board, so in every North African port, he sent the cadets on a goat hunt. They returned empty-handed—until Alexandria. We were there about ten days, and one day they brought a black-and-white billy goat up the gangway, tethering him on deck under an awning. It was the deck cadet's job to care for him, wash and feed him. The deck cadet even named him—Robinson. It's three days from Alex to Italy, and we couldn't dock with a goat on board. So the chief engineer borrowed my rigger's knife and did him in, and we had our barbecue. It was very good. The deck cadet cried.

• • •

On the second trip, heading east, we picked up loads of bagged flour from Chicago, Milwaukee, and Green Bay, then spent the week before Thanksgiving in the small port of Buffalo, New York. There we were loading 260 six-cylinder Dodge trucks, all light blue with the Jimmy Carter handshake on the doors, to give to the Egyptian government. To satisfy the bill of lading, they had to be aboard by midnight on a particular date. We had no time to put them where they needed to be, lashed down or secured. We just put trucks everywhere. Next day we went back and off-loaded them, then reloaded them where they belonged.

Loading was not without mishap. The number five hatch was the only one without hydraulic tween deck hatch covers. That meant we had to put steel beams across the open hatch and cover it with pontoon deck covers. We loaded the lower hold with trucks, then started beaming up. But the longshoremen were not used to this. The sling for the beam was not rigged correctly and, as they were straddling the hatch, they dropped the beam right smack down the middle of one truck. That popped the doors out, the windshield and back window out, and put a crease down the top. We left the truck there, put the pontoons in, and finished loading.

The weather was quite severe, and we waited a week in Lake Erie for transit through the Welland Canal; because the canal closes 15 December, the grain ships had priority so they could still make another run. The weather was so rough we couldn't hold anchor, so we were basically steaming back and forth. En route to the Med, again we encountered severe weather, which took its toll on the trucks parked on the fantail on deck. Heavy quartering seas took the tires off the hubs, bent the frames, left fenders perpendicular to truck bodies.

When we reached Alexandria, Egypt, those trucks were a sad sight. Then the Egyptians started off-loading them. Because the spreaders on the sling for off-loading the vehicles were too narrow, when the sling picked up a truck it began to bend in the fenders. The chief mate, Mark Robinson, stopped the off-loading. He wrote a letter asking the Egyptians to accept responsibility for any damage to the trucks that was due to their use of an improper sling. They did. But what chaos: collisions with the trucks on the dock, dropping containers on top of them. The longshoremen would finish work, and a bunch of them would just drive off in a truck!

I like to remember Alexandria for the Khadoura, one of the best restaurants in the world, and not the other Alex, which is poor, dirty, noisy, hot, with congested harbor and congested port—and horrendous winter storms.

The worst time we ever had there was that second trip. First we discharged the trucks. Then we shifted the ship to the flour docks, which were 385 feet long. The ship, 595 feet long and docked starboard side to, overhung the dock by 217 feet, so the two aftermost hatches were not alongside the dock. We had to work hatches one, two, three, and four, then turn the ship around and work the other two. Because of this configuration, plus the lack of bollards on the dock to accept mooring lines, we had to drop our offshore port anchor to assist in docking and to act as the forward spring line. The stern lines became after spring lines because they were leading forward instead of aft. For stern lines we ran lines out through a midship chock to the aftermost bollard on the dock. Across the dock was a Russian ship we befriended; across the slip opposite us, the Greek ship *Fanis.*

When a low hits the eastern Mediterranean, it just hangs there. The harbors close. Nobody sails in or out. One night a terrific winter storm went through. During the worst part of it, ships were dragging their anchors in the inner harbor, with sparks flying as they hit each other. You could hear calls on the VHF radio for pilots and tugs for assistance.

The stern end of the ship is always the most vulnerable, because the propeller and rudder are there. That's why in maneuvering, you always turn the bow toward the danger. In the best of times there, the harbor is so congested that barges for off-loading ships were always hanging around the stern, hitting the rudder, prompting us to rig up a fire hose and spray them with water to push them away.

The *Marjorie* had seventeen mooring lines out, probably every line we had. Eight is the minimum, ten usual. Jack ordered twenty to forty RPM (dead slow to slow ahead—sea speed is about eighty-seven RPM) on the engines all night just to keep us there. It's highly unusual to do that—in fact, that's usually the last thing you do. The movement of the ship from the storm surge kept chafing the lines and parting them throughout the night, with the crew resplicing them on the spot. Because the ship ran the Great Lakes, on either side of the hull at different levels were welded about four steel pieces, each about fifty feet long, to act as fenders for tying up in the locks. So each time the ship drifted in against the dock and back out, those fenders slipped underneath the dock and lifted the concrete. When the storm was over, the port of Alexandria hit us up for dock damage, but didn't hit up the Russian ship, with an armed guard at its gangway, for anything!

In order for us to turn the *Marjorie* to work the last two hatches, we had to wait for the *Fanis* to sail and clear us. The *Fanis* had her starboard anchor down, with the tug *Zamzam* tied to the stern to assist in the undocking. And the wind was a problem, blowing on the port bow. She was going full astern and the tug was hauling her out full bore, when the wind caught her and blew her down on us. Before she could haul up her anchor, it caught on our port anchor chain. First her bow hit us on the port quarter, then came around and hit us on the starboard quarter. Because we had steam on the engine in preparation to shift the ship, the propeller shaft was slowly turning. (Once the engine is hot, the shaft must turn or it will warp due to uneven heat.) When it was over, we had five turns of her anchor chain around our propeller. Jack sent Mark to the *Fanis* with a letter of responsibility, which covers damage to the vessel and also delay in any cargo operations. Mark climbed the pilot ladder to go to the Greek captain with the letter and reached the captain's office, only to find the Egyptian pilot and the Greek captain going over the bell book. It appeared they were trying to correct the bell book to show there were no full astern bells, turning aside the captain's responsibility.

Mark returned, and for the next two days Egyptian divers were in that disgusting, polluted water cutting those five turns of anchor chain from around our prop with an underwater torch, doing the whole operation from the *Marjorie*. The trick was to cut only their chain, not ours. I will never forget that when they got it untangled, the Greek who had to climb over the side in a boatswain's chair and reattach their anchor chain was the captain. We felt sorry for him.

Because the prop on the *Marjorie* had been turning as the anchor chain rolled on, it sustained very minor damage. But the authorities put the Greek ship at anchor in the inner harbor. In a turnabout, a week after the accident the Greek captain tried to come aboard with *his* letter of responsibility. He was met by Jack, who read it to find out who owned the *Fanis* and handed it back, but wouldn't let him come aboard.

Eventually the case wound up in litigation in court in the United Kingdom. It was the worst accident I ever experienced in Egypt.

The best view of Alexandria is over the stern heading for the next port.

In 1980, I was second mate during a six-month run on the *Jean Lykes,* a sister ship to the *Marjorie*—two of five ships on the Great Lakes to the Mediterannean run. The captain was Robert Kay, whose main interest was taking care of the passengers. A Kings Point grad and captain in the U.S. Naval Reserve, he was a very large man. He liked to wear his old uniforms, and the front of his shirt didn't quite meet as he sat at the captain's table with the passengers as his guests. Leftovers and dirty plates were always sitting around his office. I have never seen so many roaches on a ship. We caught thirty-five rats in number five hatch alone. It was a filthy ship.

We started the run in Milwaukee. On Labor Day, a pilot was taking us through the St. Clair River, which leads to the Detroit River, between Lake Huron and Lake Erie. Because we were short a third mate until we reached Detroit, I was temporarily standing the midnight-to-four watch and, on my way to the bridge, ran into Captain Kay in the pantry.

"The crazy pilot just sunk a boat," he said.

"Did what?"

"We just sunk a boat," he repeated.

Sure enough, the pilot was on the VHF radio with the Coast Guard reporting the incident. The boat had been anchored smack dab in the middle of the channel, with no lights on and a father and son aboard, drunk. Because it was Labor Day night, boats were everywhere. Our lookout had reported something, but nobody could see the boat, which we hit. The boat sank. The Coast Guard picked up the two occupants, who survived. Next day the headlines of the local paper said a Lykes ship had sunk a boat anchored sixty feet off the beach. That's impossible. Sixty feet offshore it's eleven feet deep, and our draft was twenty-five. Small-boat owners either don't know or ignore the fact that, because the ship is confined to the deep-draft channel, she has the right-of-way. Besides, the ship can't swerve around a small craft—even if we can see it—without the danger of going aground.

A year later the father filed suit against Lykes for everything from loss of the boat to reinjuring his back and nightmares about a big, black bow bearing down on him. Lykes was exonerated.

• • •

That trip was the first stop for all of us, ship and crew, at Assab, Ethiopia, at the mouth of the Red Sea. Russian ships called there, and I think the flour off-loaded from us was taken over to the Russian ships on the other side of the harbor.

As captain of the first Lykes ship there, one of Captain Kay's jobs was to write a port information report about what he found—water depths, gratuities expected, stevedores, required paperwork, all that stuff. It's supposed to augment the Entry to Port Guide, an international publication on all ships. Captain Kay's report was to be sent to the office, and in turn made available to each Lykes ship calling there. It's the captain's thing to do, but he made me write it, so I put in overtime for doing it. I wasn't asked again.

Assab was a most unfavorite port. The air is hot, and the sea temperature is so hot you have to wear gloves or burn your hands on the handrails in the engine room. It must have been 120 degrees in the engine room. In fact, that was the only trip I was so hot I wore a skirt to the bridge for watch.

There was nothing to see, it was filthy, and the flies were horrendous. I think I had one beer the whole ten days we were there. When you opened one, you had to keep your hand over the top of the bottle or it would be full of flies. I lost my appetite, and lost twenty pounds.

For me it was a tough time anyway. Jack was on the same run, but at the opposite end of the world.

After the *Jean Lykes,* I made trips on the *Solon Turman* from the Gulf of Mexico to the Mediterranean, and Jack and I finally found time in 1980 to take a honeymoon, driving to Mexico. I finally landed a permanent job, which lasted only three months until I lost it for lack of union seniority because so many ships were being laid up and crew laid off. Other tours on other ships followed until 1983, when I got a forced "vacation." Jack and I hadn't spent time together for ages, and I refused a job as chief mate on the *Ashley* so I could see Jack. As punishment, Captain Manchester wouldn't give me another job for eleven months. I was figuratively and literally on the beach during that time. We were living in Cape Cod, and I spent most of the eleven months there. But I was still on Lykes's select list—chief mates who worked only for Lykes—so when shipping got busy, he called me. He knew he had to keep pushing me, too, because I was Lykes's token woman.

I remember another trip on the *Marjorie,* chiefly because we carried a Brahman bull.

I was chief mate this trip, about 1984; third mate was Walter Graf, a Kings Point grad, a good mate and good friend I still hear from today. Walter was really good with the passengers. He even talked two couples from Seattle who were traveling together into painting the picnic table—with a fancy blue "L" for Lykes on top and candy-striped stanchions.

We were sailing foreign from New Orleans, but the bull was loaded in Houston first. They brought him in a truck, along with a wooden pen to put him in. It was boarded solid on the back, with planked sides. It had no door. They just nailed it up after they got him in it. Then they lifted him in the pen onto the ship. At first he didn't want to walk down the ramp from the truck into the pen, but had to be prodded. Once he was on the ship, he was fine.

The bull had to be tended to daily, given water, feed, and clean, dry hay. I thought it would be a problem having him there, but it wasn't. A lot of feed and hay were aboard but no vet, so the boatswain and the day man took care of him. The day man was the boatswain's right-hand man then—it's a rating that's since been done away with. In this case the day man was Clifford Dixon, the brother of the boatswain, Rudy. They're Hondurans, who, I think, make the best sailors because going to sea is in their tradition.

We'd secured the bull, which we nicknamed Ferdinand, out on deck on the port side of number six hatch. He was sitting so he faced across the hatch. Several days into the trip, going through the Caribbean, we got tangled up in some nasty weather. About 1600 one afternoon, over the port quarter we took a pretty good sea that stove in the forward part of the pen. We cleared out all of the broken boards and put up a tarp to protect Ferdinand from the sea for the night. The next morning we moved him on top of number six hatch for the rest of the trip.

After we off-loaded the bull in Capetown, he was taken by train to a farm where he was quarantined for thirty days before he could be used for breeding.

That same trip, Jack followed his usual routine of going to the bridge to act as lookout while the second mate took morning and evening stars. On the horizon to port, Jack noticed what looked like a handkerchief. Taking up the binoculars, he made out a small boat with a makeshift sail. Immediately he changed course and steamed toward her. The boat was an eighteen-foot dugout with an outboard engine. The three men aboard said they needed assistance. Jack turned the ship around, ordered the engineers to slow down, and got the men onto the *Marjorie.*

One was naked, the other two in rags. Their bodies were covered with saltwater ulcers. I was medical officer, and initially I was concerned that they might be pirates, might be armed, whatever. They'd been adrift twenty-two days. They had gone fishing on a Sunday afternoon from St. Lucia in the Grenadines, had gotten stuck in a strong westerly current, and had been unable to restart their engine. They claimed that despite burning their clothes to attract attention, fourteen ships had passed them by. They'd lived off raw fish. When we found them, they had drifted 535 miles west of home.

We were headed toward Trinidad on our way to Capetown to avoid a tropical depression further north, but to drop them off close to home we made for St. Vincent, the first island south of St. Lucia. During the day and a half they were on board, I treated their ulcers. We fed them and took up a collection for them. The oldest was about thirty-five; the younger two, twenty and twenty-two. Neither of them wanted to leave. We'd alerted the port of Kingstown we were coming, and it was a big event to have a ship that size there. I was familiar with the island because I'd been to St. Vincent with my family on our way to visit friends who lived in Bequia, the next island south. But I'd never sailed in on a freighter, and at night. We reached Kingstown just about midnight. The *Marjorie* had no charts for the place, but Jack got us in there just long enough to greet the officials and off-load the three fishermen into the customs launch. They were gone within twenty minutes—on a banana boat back to St. Lucia—and so were we. For rescuing them, Jack should have received the AOTOS Honored Seamen Award, but he didn't.

It was up to his boss, Captain Manchester, to propose it. But Captain Manchester explained away his negligence: "Aw, Jack, I forgot about it."

From New Orleans to Capetown takes eighteen days, and it wasn't the bull so much as the second electrician who provided the excitement on the crossing. Harry had been on the ship for a while before he came to me as the medical officer and told me he was bleeding rectally.

"Are you drinking?" I asked. Emphatic no.

We had twenty-four-hour contact with medical advisory state-side, and Harry wasn't getting any better, so we finally decided we had to land him. We considered Ascension Island, but there was no way to lift him off of there if he needed more help than Ascension could offer, so we continued east to the next closest place with better medical facilities, the island of St. Helena in the middle of the South Atlantic. That was a day and a half further. We arrived in the middle of the night, and again it was a big event bringing a 595-foot ship in there. I'd talked to the doctors on St. Helena on the single sideband radio while we were a day out, and they also asked me if Harry drank. No.

We had no charts. Jack was on the VHF radio with the harbor master, who was talking us in. I was on the bow ready to drop the anchor. Looking around, I could see we were really getting in among small boats, and I got concerned about going aground. So Jack backed that sucker out into deeper water, and I dropped the hook. The officials all wanted to come aboard, and they were in Jack's office while I took the doctor to see Harry.

"Do you drink, Harry?" he asked.

"Um, a little."

"What's that?"

"Only about six ounces of vodka a day."

They took him to the hospital, and after two weeks he sailed to Capetown in order to fly back to the States. When we reached the States, Harry climbed back on board and returned to his permanent job.

In 1986, I served a full tour of 180 days as chief mate on the *Louise Lykes,* a Clipper class ship—535 feet long with six hatches. Built as a breakbulk ship, she had a jumbo eighty-eight-ton staulken boom, which can work two hatches, flipping from number two to number three hatch. Each of the other hatches had four twenty-ton booms. The ship was automated and nicely laid out, and when not under charter she carried only four passengers. I sailed three voyages on MSC charter from the West Coast. The ship started in Oakland, called at Port Hueneme and San Diego, then sailed to Pearl Harbor, Midway Island, and (usually) three ports in Japan; Naha, Okinawa; Pusan, Korea; Subic Bay, the Philippine Islands; Guam; Pearl Harbor; along the West Coast to San Diego, Port Hueneme, Tacoma, and back to Oakland in about forty-five days. Those were the days before we were reduced to three-mate ships, so the chief mate was still a day worker, and because it was a military charter, in all ports we only worked 0800 to 1700. So I could play after 1700.

In Pusan, the first assistant engineer took me to the Texas Bar to show me Texas Street, the red-light district. He also wanted to see his girlfriend, which he did. Unfortunately for me, the girls were all over me, too. I even was propositioned by one. That was too much. My last words were, "Get me out of here," as I fled.

The ship was carrying sixty-foot creosoted pilings, landing craft, helicopters, containers for the military. And soda, made from guava and papaya, that had been in Rota, Spain. The soda had not been used by the military, so it was shipped back to the States from Spain. We were taking it on to Japan. The *Louise* began to roll quite a bit with quartering seas, and that stuff was just stacked below, pallet on top of pallet on top of pallet. When we started rolling, the aluminum cans started shifting and collapsing, and we had sticky, sweet-smelling soda all over that hatch. At Midway we stuffed what wasn't ruined in an empty twenty-foot container. I found it totally typical of dealing with the U.S. government—you feel like your effort is wasted.

In working for the military, nobody cares about maintaining a schedule—there's no push to get cargo on or off, to follow set schedules in bad weather. It is extremely lucrative—remember when the U.S. military chartered the *Lyra,* it paid Lykes $35,000 per diem plus fuel. Many charters pay 10 percent over cost. When the *Lyra* was under charter from 1981 to 1986 in Diego Garcia, it was a very bad time financially for Lykes, and that charter carried Lykes through.

Midway was fun, though. The channel is narrow coming in between the reefs. The dock is only a thousand feet from the beach, providing opportunity for a quick swim during coffee time. And the island is covered with gooney birds, a black-footed variety of albatross, on the nine-hole, par-three golf course—everywhere. They have to pick up the birds and get them off the runways before planes come in. A lot of chicks don't survive.

The nature of the merchant marine means we're always on the move, from ship to ship, port to port, memories of crews and voyages running together after a while. But the strong impressions of ports and peoples remain.

Like Alexandria, Tamatave, Madagascar, is also on my less-than-favorite list. Dar es Salaam, Tanzania, where I spent thirty days discharging rice, is another. East Africa is so poor, and like Assab, Ethiopia, or Tamatave, all of the poorest ports were the most trouble; conditions were so miserable for working. Every day brought problems, and it's unpleasant dealing with them.

One time when Jack captained a ship into Assab, two of his three cadets spent a night in jail for stealing an Ethiopian flag from a government building. The police chief prevented Jack from sailing until he paid their fines. When he visited the cadets in jail, each cried, "Get me out. There are rats in here." When they returned to the States, the fines were deducted from their wages and they were expelled from their respective schools.

Arzew, Algeria, was the worst in the world. It was filthy. We only went ashore one day. Algiers was scary because of customs. The customs people would come aboard the ship whenever they wanted, tear through everybody's gear, count cigarettes one day, come back and recount the next, just harassing you. Everybody hated to go there because of customs problems.

Working on the northern Europe run brought its own concerns. Bremerhaven was easier to get into, for instance, than Antwerp, nine hours' run up the Shielde River. In Felixstowe, we always had a problem with British customs over bringing in pornographic material. Besides, the British pilots weren't the best, and the longshoremen walked off the job if the mate said a bad word to them. Rotterdam is a busy, modern port, and it's fun to ride a bike there from the ship to local restaurants.

In the Med, Izmir could be a difficult port to sail because of fishing traffic, and high winds in summer. Haifa was the easiest port to sail into—a half mile from where you take arrival and you're there—and it had phenomenal tugs and excellent pilots. But in winter it is exposed to storms and surge. And Italy—Livorno was easy sailing except during rough weather. Then it's difficult. Anchoring was difficult at Naples because the harbor is so deep. Alexandria was tough: the ship usually couldn't pick up a landmark, and the navigational aids were not there. Piraeus, Greece, was hard to get into and out of, and a hard spot to anchor because the water is so deep.

My perspective of the Far East is different, because I never sailed there as captain. As chief mate, I was working cargo around the clock and I almost never got off the ship. But the experience left me with very different impressions of the work ethic country to country.

I particularly liked the people I worked with in the Philippine Islands: The Filipino workers had nothing and were anxious to work just to get to the next step. We had a good relationship with the dock workers there, and they went out of their way to help me. I met one gentleman in Subic who must have had a zillion kids. He'd bring pictures of his kids to show me, bring me lace. In return I brought him Hush Puppies and cigarettes.

You can't beat Japan. Japanese customs people were nice. And it's clean. The docks were clean—the stevedores swept the docks and the ship. The stevedores were in uniform and could teach everybody about line handling. I always remember them playing ball on the dock at lunch. The ports where we called—Yokohama, Kobe, Kudamatsu—are all very busy waters; being an island country, Japan has a lot of water traffic. I admire the fact that they do so much with so little, every single inch is used. It seemed very safe; in Kobe they didn't even lock up things.

In contrast, in Indonesia I was afraid. Our agents, old Lykes people, were very good there. But I never left the ship because the longshoremen had a reputation for harming chief mates or crew from ships. As chief mate, you're always walking through the ship alone, checking cargo, checking for stowaways, but not there. I always made sure I had someone with me.

I liked shipping into some U.S. ports better than others. I liked the Great Lakes in summertime. East Coast ports were better than Gulf ports, with their mosquitoes and oil rigs to dodge. The approach to Ambrose Light, outside New York City, with three lanes leading into the pilot boarding area, could be confusing. Charleston, South Carolina, had an easy approach; Norfolk was not bad but not as easy. The Mississippi River was not easy because of fog and the oil rigs—in Houston and Galveston, particularly, the sea buoys are overshadowed by the myriad of other lights and lots of fog. San Francisco, too, could be difficult due to fog, and quite a bit of traffic, which is extremely controlled through lanes. I've been into Long Beach on a containership, and there's not much to that. San Diego also was not very difficult. Puget Sound was easy just because there is so much water and so much area.

Get to know any port, and it's easy.

Landlubber's Log
7–12 March 1994

Monday, 7 March

Debbie says this is moderate weather—which gives the passenger an inkling of what heavy weather is like. We're down to fourteen knots, due to swell and wind. To be expected.

After breakfast, get pictures of Milton in the pantry and the steward in the galley, then work. At coffee, chart the weather on the map with the yellow grease pencil.

You can tell the voyage is nearing an end. With the dawning of Monday morning, it's definitely a work day—reports to complete, money to give and get. The captain is walking around again with record books and pouches full of greenbacks. Not everyone will get an advance until we arrive in New York—the captain has had to order more money. Crew can be paid by cash or by check at payoff in Galveston, but not both, so those who want some of each must take cash as a draw before we reach New York.

After lunch and work, it's time to walk—too windy after a half around outside, and we opt for the tunnel and, of course, a lesson in the piping system. In case anyone ever asks, the ballast pipes are the lowest, those carrying fuel above them. Everywhere are sounding tanks—green for ballast, the international color, and usually black for fuel. Even if they aren't painted that color, they eventually become black! We even crawl back into the opening to the pump room, which is down several ladders, the last being vertical, and I take the captain's word in the pitching weather that the pump room is still there. Only see one ship, her booms for working cargo visible, about 1600. A welcome hour to read before cocktails. Cribbage—I get beaten two of three—and the last of the mozzarella, dinner, and a double feature with chocolate and vanilla gelato from Livorno. Retard clocks, and to bed. The swell has subsided dramatically, which means a good night for sleeping.

Tuesday, 8 March

Wake early, before 0600, to a bright, sunny sky and smoother seas. We're doing 16.4, but the water temperature has changed, first cooler, then warmer because we're in an eddy. Certainly the air temp has dropped—no blankets two nights ago, last night three blankets, and glad for them. See one red fishing buoy out the port side. Laundry before breakfast, and work after it—then coffee (peanut butter) on the bridge and last boat drill at 1030. It's up to me to chart the weather again today.

Work, then lunch, teach Debbie to play Tetris on the Mac, walk the slalom and giant slalom/obstacle course; more buoys. At fifty-eight degrees in bright sunshine, it's sweatshirt weather outside, with strong whiffs of exotic spices from a container as we round a bend in the course. High cirrus clouds—the captain says that means in twenty-four hours the next low pressure system will be here.

More work, then cribbage (I lose again), cocktails and a lovely barbecue of hot dogs and hamburgers aft. Call home on the ham radio, thanks to Steve. We give Amy and Don a cribbage rematch, and lose big-time, again.

Wednesday, 9 March

Gray today, with sprinkles off and on. We're doing poor speed—twelve knots with the wind against us. Then, whoosh, a front comes through about 1130, and suddenly the wind is behind us and our speed shoots back up. We're plowing through the Gulf Stream, so it's warm and muggy. Water temp is seventy-two. Coffee on the bridge (pecan), chart the weather, and talk about the Buys Ballot law of how to figure where a low is located—in the northern hemisphere, find the wind, go 120 degrees to the right, and there it is.

After a quick, early lunch, in quick succession: telephone and Tetris, nap, walk, and take water pictures. It may be the last chance for photography outside, because tomorrow afternoon we anticipate force nine winds. And just in time to get into New York—ETA: 2200, 10 March. Maybe. We can't dock from 2400 until 0600. We anticipate receiving a message to delay arrival until 0300.

Coffee and work, then cocktails, cribbage (3–2, in my favor), and dinner. We throw over the last wine bottle, noting that instead of a dull splat, it sounds more like a crack when it hits, but it's dark so we don't know what happened to it. At 2000 we climb up to the mellow darkness of the bridge.

In conversation, I comment that most people are referred to by their title on the ship, and that no one calls the captain anything but captain.

"They'd better not," she answers.

Retard clocks for the last time, and to sleep.

Thursday, 10 March

After a lulling night, we wake this morning before 0600 to building seas and wind. Then the ship lists to port for a long time, maybe fifteen minutes, and the sun is moving by. What's up? After reading for a bit, I get up and the captain explains the mystery. Just before 0700 the ship did a round turn, just to make sure the gyro repeaters would follow. They did.

After breakfast, some work. Don decides today is his day to learn to play Tetris, and with my encouragement, he comes to my "office" to play on the computer. Then coffee (chocolate chip) on the bridge. The weather plot shows the deepest low is right smack dab over New York, right where we're heading, and the barograph is nose-diving. We've slowed the RPM to one hundred for timely arrival when the chief reminds the captain that slowing down is what makes the number eight piston leak, so the alternate plan is to keep steaming, then begin to drift without engine at 1700 for about five hours or maybe fifteen miles, either before or after we take arrival at 0300. I finally get to blow the horn on the bridge wing at coffee, even though we don't need it. No big deal.

After lunch we check the bridge to find wind and seas are both coming up, when right through them swim some porpoises. Beautiful. Nap, and wake to find rain and zero visibility and, reassuringly, the sound of the foghorn every few minutes, when we certainly do need it. Even with land not far off, the problems the captain has to deal with continue—there's ballast water everywhere it shouldn't be, and she's got the chief pumping to get rid of what he can before New York so the ship won't be over her marks.

I work, the captain works, and we finally break about 1700 for cocktails and cribbage (we split two games), then dinner. Time for paperwork, including arrival-dating reams of reports and documents. At 1830 the captain stops the ship, to drift, for five hours. It's a very weird feeling to be on a dead ship drifting in the Atlantic. Lights are turned on outside on the hull, including two red-over-red ones above the flying bridge that let other vessels know the ship is not under command, or cannot maneuver. We sleep quickly, and about 0230 my door opens.

Friday, 11 March

"We're just about to pick up the pilot," Debbie says on her way by.

I jump out of bed and throw on my clothes, grab coffee cup, granola bars, binocs and flashlight, and head for the bridge. About 0300 we take arrival at Ambrose Light, the center of a seven-mile circle where the traffic lanes for ships going into New York converge. In spite of slowing for twenty-five hours and thirty minutes, including stopping for five hours and eighteen minutes, the *Charlotte* averages 16.53 knots in ten days, fifteen hours, twenty-four minutes, the fastest westbound crossing since the vessel has been on the Med run.

The pilot—again Brian Mercereau—is aboard, with a *New York Times* and lots of conversation. We hear firsthand about the awful winter weather New York has had in our absence. It's beautiful tonight, all glittery and bright, including the symbolic Statue of Liberty. The dredge once again has promised to be farther out of the channel than it is, but we make our way around it anyway. The channel looks familiar, after traversing it twice before.

Docking master is Simon—again—and cordial greetings are exchanged.

The sky lightens, and about 0630 we're literally inches from tying up at Berth 80, Maher Terminal (we're the inaugural Lykes Lines vessel at this new berth), when someone from the harbormaster's office comes running out to the dock, waving his arms: "No, you can't dock starboard side to."

Never has this happened before, ever. We're told, with lines ready fore and aft, to take the ship out again and turn her around to dock port side to. Tugs are still fast fore and aft. Then, no, orders are to dock starboard side to for repairs. Finally, as the sea pilot reads the *Times* opened onto the chart table, and jokes that it's a good thing the ship only has four sides, it's agreed that it will be starboard side to. The strong northwest winds we'd anticipated never arrived as the ship made her way toward New York, but are apparent as we're trying to dock, with the tug holding us fast at the stern end as we put out lines as quickly as possible. About 0700, we're tied up three and one each end.

Then the immigration officer is aboard; she needs to see the passenger and compare her with her passport, then each seaman and his or her Z card in the officer's lounge. Customs man peruses each slip, filled out previously, and needs to see two crew members so they can verbally confirm where purchases were made. The customs official says only the cases of wine are subject to duty, but in this case he'll overlook it. George Rolando, the agent with U.S. Navigation, is aboard next, with a box of doughnuts. He says that, in fact, the one-way loading pattern on the dock makes it much quicker to load the ship if it docks port side to. In this case, we docked the other side to so the lifeboat motor could be worked on (even though the motor wasn't going to be worked on, and the Coast Guard did not want to come inspect it even if it were fixed). The captain warns that on the return trip in ten days that may be the case.

Finally we have a quick bite of breakfast, and Milton, the crew messman, tells the captain he's decided he's tired of being picked on by the steward, who's known him since he was two; tired of being called "Roscoe" and stupid, and has decided to get off in Norfolk where his girlfriend lives. The captain says she'll change the paperwork, and does he want a draw so he'll have enough until his paycheck comes through? Then George is back to take us to the agent's office, where the captain makes the rounds in New Orleans via phone. It's 1000, then 1100, then 1200, then 1300, and finally about 1350 we grab another ride back to the ship. Much of the conversation is about repairs not done; the fact that the money for draws came half in fifties, the rest in loose twenties, not all in fifties as requested; some personnel consultations; making sure the schedule is accurate for payoff on Thursday, the 17th; conversation with the other permanent captain, Karl Fanning, at his ranch in Colorado so he's aware of the schedule.

Arriving back, we grab sandwiches from a lunch wagon on the dock, then head for the captain's office. We come across a crewman who was told his father passed away while we were at sea and wants to get off for vacation in Galveston. The captain says she'll change the paperwork, making sure his replacement is ordered. The second mate's wife is aboard, and there's lots of visiting—will he get off and try to sail chief mate this summer, or stay on? He puts his guitar and stuff in her car, contends with the jitters that the prospect of a new job brings, is warned not to explain to any other officers what may be transpiring, only to have Debbie receive a call saying it's not possible, and everything is undone. He's philosophical. He calls New Orleans and is told that Captain Dempsey seldom makes a personnel recommendation—she's not the easiest person to work for—so the office listens very carefully when, as in this case, she does.

Cargo is finished at 1505, earlier than anticipated, including loading only thirty-five empties for Norfolk—everyone thinks the new terminal is trying to make a good impression, but is skeptical about whether it will last. At 1700 we finally eat our sandwiches, awaiting the agent and the paperwork to sail.

Simon the docking master is aboard again, relaxing in the captain's office until it's time. He's had two more ships since he docked us that morning, but we're his last for the day, and then he can go home and have a late dinner with his wife and see his two-year-old son. He likes his job, and the lack of travel is made up for by the closeness to family. It's a trade. His dad was in the business before him, and traveled, but never saw anything except maybe a newsstand.

Finally Troy arrives from the office with the paperwork, talking about his anticipated vacation with his girlfriend and her family in Florida. A last good-bye, and we head for the bridge. There's that sinking feeling when the process of undocking is complete and, with the last line, the captain repeats, "All gone." So is the adventure.

It's just after 2030 when the last lights of New York fade, we're beyond Ambrose Light, and off the quiet of the bridge at night for the last time. Dinner is cheese and goldfish crackers and gin and beer in the captain's office; the passenger falls asleep on the settee, and finally decides to sleep with clothes and with heat (none tonight on the passenger deck), right there.

Saturday, 12 March

About 0100 the phone rings in the captain's office. It's Amy, from the bridge. In switching from one chart to the next, either the course has been drawn wrong or we're ten miles closer to the right coast than we should be. The captain is in her clothes and on the bridge in a flash, walking Amy through the steps. The course just was drawn wrong, but the captain says she doesn't show even an ounce of disgust—she'd always rather be called and not needed, than needed and not called. Back to sleep, and the phone rings the wake-up call at 0500.

Time to pack—frantically—and haul boxes and baggage down four decks to the hospital, where some has been stashed earlier. We run through military traffic on maneuvers, listen to them on the radio, but encounter no problems. At 1000 we take arrival at Norfolk. Then we lose the plant (the engine quits), so the ship does not react to the astern test, just as we reach CBJ—Chesapeake Bay Junction—and the red and green marker that signals the center of the two-mile circle where several traffic lanes converge outside Norfolk. The captain calls the engine room and receives an abrupt "We know!" before the phone goes dead. Momentarily she loses her cool.

She dials the engine room: "You damn well better not hang up on me again!"

Then the problem is fixed, and shortly the pilots are aboard. Two young men, both looking very Virginian in khakis and blue blazers. One of their own is getting married this afternoon, and as soon as they dock the *Charlotte* they're attending the wedding. The *Jean Lykes* is docked just adjacent to our berth, and there's some question whether we'll stay off for twenty minutes or so, letting her leave first, but when we round the bend past the navy ships it's clear the crane is still down, working the ship, and we head for the dock. It's just past 1200, and gangs are ordered for 1300, only four hours' work, with the ship due to sail at 1700.

Between trips hauling stuff off the ship there are hasty good-byes—the second mate has a hug for me at the door to the captain's office, the chief mate a handshake in the corridor; engineers Stu and Russ come by and shake hands, Brendan has a big hug on deck; Mitch, the OS, a cordial good-bye; Amy has a hug on the dock, Janie, the BR, a friendly farewell. The chief engineer, Don Forbes, sees me on the dock and says, "Well, Joanne, had enough of us?" That's about the most he's said and most direct he's been in forty days. Third assistant engineer O'Neill Vanderhorst, many a morning's political analyst at breakfast, says good-bye as we head for the car.

A quick lunch at Uncle Louie's—we've come full circle. Then we part, me to go home and Debbie back to the ship. The *Charlotte* never stops—she's sailing without me, a fact that causes me more than one twinge and tear. I know a second trip won't be the same, but before I'm even back on land, I'm determined to do it again.

Epilogue:
Is There Life After Lykes?

*T*he business of commercial shipping is shrinking. The enormous cost of replacing aging vessels is forcing American shipping companies to request greater subsidies from the government or to try to go "foreign flag" to save money or, if necessary, to sell off aging ships and not replace them. The result is fewer jobs available to merchant seamen. It is a serious concern. Licensed captains like me, sailing on U.S. flagships, owe their jobs to the unions, not the companies for which they work. The unions set the pay scale as well as the working conditions. Salaries are based on the class of ship and the job description, not merit. Even for a captain, it is not a secure working life. For security I must work twenty years in order to collect my union pension. It's not that I'm unwilling—it's that I could see, before those twenty years are up, there might not be a ship for me.

Tabulations show the 1995 fleet of merchant ships flying the U.S. flag at only 351, compared with 3,644 in 1948. As a result, the Stars and Stripes' share of the world's ocean-shipping trade has dropped to about 4 percent; in 1950, it was 42.6 percent.

And the American merchant marine faces increasing competition from foreign-flag carriers. U.S.-flagged ships cost more to build stateside because our shipyards are no longer subsidized by the federal government, as they are in other countries. More stringent Coast Guard safety rules bump up costs. The Oil Pollution Act of 1990 (OPA 90), for example, now requires double-hulled tankers, obviously more expensive to build.

If U.S. ships are subsidized by the federal government, they cost more to operate because they must have U.S. crews. Wages are part of the higher cost. Some of Lykes's ships, for instance, were more than thirty years old and not automated, so they required twice the crew that the new automated ships do. But insurance is even more significant. The insurance is astronomical because if you have an American citizen aboard when calling in U.S. ports, the ship is subject to laws that protect that one sailor—to the point that, in an extreme case, a lien could be put on the ship. So, to compete, the shipping lines have come to depend on the maritime subsidy program for operating. Even U.S. ships that are now ineligible for federal subsidy satisfy U.S. cargo-preference rules immediately for U.S. military shipments, and after three years of operation, for Agriculture Department food relief shipments. But a central issue is that with drastic reductions in U.S. military shipments, there's not enough government cargo around to support the U.S. merchant marine, so there's no longer an advantage to being a U.S.-flag carrier.

Those subsidies expire in 1997, as construction subsidies for U.S. shipyards did in 1981. So unless federal subsidies are renewed, carriers will re-flag their oceangoing fleets with the flags of convenience—Panama, Liberia, Cyprus, or the Marshall Islands, for instance. That means their crews will be foreign as well.

I'm lucky. The fact that the U.S. merchant marine was under pressure to give greater opportunity to women at a time when I was able to take advantage of that opportunity has meant an exciting and rewarding career, beyond what I ever dreamed possible.

A high point came in May 1994, when I received an honorary degree from Maine Maritime Academy, an award I treasure. I hope the U.S. maritime industry does not decline to the point that the title "captain" becomes only honorific.

I'm not optimistic. I can see the direction the American merchant marine is going: with the new Congress in January 1995 came the disbanding of the House Merchant Marine and Fisheries Committee, the congressional focal point for all maritime issues since 1887. What's left of U.S.-flag commercial shipping is now under the jurisdiction of the House National Security Committee.

At the same time, Lykes's star seemed to be dimming. In 1993, numerous captains as well as other key employees took retirement when a decent package was offered. Other key people were let go in the next two years. And because Lykes was dumping ships and not replacing them, by July 1995 the company was down to a total fleet of fourteen ships.

The Lykes Bros. Steamship Co. began in 1899 with the seven sons of Dr. Howell Tyson Lykes shipping cattle in a wooden schooner from

Florida to Cuba; by the 1950s, with fifty-four ships, Lykes had the largest privately owned American-flag cargo fleet under a single management. In October 1995, the company filed for bankruptcy.

The uncertain future of both the U.S. merchant marine and Lykes, and subsequently of my future with Lykes, forced me to turn in another direction. The tag line at the bottom of a Lykes employee information sheet certainly was clairvoyant: "In the long run, the race belongs not merely to the swift, but to the farseeing, to those who anticipate change."

A marine engineer has a skill that more readily translates to a variety of shoreside jobs, not necessarily in the maritime field. For a deck officer, choices are slimmer. A port captain's job is less than appealing; it's all the drudgery and paperwork combined with long, irregular hours, without the joy of being at sea. The other possibility is a piloting job. Coincidentally, the Columbia River Bar Pilots Association was looking for a woman at the same time I was looking for a secure future in the industry.

I've always wanted to pilot—for masters in my position the natural progression is piloting, handling ships all of the time. Certainly the fun part of being a master on a ship is the ship-handling end of it.

As with any maritime job, you have to go through the steps to be certified. In September 1994, I started working to get a federal license. It required fifteen round trips over the bar, plus passing a grueling two-day written exam.

Once the federal license was in hand, I needed one hundred one-way trips to obtain my state license. I managed to complete the whole process in about two months—by 20 December 1994, to be exact. On 21 December I started work.

It's not a glamorous job; I'm hard put to dress nicely for work. My outfit is a far cry, for instance, from that of the super-proper pilots I've had in Japan, who always came aboard wearing ties, white gloves, and hats. The male pilots can at least wear a tie and cardigan. I wear slacks, dark-colored because I get them dirty climbing the ladder, and usually a turtleneck and a sweater vest. I layer so as to be cool enough in the warmth of the pilot boat and warm enough when I take off my jacket on the bridge of the ship.

In some ways a pilot's job means a more regular life than that of an international captain. There are twenty-two pilots in the association; each is "on the board" twenty-two days and off twenty-two days. It's certainly different from international shipping with its long voyages and exotic ports.

The job of a bar pilot is to bring ships from the Pacific Ocean over a four-mile-wide sandbar across the mouth of the Columbia River. The routine is to board a ship three miles seaward of the bar and pilot it seventeen miles up the river to Astoria, Oregon. The bar pilot, in turn, is relieved by a Columbia River pilot who takes it to Longview, Kalama, or Vancouver, all ports in Washington, or to Portland, about ninety miles.

The channel through which the ships sail is about 1,200 feet wide at the entrance, narrowing down to about 600 feet; the average ship is from 80 to 140 feet wide, and varies in length from 400 to 1,200 feet. The channel goes from 55 to 42 feet deep, so the maximum draft of the ships we handle is 40 feet.

The job requires precision. We're sometimes required to anchor grain or log ships that are waiting for berths or cargo along a two-mile stretch on either side of the channel, but within 0.02 mile outside the channel, when a Panamax grain ship of 738 feet is itself longer than 0.1 mile. It's easy to go aground there, although the bottom is mud and quite forgiving. Current plays a big factor. The ebb current is very strong: average of four knots, as much as seven knots. It's not too bad anchoring on an ebb current, but very tough on a flood current because the ship tends to continue upriver with the current while you are trying to anchor it.

Also, because Astoria itself is a port, maybe once a month bar pilots dock ships there as well. It used to be quite a fishing port, but now it's mostly used as a logging port and an inspection port for U.S. tankers.

A fast transit is about an hour from when I get on inbound at Buoy Two to the Astoria port docks. An hour and a half is average, two hours not unheard-of, if you're fighting a strong ebb current. An anchor job is at least two hours. When you leave the office for an outbound job, one way, and come back in on the pilot boat, you can figure three hours—if you don't have to wait for anyone. If you have an outbound job, followed immediately by an inbound, figure three or four hours. And if you're taking a low-powered log ship out in bad weather, with an ebb current opposing the southwesterly winds and building seas, it can take four hours just to travel three miles. You can be gone up to eight hours, with maybe four of them sitting in the pilot boat. That's a very long time if it's rough water. It'll take a couple days to recover from it.

The weather is the big factor that keeps the Columbia River Bar pilot's job anything but routine. It is considered one of the most dangerous pilotages—if not *the* most dangerous pilotage—in the world. Seas can be forty foot. Yet the bar is closed only five or six days a year; they *think* about closing it when swells exceed twenty feet. And it's not uncommon to have sustained winds of sixty knots. Under those conditions, accidents happen. The last time a pilot was lost there was in 1971. Capt. Bill Quinn was trying to disembark from a ship onto the pilot boat in a pretty good-size swell. The ladder was too long, he wound up in the water, and they couldn't get him out in time. They also had a pilot, Mike Dillon, in the water in February 1994, but he was rescued.

The most difficult part about the job—and what the Columbia River Bar pilots are known for—is getting on and off the pilot boat, the eighty-seven-foot *Peacock,* in rough weather. Built in Germany in 1967, the *Peacock* is a North Sea rescue boat with rounded sides, so she can't go alongside the ships themselves. She's made to be able to turn turtle, which she hasn't, but she has twice turned ninety degrees, flooding the interior. Pilots are transported to the ship on a twenty-three-foot daughter boat launched off the stern of the *Peacock.*

The daughter boat is very light, rising and falling rapidly with the sea condition, which can be at its worst when we're working—twenty-four-foot swells, with sixty-five-knot winds, visibility half a mile, pouring rain. The pilot ladder is made of rope, with two-foot-by-four-inch steps every fourteen inches. It hangs over the side of the ship, like a Jacob's ladder, with spreader bars to keep it from spinning. The trick is to catch the ladder as the daughter boat falls away from the ship, then to scamper up anywhere from six to thirty feet of freeboard as quickly as possible to get aboard. The ladder is rigged so the bottom is one meter from the water. At all costs you hang onto the ladder—even when, sometimes, it drags in the water and you with it, a scary feeling as the water tries to pull it away from the ship.

Disembarking is another story. It's too dangerous to try to climb all the way down the ladder and into the boat—whether it's the daughter boat or the other pilot boat, *Columbia,* a heavy eighty-seven-footer that can come alongside in fair weather—when both the ship and the boat are rolling and rising, six feet, nine feet. You have to use manropes—one or two. A manrope is a manila line three inches in circumference, rigged so it hangs lower than the pilot ladder. Some prefer to use one, some two. You climb down the ladder until you're about six feet above the deck of the pilot boat when she's on top of a swell, then you hang onto the manrope, kick away from the ladder, and slide down the rope onto the deck of the boat.

Helicopters, in use on a trial basis in late 1996, certainly do shorten trips. It remains to be seen whether using a helicopter instead of a pilot boat to embark and disembark pilots will also prove safer under certain weather conditions.

Ship captains and pilots often get involved in an intricate gift-exchange tradition.

Ships I have worked sometimes offer the pilots liquor: Johnnie Walker Red Label Scotch; from a Greek ship, brandy in a fancy bottle; ouzo. Some pilots won't take it, however, because if you get caught by customs, there's a huge fine. Some hide it when they get off the launch boat and, after finishing their paperwork at the office, then take it home.

American cigarettes, of course, are an international commodity. After years of giving out cartons of Marlboros—and heaven help me if I ran out—now as a pilot I get them! I don't smoke, so I pass them on to the launch drivers, who do.

I asked one captain, "How many cartons do you give out going through the Suez Canal?"

"About twenty-five," he said. I had done the same.

Unlike the Japanese pilots, I do not come bearing gifts. The Kobe pilots, for instance, one time brought me a triangular box of wooden matches, which are great for lighting a fire in the fireplace, and another time an abacus—nice little mementos tourists would pick up in town.

Generally, I just show up with a bag of carrot sticks to munch on, and go to work.

After I earned my state license, for Christmas Susan Johnson, administrator for the Oregon Board of Maritime Pilots, had stationery printed for me that reads, "from the desk of . . . Capt. Deborah Dempsey, Columbia River Bar Pilot. It's not just a job—It's an attitude."

That says it all.

Glossary

AB Able seaman; acts as quartermaster at the wheel or lookout for traffic on the bridge wing.

Amidships or **Midships** Helm order meaning to center the rudder parallel to the ship (with the rudder-angle indicator showing 0); to steer straight ahead.

Athwartships From one side of the ship to the other, as opposed to fore and aft.

Ballast Tanks of water, used to balance fuel oil and cargo on modern freighters.

Bearing "The situation or horizontal direction of one point with respect to another or to the compass." (Webster's) The navigator takes compass bearings of objects on shore to find the ship's exact position; the captain fixes the position going into Haifa by taking a bearing on Rosh ha Karmel.

Beaufort Wind Force Scale
force 0 wind less than 1 knot (1.15 MPH)
force 1 wind 1–3 knots, wave height .25 feet
force 2 wind 4–6 knots, wave height .5–1 feet
force 3 wind 7–10 knots, wave height 2–3 feet
force 4 wind 11–16 knots, wave height 3.5–5 feet
force 5 wind 17–21 knots, wave height 6–8 feet
force 6 wind 22–27 knots, wave height 9.5–13 feet
force 7 wind 28–33 knots, wave height 13.5–19 feet
force 8 wind 34–40 knots, wave height 18–25 feet
force 9 wind 41–47 knots, wave height 23–32 feet
force 10 wind 48–55 knots, wave height 29–41 feet
force 11 wind 56–63 knots, wave height 37–52 feet

Bell Book Kept by the mate on watch, a record with the times of all changes in course and speed, navigation lights and landmarks sighted, bearings taken, compass comparisons, and other incidents that may affect the safety of the ship, cargo, crew, or passengers.

Boom (noun)—Device used to lift cargo on a freighter; (verb)—to float a barrier around a ship to contain a possible oil leak.

Bowditch Nathaniel Bowditch (1773–1838) wrote the *American Practical Navigator,* first published in 1802. American seamen still consider it the bible of practical navigation.

Bow Thruster Powered mechanism that gives a ship greater control in docking and undocking.

Breakbulk Freighters that carry a variety of loose cargo in the holds, as differentiated from containerships, which haul cargo pre-stowed in containers; tankers (liquid cargo); or car carriers.

Bridge The topmost deck but one (the flying bridge is above), with an open wing on either side. It is an enclosed space running athwartships, with picture windows nearly all around offering a virtually unobstructed view. The ship is navigated from there, and activities on deck can be seen and controlled by the captain or officer on watch. Bridge equipment includes the steering wheel, magnetic compass and repeater from the gyro compass, engine and bow thruster controls, chart table, radar scanners, coffee pot, and captain's chair (other crew stand, to stay awake).

Bulkhead Vertical partition (on land, a wall) dividing the hull into separate compartments.

Bunkers Fuel oil.

Conn Control.

Container Reusable metal box, twenty or fourty feet long, that can be packed with cargo, sealed, and transferred from ship to dock and loaded onto trucks or trains via cranes or booms.

Course Line Line drawn on the chart for the vessel's intended direction of travel.

Drag Amount by which a ship floats lower aft than forward; on the *Charlotte,* the optimum drag for best speed was about four feet.

Elephant Feet Devices designed especially to lift hatch covers.

Fetched Up The anchor is holding the ship.

Fo'c'sle Short for forecastle, a short raised deck forward on the ship. The Forecastle Card, also known as "articles," is the contract a merchant seaman signs before shipping out.

FWE Finished with engines; the engines and steering gear are turned off.

Gimbals Metal rings that form the mounting and suspension for such objects as compasses, cooking stoves, and hospital beds on ships, allowing those objects to remain level regardless of the rolling or pitching of the ship.

Great Circle Sailing On transoceanic voyages, a method of navigating a ship along the shortest distance between the point of departure and the point of arrival.

Halyards On a freighter, lines (never called ropes) used to raise flags indicating the country the ship is from and where she is calling, the company she sails for, or that a pilot is aboard. A halyard can also fly a day shape giving other information, such as that she is being towed.

Hanging Locker Closet with a rod to hold hangers.

Hatch or **Hold** Large compartment below deck for stowing cargo, covered with a hatch cover. Additional cargo, such as containers, can be placed on the hatch cover, in locations designated by row, bay, and tier.

Hawsepipe Opening in the foredeck through which the anchor chain runs from the deck to the water.

Heading The vessel's actual compass direction, expressed in three figures denoting the 360 degrees of a circle; 000 is due north; 090, due east; 180, due south; and 270, due west.

Heave Pick up the anchor.

Heave To Hold position by moving slowly in bad weather, as opposed to anchoring.

House Superstructure of the freighter. It contains the crew's living and working quarters.

Lashing Gear Twist locks (that secure the containers to the deck and to each other, one at each corner), turnbuckles, shackles, chain; all are used to secure the cargo.

Lee The side of the ship opposite that from which the wind blows; the protected side.

Make Up To or **Make Fast To** Attach with lines. Tugs often make up to ships; in some ports, such as Alexandria, they push the ship to or from the berth without attaching to it.

Maneuvering Speeds Dead slow (35 RPM, 6 knots); slow (55 RPM, 9 knots); half (80 RPM, 12 knots); full (105 RPM, 16 knots).

MARAD U.S. Maritime Administration.

Merchant Marine Commercial (as opposed to military) ships and seamen.

MITAGS Marine Institute of Technology and Graduate Studies, in Linthicum Heights, Maryland.

MSC U.S. Military Sealift Command.

Noon Slip Kept by the third mate, it shows past day's run, latitude and longitude, speed made good, course made good, total distance, distance to go, and number of hours in the day. Remarks may include weather warnings or whether clocks need to be advanced or retarded.

On The Beach A seaman who is not currently employed aboard a ship is on the beach.

OS Ordinary seaman. An unlicensed position, one notch below AB. Other unlicensed positions are boatswain; steward, cook, or utility; electrician, engine maintenance, or wiper.

Pilot An expert at navigating a particular piece of water, such as into a port, through a strait, or over a sandbar. The pilot has the conn (control) when aboard the ship, even though the captain is still responsible for the ship. In some ports, such as New York, a docking master replaces a pilot to dock or undock a ship.

Pitching Movement of the ship fore and aft, as opposed to rolling (from side to side).

Port Left-hand side of the ship, as viewed facing forward.

Port Captain Employed by a shipping company to handle its ships' business for the ship captains while they are in that port.

Port Engineer Employed by a shipping company to oversee the maintenance and repairs of its ships in that port.

Rhumb Lines Chords of the Great Circle track that appear as straight lines on a Mercator chart. If a ship alters course, straight line to straight line, she can keep as close as possible to the great circle joining the two points. Doing so means sailing the shortest reasonable course between them, thus saving fuel and time.

SBE Stand by engines; engineers are standing by, immediately available for maneuvering.

Shot Ninety feet of anchor chain.

Slop Chest A stock of incidentals maintained and sold by the chief mate to the crew during a voyage. (It is not actually a chest, but a space where everything can be locked up when it is not being sold.)

Slops Drippings from the engine, oil leaks, bilge water, pumped into the slop tank and held until they can be off-loaded onto a barge.

Spreader Bars Heavy steel bars used to lift cargo on or off the ship.

Starboard Right-hand side of the ship, as viewed facing forward.

Stiff Condition of a ship when her bottom is full of fuel oil and ballast and there is no balancing cargo above. Bottom-heavy, she rides high in the water and is subject to quick snap rolls. Opposite of tender.

Stop Engines Stop the propeller from turning.

Supercargoes Military personnel being transported aboard a commercial freighter. They superintend their cargo during the voyage.

Take Arrival or Take Departure Pass the official spot that marks the entrance to the channel that leads to a port (such as Ambrose Light entering New York harbor) when arriving or departing.

Tender Condition of a ship when she has cargo to balance the fuel oil and ballast in her bottom; she rolls gently. Opposite of stiff.

To Haul Maneuver for other ship traffic or stationary obstacles, such as oil rigs.

Traffic Other ships or boats maneuvering in the area.

Way Point Predesignated place where a ship changes course from one line to another.

Z Card U.S. merchant mariner's document. A Z card substitutes for a passport when a seaman sails foreign.

ABOUT THE AUTHORS

Debbie Dempsey's love for the sea comes from generations of sea-farers starting with Deacon John Doane's landing in Eastham, Cape Cod, in 1629. She was raised in Essex, Connecticut, on the mouth of the Connecticut River, where her family and community are very active sailors. Sailing remains her preferred mode of transportation.

Her love and respect for the discipline of working and surviving the elements of the sea were shared for eighteen years with her husband, Jack, until his death in 1996. Her lifelong dream remains to create an offshore sailing school, to share with children and instill in them that same love and respect for the sea. She lives in Astoria, Oregon, with her companion, Gehrig, an eighty-eight-pound rottweiler.

Joanne Foster's writing and traveling have taken her to exotic and unusual destinations. A Denver native, she earned a bachelor's degree in English from the University of California at Berkeley. She began as a reporter on the Denver *Rocky Mountain News,* subsequently wrote for the *National Observer* and *The Washington Post,* and traveled with her foreign correspondent husband to Vietnam, Cambodia, and other Asian datelines.

For more than twenty-five years, Foster has been drawn to a variety of islands, seas, and sailing vessels—from marriage in Hong Kong, to summering on Hilton Head, to living on Chesapeake Bay. This book is her first chance to connect all of these interests. Today she writes and edits books at her home just beyond "End of State Maintenance" at White Stone, Virginia. Her husband, Jim, edits a circus magazine, and their daughter, Julie, works in London for an international bank.